D1527163

Export Development and Promotion: The Role of Public Organizations

Export Development and Promotion: The Role of Public Organizations

Edited by

F.H. Rolf Seringhaus
Wilfrid Laurier University

Philip J. Rosson
Dalhousie University

Kluwer Academic Publishers
Boston   Dordecht   London

Distributors for North America:
Kluwer Academic Publishers
101 Philip Drive
Assinippi Park
Norwell, Massachusetts 02061 USA

Distributors for all other countries:
Kluwer Academic Publishers Group
Distribution Centre
Post Office Box 322
3300 AH Dordrecht, THE NETHERLANDS

Library of Congress Cataloging-in-Publication Data

Export development and promotion : the role of public organizations /
   [edited by] F.H. Rolf Seringhaus, Philip J. Rosson.
      p.   cm.
   Includes bibliographical references (p.   ) and index.
   ISBN 0-7923-9090-3
   1. Foreign trade promotion—Government policy. 2. Commercial
policy. 3. Public administration. I. Seringhaus, F.H. Rolf,
1942- . II. Rosson, Philip J.
HF1417.5.E9   1990
382 ′.63—dc20   90-47829
                                                              CIP

Copyright © 1991 by Kluwer Academic Publishers

Printed on acid-free paper.

Printed in the United States of America

This book is dedicated to

Elizabeth Seringhaus

and

Tom and Michael Rosson

TABLE OF CONTENTS

Table of Contents   i x

LIST OF FIGURES

LIST OF TABLES

ABOUT THE EDITORS

F.H. Rolf Seringhaus is Associate Professor of International Marketing at the School of Business and Economics of Wilfrid Laurier University in Waterloo, Canada, where he is also chairman of the International Business Unit of the Laurier Institute for Business and Economic Studies. He studied at York University in Toronto, where he received his MBA and Ph.D. in International Marketing. He has researched and published internationally in journals and books in the areas of export marketing management, international marketing strategy, and government export promotion. The most recent book to his credit is **GOVERNMENT EXPORT PROMOTION: A GLOBAL PERSPECTIVE,** published by Routledge in 1990. Dr. Seringhaus has been visiting professor at the Institut fur Absatz, Handel und Marketing at the University of Innsbruck, and Scuola Superiore di Studi Universitari e di Perfezionamento S. Anna, Pisa. Prior to his academic career, Dr. Seringhaus spent twenty years in managerial positions in marketing and finance with major international corporations in Canada, Switzerland and Germany. Dr. Seringhaus also consults to industry and government in matters of marketing strategy and research, export development and export promotion.

Philip J. Rosson is Professor of Marketing at the School of Business Administration of Dalhousie University in Halifax, Canada, where he is also Director of the Centre for International Business Studies. He was educated in England, obtaining an M.A. and Ph.D. in Marketing at the University of Lancaster and Bath, respectively. He has taught at universities in Scotland and New Zealand and lectured in Italy and West Germany. His research interests currently embrace export methods and strategies in smaller firms and marketing in high technology environments. He has published widely in journals and book collections, and has three books to his credit, including **MANAGING EXPORT ENTRY AND EXPANSION (1987).** Dr. Rosson has seven years of marketing experience with organizations in England and East Africa. He consults for government and business on export and technology marketing matters.

CONTRIBUTING AUTHORS

Jim Bell is Senior Lecturer, University of Ulster at Jordanstown, Jordanstown, Northern Ireland.

Mary Brooks is Associate Professor, School of Business Administration, Dalhousie University, Halifax, N.S., Canada.

David Camino is Assistant Professor, Faculty of Economics and Business, Universidad Autonoma de Madrid, Madrid, Spain.

W.M. Clarke is Head of Department of Banking and Commerce, Faculty of Business and Management, University of Ulster at Coleraine, Coleraine, Northern Ireland.

Charles Pahud de Mortanges is Assistant Professor, Faculty of Economics and Business Administration, University of Limburg, Maastricht, The Netherlands.

Adamantios Diamantopoulos is Senior Lecturer, European Business Management School, University of Wales, Swansea, United Kingdom.

Luis R. Dominguez is Professor, School of Business, University of Miami, Coral Gables, Florida, USA.

Antonio Francés is Associate Professor, IESA - Instituto de Estudios Superiores de Administracion, San Bernadino, Caracas, Venezuela.

Nigel Hamley is at the Centre for International Business, Monash University, Clayton, Melbourne, Australia.

Karen Inglis is a Consultant with CACI Inc., Edinburgh, Scotland.

Riccardo Lanzara is Associate Professor, Scuola Superiore di Studi Universitari e di Perfezionamento S. Anna, Pisa, Italy.

James D. McNiven is Dean, Faculty of Management, Dalhousie University, Halifax, N.S., Canada.

Maurice Murray is at the University of Ulster at Jordanstown, Jordanstown, Northern Ireland.

John Onto is Associate Professor, School of Business Administration, Georgetown University, Washington D.C., USA.

Roberto Sbrana is Professor, Dipartimento di Economia Aziendale "Egidio Giannessi", Universita Degli Studi di Pisa, Pisa, Italy.

Bodo Schlegelmilch is Professor, European Business Management School, University of Wales, Swansea, United Kingdom.

Carlos G. Sequeira is at the INCAE - Instituto Centroamericano des Administración de Empresas, Alajuela, Costa Rica.

Monica Siena Tangheroni is Research Fellow, Dipartimento di Economia Aziendale "Egidio Giannesse", Universita Degli Studi di Pisa, Pisa, Italy.

Aart P. van Gent is Professor, Nijenrode, Netherlands School of Business, Breukelen, The Netherlands.

Riccardo Varaldo is Professor, Scuola Superiore di Studi Universitari e di Perfezionamento S. Anna, Pisa, Italy.

Patrizia Zagnoli is Assistant Professor, Scuola Superiore di Studi Universitari e di Perfezionamento S. Anna, Pisa, Italy.

PREFACE

Companies succeed in international markets because of their competitive competence which, in large measure, is based on the level of knowledge and skill they bring to their international marketing activities. Public organizations in the export development and promotion field play a facilitating role in this process. Their mandate is to enhance the know-how of exporters and thereby assist foreign market entry, development and expansion. The interaction between these public organizations and the companies they exist to serve is the subject of this book.

The book is wide-ranging and up-to-date. The work of researchers from 11 countries (in both the developed and developing world) is represented which means that a variety of perspectives are contained in the book. These contributions present the latest thinking on this important matter. The authors of each chapter are objective in their approach. Consequently, considerable attention is paid to the performance of the public organization support programs and activities. Each researcher comes to his/her own conclusions based on the individual work undertaken, but readers will find that certain common themes run through many of the chapters.

The key objectives of the book are:
1. To provide academic researchers with a current and comprehensive treatment of the role played by public organizations in export development and promotion.
2. To expose professional readers (officials in relevant public organizations, consultants in the private sector or in international agencies) to a view of their field of interest that might be broader and more critical than normal.
3. To expose students of exporting and international business to issues and perspectives on the topic of export support and public organizations, as well as to our present level of knowledge in this field.

The book has 14 chapters that are organized in five parts. Each part is highlighted below, so as to provide a sense of what follows. In Part I—*Export Development and Public Organizations: The State-of-the-Art*—the critical issues are outlined and both developed and developing world contrasts and experiences are introduced. Part II is entitled *Challenges in Export Development: Some Regional Perspectives*, and focuses on the export situation and problems in various Latin American and European nations. The topic covered in Part III is *Evaluating the Role of Public Organizations in Export Promotion,* and findings from studies of the performance of a variety of export promotion programs in different nations are presented. Attention turns to the future in Part IV—*A Case for Successful Intervention: Some New Initiatives,* where several promising departures from normal export support practices are described and examined. Part V has the title *Research Directions in Export Development and Promotion,* and provides an assessment of present knowledge from studies in this area, as well as ideas for future research activity.

It is hoped that the book will contribute to a better understanding of the role played by public organizations in equipping companies to compete more effectively in the international business arena.

F.H. Rolf Seringhaus

Philip J. Rosson

Waterloo, Ontario

Halifax, Nova Scotia

August 1990

ACKNOWLEDGEMENTS

We wish to express our gratitude for the support provided by our universities, Wilfrid Laurier University and Dalhousie University, respectively.

We also wish to thank Elsie Grogan and her word processing team at Wilfrid Laurier University for secretarial assistance in preparing the manuscript. Rob Hyndman of Dalhousie University also deserves our thanks for his assistance in producing the final tables, figures and text pages for publication, as well as for the cover design.

PART I

Export Development and Promotion and Public Organizations: The State-of-the-Art

INTRODUCTION

Part I sets the stage for the discussion of export development and promotion, identifying many of the issues that are explored in detail later in the book. It begins with an overview of the topic and then goes on to review export promotion in developed and developing world contexts.

In Chapter one, Seringhaus and Rosson provide an essential guide to export promotion, how it relates to the export development process and how public organizations participate in and contribute to this process. They describe how export promotion programs help companies overcome barriers and compete in international markets. Seringhaus and Rosson conclude that there is no "best" form of export promotion or public organization. The particular situation in each setting determines program offerings and delivery. However, similarities exist across countries. A common need is that of better evaluation of the impact of public organizations' export efforts.

McNiven examines the emergence and increasing influence of export development efforts at the state level in the U.S. in Chapter two. He provides examples of available state programs for increasing exports through economic and marketing incentives, and argues that states have seized the initiative largely because of program deficiencies at the federal government level.

Moving to the developing world, Seringhaus provides an analysis of the characteristics and operations of export promotion organizations (EPOs) in 70 developing countries. In Chapter three, he draws the link between export promotion, export development and economic well-being. A profile is provided of the organization and functions of EPOs, showing their important role as a bridge between public policy and the private sector.

CHAPTER ONE

Export Promotion and Public Organizations: State-of-the-Art

F.H. Rolf Seringhaus and Philip J. Rosson[*]

SUMMARY

This chapter provides an overview of the topic explored in this book. It defines what is meant by the terms "export promotion" and "public organization" and explains why companies often need support and assistance in their exporting endeavours. Although there are many similarities in company needs and program offerings around the world, because of their different settings, developed and developing countries show some contrasts – in orientation, organization, and methods. The similarities and contrasts between developed and developing countries are briefly described. When public funds are used to support private sector initiatives, effectiveness is always an issue. The chapter highlights what we know about this matter, in the process pointing to some of the measurement problems involved.

INTRODUCTION

Exporting is an activity of growing importance for companies and countries worldwide. More and more companies realize that foreign markets provide either avenues for growth or means for survival in an increasingly competitive and international economic environment. Because many companies

---

[*] Wilfrid Laurier University, Waterloo and Dalhousie University, Halifax respectively.

lack the motivation, information or resources to exploit foreign market opportunities, national governments and other public organizations have evolved programs of support and assistance. Essentially, these programs attempt to improve the competitive competence of participating companies and, thus, bolster their chance of international market success. This should, of course, lead to more employment and wealth creation.

Our interest in this book is the exporting process and the form and effectiveness of company-public organization interaction. We should elaborate what we mean by the term "public organization" before going any further. In the context of exporting, most public organization activity is undertaken by departments of government such as the U.S. Department of Commerce and the Department of External Affairs in Canada. Also included within our definition are quasi-government organizations like the Swedish Trade Council and the Austrian Bundeswirtschaftskammer. Non-governmental organizations such as industry, export, and trade associations also qualify, as do chambers of commerce. These types of organization are found in West Germany and the Netherlands, as well as elsewhere.

This chapter provides the necessary introduction to the topic. We hope that it also permits readers to integrate the individual contributions that follow. The chapter is divided into four sections. In the first, the reasons that explain public organizations' support for exporters are identified and discussed. Attention then turns to a description of the situation in the developed and developing world, highlighting some points of difference in public organization roles and mechanisms employed. In the third section the issue of effectiveness is raised and discussed. An attempt is made to summarize what we presently know about the impact of public organizations' export promotion programs. A number of problems that bedevil evaluation are also noted. In the fourth and final section, some conclusions are drawn.

 THE NEED FOR EXPORT PROMOTION

Since the mid 1960s to 1989, world merchandise trade has grown from $200 million to $3 trillion – that is by a factor of fifteen thousand[1] (Economist 1990). As well as this absolute measure of the importance of trade, consider

---

[1] In addition, global trade in services amounted to approximately $600 billion in 1989.

also that world trade is growing more quickly than industrial output. This points to the increasing importance of trade in relative economic terms.

The developed nations lead the way in trade. In 1986, industrial Western countries accounted for 85 percent of world manufactured exports. Furthermore, these nations are their own best customers: 75 percent of world manufactured exports take place between countries in this grouping. This figure has increased in recent years, indicating that, as a group, developing countries are not maintaining their share of exports to the West. However, experiences vary in this regard. Some countries (South Korea) have penetrated Western markets with their products. Others have not been so fortunate and have had to find alternative markets to offset the loss of developed world business – often through trade with other like countries.

Part of the reason for the sharp growth in world trade is the lower import tariffs that have resulted from successive rounds of the General Agreement on Tariffs and Trade (GATT). For the companies of any single nation this development has created foreign market opportunities, but it has also meant that those same companies have less protection in their own domestic market. Thus, tariff reductions have proven to be a double-edged sword – throwing up both opportunities and threats.

These developments mean that regardless of where the export company is located, the industrial sector it is a part of, or the area of the world to which its marketing activities are directed, there is one generic requirement, namely its competitive competence. Although a common requirement for all companies, because of their resource limitations, small and medium-sized companies need to be as fit as possible when taking on foreign competition. Few smaller companies will be able to sustain foreign marketing operations that are not "right" for very long, whereas larger companies have greater staying power. For smaller companies in particular then, the export promotion programs offered by public organizations provide a ready means to acquire or enhance the skills that are needed to become an effective competitor in foreign markets. We should at this point define what is meant by "export promotion programs". These are public policy measures which actually or potentially enhance exporting activity at the company, industry, or national level (Root 1971). This involves "the creation of awareness of exporting as a growth and market expansion option; the reduction or removal of barriers to exporting; and the creation of promotion incentives and various forms of assistance to potential and actual exporters" (Seringhaus and Rosson 1990).

In summary, we can say that the following factors help explain why companies seek export promotion support and why this is provided by public organizations:

1. The growing importance of international trade.
2. The increasing intensity of international competition.
3. The necessity of participating in the global expansion of trade in goods and services.
4. The need to strengthen domestic industrial sectors.

Having explained why export promotion programs are needed and offered, next we turn to the question of design and delivery. Clearly these programs will only assist exporters to the extent that they meet real needs, which vary depending on a company's stage of export involvement. The idea that companies vary in terms of the extent and intensity of their export involvement, and that their needs are related to such involvement has been discussed in the literature (Sheth and Schoenfeld 1980; Czinkota 1982; Cavusgil 1984; Seringhaus 1987). Figure 1.1 provides a convenient summary of the stages of export involvement, corresponding company needs, and export promotion program responses.

Another way of understanding how public organizations might address company export needs is through considering the barriers faced in international trade. Numerous studies have been conducted over the last two decades into this matter with a broad range of factors considered. Most of these employ different lists of factors, with emphasis given to task factors such as export documentation and financial constraints. However, the root of the problem appears to lie elsewhere. Our view is that the crucial barriers to increased involvement by companies in foreign markets are managerial motivation, knowledge and resources.

Non-exporters often view exporting as more risky, costly and time-consuming than domestic business. This perception, although partly true, is incomplete. Exporters find that entry to foreign markets frequently generates good returns, spreads market risks, and provides opportunities for growth and expansion (Brooks and Rosson 1982). Thus, many firms need motivation before they are likely to start exporting. This is the first barrier to be overcome. Advertising, testimonials and seminars are frequently employed to achieve this goal.

Informational barriers are the second hurdle. Many companies do not know where to begin – they lack both an appreciation of the information that

Figure 1.1: Company needs and export promotion programmes

Type of export involvement	Key questions	Company need	Export promotion focus and typical initiatives			
			Motivational	Informational	Operational/Resource
Non-exporter	Should we even consider exporting?	To be made aware of opportunities	Advertising Local seminars Export weeks/months	-	-
New exporter	Should we initiate exporting? Which market should we investigate?	To determine feasibility of exporting	Seminars Export bulletin/newsletter	Market reviews Supplier/Buyer newsletter Custom market research	Trade missions Financing, insurance
Expanding exporter	Which new market should we enter and how?	To select the most promising market and the best market entry method	-	Market visits Export seminars/meetings Export newsletter	Trade fairs Trade missions Financing, Insurance
Continuing exporter	How can we achieve better performance?	To improve and fine tune existing operations	-	Export seminars/meetings Export newsletter	Trade fairs Foreign buyer visit Sales offices Financing, insurance

Source: Prepared by authors.

should be collected, where it might be found and, in the event that these problems are surmounted, how it should be analyzed.   Again, public organizations play a role in this area, providing standardized economic data on markets around the world, more specific data by product ("Export opportunities for automobile parts") or country ("Doing business in Thailand"), and assistance in interpreting data collected (through sectoral and geographic desks, foreign trade posts, seminars, and consulting assistance).

Operational or resource barriers mean that companies suffer from a shortage of the time and/or money that must be invested if export markets are to be seriously developed.   As argued above, although critical to success, managerial knowledge of foreign markets and marketing is typically lacking in the novice exporter.   Again, public organizations frequently help companies to deal with these barriers through, for example, such vehicles as cost-shared market visits, trade missions, and trade fairs.

A review of export promotion programs around the world indicates that public organizations in the developed world have created broadly similar services so that companies might overcome motivational, informational and resource barriers (Seringhaus and Rosson 1990).   We now examine these programs more closely, as well as those found in the developing world.

EXPORT PROMOTION IN THE DEVELOPED AND DEVELOPING WORLD

Although trade is as ancient as mankind, export promotion by public organizations has primarily evolved because of the surge in trade activity over the last 20 years.   Today's export promotion programs often provide comprehensive and sophisticated services to the business community. We distinguish here between export promotion in the "First World" and the "Third World".[2] Not surprisingly, these different trade settings have thrown up varying approaches to export promotion.   In the developing world, export promotion is

---

[2] In the "Second World" of Eastern Europe and China, government has to this point handled all exporting activity through foreign trade organizations.   This makes for a very different form of company-public organizational interaction, and one we do not attempt to deal with here.   Although events are changing rapidly in many of these Socialist countries (in the Soviet Union for example, enterprises and Ministries are now able to export), it is too early to tell what lasting effect these initiatives will bring.

generally viewed as an instrument of economic development. In the developed world, however, the emphasis of export promotion programs is one of strengthening the competitive competence of individual companies. This is not meant to imply that developing countries do not seek to strengthen companies. This is a goal, but it is tied to the more fundamental issue of economic development. Figure 1.2 serves as a guide for both the terminology and the positioning of export promotion in the economic development process.

Developed Countries

We have noted above that broadly similar programs of export promotion are evident in the developed world. This primarily reflects the fact that companies from these nations are competing in the same sectors and markets, and have roughly common needs as exporters. To this end, many of the industrial nations offer an array of standard services to client companies (Seringhaus 1987). At the same time, however, differences are evident from country-to-country. These differences mirror the prevailing philosophy concerning business and government responsibilities and interaction. What this means is that the (largely) standard export promotion programs are provided by different bodies. In some cases government plays the lead role, while in others it is shared between government and private sector organizations, and in still others the private sector dominates. In addition to these differences regarding responsibility and delivery, Figure 1.3 shows that export promotion varies in the approach taken in different countries. In some cases the programs are only loosely coordinated, whereas elsewhere an integrated or strategic approach prevails.

Government-led export promotion initiatives are found in countries such as Australia, Canada and France, with the latter showing a much more strategic focus than the others. A second group of countries prefer to involve government as a partner in the planning and implementation of programs. Thus, in the Netherlands export promotion draws support from government but is largely carried out by independent organizations. A certain independence from government is also preferred in Sweden. In contrast to the Netherlands, however, export support is more strategic in its approach, in that companies are assisted for a specific period of time on particular foreign market projects. The third group of countries is characterized by private sector-led approaches. Germany and Austria, for example, exhibit minimal government involvement. Within

Figure 1.2: Economic development process

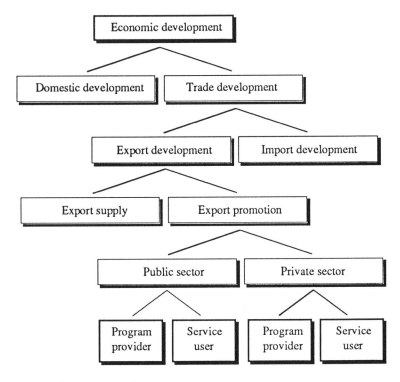

Source: Prepared by authors.

this group though, contrasts are still found. In Germany, government's attitude towards business is essentially laissez-faire. This means that Germany does not have the broad and integrated private sector-led export promotion structure of Austria, but rather depends on individual efforts mounted by trade and industry associations.[3]

Although developed countries exhibit differing export promotion structures, we cannot assume that one form is ideal. The role played by government and the private sector in various countries reflects varying philosophies and histories of business-government interaction. One might argue, however, that differences in the strategic orientation of export promotion

---

[3]   We should point out that in North America private sector organizations such as chambers of commerce, and trade and industry organizations, generally play a more passive role in export promotion than their European counterparts.

Figure 1.3: The organization and approach to export promotion

Dominant player(s)	Organizational structure and channel:	Approach to export promotion effort:
Government	Government departments or government controlled organizations	Co-ordination among different levels (Canada, Australia)
		or
		Strategic planning and goal oriented (France)
Government/ private sector	Government departments or organizations, chambers of commerce, industry associations and trade promotion councils	Restricted government involvement, often carrying out own separate activities (Netherlands, Italy)
		or
		Organized partnership approach with extensive sharing and cooperation (Sweden, U.K.)
Private sector	Chamber of commerce, industry associations	Institutions mainly influenced by business membership and act in its interest (Germany)
		or
		Obligatory, structural ties with business community, strategic planning approach to international business process (Austria)

Source: Prepared by authors.

programs are more significant. To our minds, if companies are to gain or keep an edge in the tough competitive trading environment of the 1990s, then planned and strategic export promotion programs will probably outperform those that are more loosely coordinated.

Developing Countries

Developing countries have achieved significant growth rates in industrial output and exports over the last 20 years. As a group, these countries now export more manufactured goods than agricultural products. That exporting is important to a developing nation's progress is reinforced by recent World Bank studies, where countries with an "outward orientation" were seen to perform better than those with an "inward orientation" over the 1963-73 and 1973-85 periods examined (World Bank 1987, Economist 1989c). Nations with a strongly outward orientation (Hong Kong, Singapore, South Korea) have developed strong exporting sectors through investment in export supply systems and infrastructure, as well as export promotion programs (Keesing and Lall 1988). Many developing countries are now following this path, initiating policies and programs to help their fledgling industries and companies to compete more effectively in the world economy.

Western governments have a part to play in fostering stronger developing countries too. Several countries have made efforts in this direction by establishing import promotion organizations to help improve market access for developing countries (IMPOD in Sweden and CBI in the Netherlands are good examples). Recent initiatives by Japan are also worth noting, encompassing attempts to create more harmonious trade flows with developing countries, greater market access by the newly industrializing countries (NICs), aid-investment that has a clearer business and industrial development focus (Economist 1989b), and the unilateral elimination of tariffs on tropical products (Economist 1989a).

Most developing countries have an export promotion organization (EPO) today. International organizations such as the International Trade Centre UNCTAD/GATT, the World Bank, the Economic Social Commission for Asia and the Pacific (ESCAP), and others, are frequently involved in establishing such units and in providing operational guidance. EPOs play an important role in export development for they help to foster an export orientation not only within the business community, but also within the public sector. In addition, they provide managerial and resource support to exporters.

As is the case in the developed world, varying national settings have produced specific and tailored organizational responses. However, a number of characteristics seem essential to the success of an EPO. These include: a voice in the creation of export policy; a specific promotional role in export development; and overall autonomy and influence (Seringhaus 1989a). If EPOs are to be effective, they must also be given a clear mandate and sufficient resources. This has happened in countries such as South Korea (KOTRA), and Thailand (Department of Export Promotion).

Figure 1.4 summarizes this discussion of developing country exporting. Seven stages of government involvement in exporting are shown, and EPOs should (and often do) play a key role throughout this process. By helping companies to transform foreign market opportunities into sales, EPOs essentially facilitate export development. With the exception of the earlier stages covering development policy and export potential (stages 1-3), these functions are carried out by similar organizations in developed countries. Because they cover more stages and generally have to do more "coaching" of companies, we might thus argue that EPOs in the developing world play a more critical role in export development than their Western counterparts. Figure 1.4 also introduces the idea that the operations of EPOs be evaluated, the topic taken up in the next section.

THE EFFECTIVENESS OF EXPORT PROMOTION

A pressing question for public organizations involved in export promotion is: How effective are the programs and services offered? The need to answer this question arises for two reasons. First, whenever public funds are involved there is a need to show that expenditures serve some good purpose. Second, beyond this macro consideration, it is important to demonstrate that the programs have a positive impact on user companies (that is at the micro level). Companies need to see that export promotion programs will help them to learn more about foreign markets and marketing and, thus, become stronger international competitors. Therefore, both organizational and user needs make evaluation studies desirable. We now briefly review what is known about the effectiveness of export promotion efforts by public organizations.

Most nations now attempt some form of export promotion evaluation. Developed nations are usually in a position to conduct their own reviews, whereas in the developing world, international organizations such as ITC and ESCAP encourage and help systematic studies to be carried out. One point that is common to many export promotion evaluations is that they frequently lack clear goals and targets against which to compare achievement. Another problem

Figure 1.4: Seven stages of export involvement by public organizations

Stage	Focus	Evaluation measures
1.	Economic development	Infrastructure and performance goals, yardsticks
2.	Export development	
3.	Export potential	Opportunity survey
4.	Export promotion	Need, learning level
5.	Export consciousness	Awareness level
6.	Export orientation	Motivation level
7.	Export marketing	Knowledge, resource level

Source: Prepared by authors.

area is that of measurement. Despite increasing sophistication, practices still leave much to be desired (Seringhaus 1986). One of the perennial difficulties is that of sorting out cause and effect. When one considers all of the activities taking place in a company and in its environment, isolating the influence of a single factor such as export promotion support is complex. This is also the main reason why public organization efforts are generally regarded as having a marginal effect on companies (Seringhaus 1990). This is not meant to suggest that export promotion is of little consequence to companies; on the contrary, the help may provide the marginal edge needed to succeed.

Looking at evaluation studies across many nations, some general findings emerge. For example, roughly one-half of potential users are aware of the export promotion programs and one in four actually use them. Among these users, managers are often somewhat ambivalent about the programs, however, their helpfulness seems greatest early in the export process when, for example, a company is completely new to exporting or is attempting to enter a new foreign market. As well as these general comments regarding levels of program awareness, use and perceived helpfulness, other studies enable us to draw some conclusions about export promotion by public organizations. Several common threads run through evaluations conducted recently in Australia, Canada, Ireland and the U.S. These include:

1. A pro-exporting attitude and commitment needs to be instilled in companies.
2. Efforts need to be made to motivate companies into taking foreign market action.
3. Companies have a generic requirement for competitiveness.
4. Room exists for better focusing of export promotion resources so as to improve results.
5. Programme support to companies on an ad-hoc basis should be replaced by a more strategic approach.
6. More specific objectives and outcome goals are required so as to determine program achievement.
7. Export promotion organizations and programs can only ever act as a stimulus and facilitator.

As well as these general conclusions, a number of comments can be made regarding first, users (companies) and, second, program providers (public organizations). As far as users are concerned:

1. If a company sees that support can benefit their exporting operations, it will be more likely to use public organization programs.
2. As companies become increasingly experienced in exporting, their needs become more specific so that general support is less beneficial.
3. Companies rarely evaluate the impact of export promotion programs on their operations because it is most likely minor and/or difficult to establish.
4. Management can help to improve export promotion support by providing feedback to the relevant public organization.

Regarding public organizations, the following summary comments flow from the evaluation studies:

1. The evaluation of export promotion programs is far from uniform.
2. The most sophisticated evaluations are conducted in developed countries and advances in approach and methods are being made.

3. Evaluations are most useful when they establish the effect of programs at the company level as well as in an overall cost-benefit sense.

4. A systematic and continuing evaluation effort is required to determine program impact over the long-term.

To summarize, the evaluation of export promotion programs is attempted in most countries. However, as the above discussion has indicated, establishing a clear measure of impact usually eludes those charged with the responsibility. The picture is improving though, and program users and providers will both benefit from better performance in this area.

CONCLUSIONS

More companies are being drawn into international markets. This usually is undertaken so as to increase the market scope of operations and meet the company's growth aspirations. Sometimes foreign market entry takes place for defensive reasons: a company may find it increasingly difficult to achieve its objectives at home, or it may feel it essential to participate in world markets so as to keep a finger on the pulse of developments in its industry. Whatever the case, going overseas creates new challenges for companies that they are often ill-equipped to deal with. In an attempt to fuel economic growth and prosperity, many government and other public organizations have developed programs of support for and assistance to would-be and actual exporters. These encourage companies to think about doing business overseas and, for those with such an interest, help to reduce the uncertainties and knowledge and skill deficiencies that exist. These programs are primarily targeted to small and medium-sized companies because, in many ways, these face the greatest problems.

As might be expected, no universal form of public organization or of export promotion programming is evident around the world. Rather, different circumstances have generated particular responses. We have seen that there is a good deal of similarity in the programs that are offered to companies in the developed nations of the West. These focus on improving the competence of companies so that they might become fitter competitors in world markets. Differences exist, however, in the application and delivery of these programmes. In some countries the programs are very carefully integrated into the foreign market plans of users, whereas elsewhere these are applied in a less discriminating manner.   As far as delivery is concerned, responsible organizations are sometimes a branch of government, in other nations a mix of government and private sector organizations, while in still others the initiative is taken wholly by private sector organizations such as chambers of commerce.   In the developing world, export promotion is firstly viewed as a vehicle for economic development, and only secondly as a means of support for specific companies.   A variety of organizational forms and programs are seen in developing countries, reflecting the economic, social and political diversity of this grouping.   Some nations have borrowed from the West and in many the influence of international organizations such as ITC is strongly evident.

The effectiveness of public organization spending on export promotion is difficult to substantiate.   Simple measures of cost-benefit can be derived from program expenditures and company exports but this begs the important question regarding the real impact of support and assistance to companies.   Many factors potentially explain a company's export sales, of which use of a specific promotion program is but one.   Herein lies the difficulty in establishing the precise level of impact of such programs, and the resulting effectiveness of public expenditures.   Despite this problem, better evaluation procedures are emerging, based on a more realistic understanding of the role played by export promotion programs in companies' overall international marketing activities, as well as more sophisticated measurement.   Later chapters dealing with the evaluation issue reflect some of these improved practices.

REFERENCES

Brooks, M.R. and P.J. Rosson (1982).   "A Study of the Export Behavior of Small and Medium-Sized Manufacturing Firms in Three Canadian Provinces," in M.R. Czinkota and G. Tesar, Eds., *Export Management: An International Context*, Praeger Publishers, New York, pp. 39-54.

Cavusgil, S. Tamer (1984).   "Differences Among Exporting Firms Based on Their Degree of Internationalization." *Journal of Business Research*, Vol. 12, No. 2, pp. 195-208.

Czinkota, Michael R. (1982). *Export Development Strategies*, Praeger Publishers, New York.

Economist (1989a). "Japan and the Third World," June 17, pp. 25-28.

_____ (1989b). "A Survey of the Yen Block: Together under the Sun," July 15, pp. 5-20.

_____ (1989c). "A Survey of the Third World: Poor Man's Burden," September 23, pp. 25-39.

_____ (1990). "GATT Brief – The American Connection," April 21, pp. 85-6.

Keesing, Donald B. and Sanjaya Lall (1988). "Marketing Manufactured Exports from Developing Countries: Information Links, Buyers' Orders and Institutional Support," paper presented at UNU/WIDER Conference on 'New Trade Theories and Industrialization in Developing Countries,' Helsinki, August.

Root, Franklin R. (1971). "The Elements of Export Promotion," *International Trade Forum*, July-September, pp. 118-21.

Seringhaus, F.H. Rolf (1986). "The Impact of Government Export Marketing Assistance," *International Marketing Review*, Vol. 3, No. 2, pp. 55-66.

_____ (1987). "Export Promotion: The Role and Impact of Government Services," *Irish Marketing Review*, Vol. 2, pp. 106-116.

_____ (1989). "Export Promotion Organizations as International Marketing Tool in Developing Countries," in George J. Avlonitis, Nikolaos K. Papavasiliou and Athanasios G. Kouremenos, Eds., *Marketing Thought and Practice in the 1990s*, Vol. 1, Proceedings of the European Marketing Academy, Athens, pp. 215-229.

_____ (1990). "Program Impact Evaluation: Application to Export Promotion", *Evaluation and Program Planning*, Vol. 13, No. 3, in press.

Seringhaus, F.H. Rolf and Philip J. Rosson (1990). *Government Export Promotion: A Global Perspective*, Routledge, London.

Sheth, Jagdish N. and Hanns-Martin Schoenfeld (1980). "How to Succeed in Export Marketing: Some Guidelines", in Jagdish N. Sheth and Hanns-Martin Schoenfeld, Eds., *Export Marketing: Lessons from Europe*, Bureau of Economic and Business Research, University of Illinois, Champaign, Ill., pp. 185-202.

World Bank (1987). *World Development Report*, New York, Oxford University Press.

CHAPTER TWO

Challenge and Response: The Rise of State Export Development Policies in the U.S.A.

James D. McNiven*

SUMMARY

The relative success of foreign export penetration in the U.S. and the apparent inability of American exporters to succeed abroad has become a major concern to policy makers. Trade deficits and job losses have prompted considerable attention at the state level to export development through the creation of marketing and economic incentives. This chapter reviews the circumstances and the evolution of government trade initiatives and their likely consequences.

INTRODUCTION

Much of the American concern over foreign industrial policies has been tied up with its relative export performance. The ability of foreign exporters to penetrate the American market, coupled with the seeming inability of American exporters to penetrate foreign markets, has generated a great deal of concern and not a little myth-making and sabre-rattling.

Export performance has traditionally been seen as a proxy for national strength and competitiveness. Strong countries export and weak countries import. The decline in American trade receipts in the early 1970's was partially

---

*   Dalhousie University, Halifax

dismissed as a simple result of commodity price increases, especially in oil, that could be corrected through conservation, new energy technology and the recycling of petro-dollars from the rich, though underdeveloped, economies of the oil exporters. No one really attributed the movement of commodity prices to a changed order in the strength of nations.

This was not the case with a second shock that took place after 1979. Rising imports of manufactured products, especially automobiles and high technology consumer and other products were not the result of some world price anomalies, but were due to the increased competitiveness of other relatively developed countries. This constituted a more direct threat to the American perception of itself in the world. Many attempts have been made to explain this shift in world relationships and these are the subject of the first section of this paper.

However, the political world does not wait for academia to register its conclusions about the meaning and cause of events. By the recession of 1981-82, action was demanded on American exports and foreign imports. The responses of the federal and state governments differed considerably. This is the subject of the second part of this paper. The federal government, at least through 1986, opted for a largely passive approach to the problem, while the states began to seriously explore more active approaches, sometimes in imitation of their foreign competitors.

Export development does not include the taking of protectionist measures to allow domestic firms to maintain or increase domestic market share. The story of such measures after 1981 is interesting, but these are outside the scope of this chapter. Instead, emphasis is placed on the attempts governments to develop exports through both marketing and economic incentives. The first includes measures taken to overcome the psychological barriers facing firms as they attempt to deal with foreign markets. These include information services, training programs, and foreign missions, among other things. The second is related to the subsidization of exports and the financing of export sales.

It should be noted that state export development policy is but one facet of a larger movement at the state level to embrace a more active role in economic development. The emergence of active industrial policies at the state level is the subject of a larger research project, of which this chapter is only a part.

THE TRADE SHOCKS AND U.S. REACTION

The impact of foreign imports on the American economy came in two stages. First, in the late 1970's came the penetration of the American economy by significant volumes of foreign manufactures, especially in the automotive field. This was paralleled by market penetration in electronic consumer durables, such as television sets and stereo equipment, as well as increased sales in other durables, such as construction equipment and motorcycles. The effect of this penetration on the whole American market was relatively small, but it came in market areas that were quite sensitive to Americans (see for example the President's Commission 1985b). The United States had traditionally seen itself as the originator and major market for automobiles, so the rising market share of foreign imports, caused in part by their relative fuel efficiency, almost seemed an affront to national pride. What was worse was that Americans themselves acting as consumers, crested the demand for these imports.

The American sensitivity was compounded by the effect of internal shifts in domestic production practices. Not only were jobs being lost to foreign competition, but new investment was moving from Rust Belt locations into the south and west of the country, compounding the problem. As well, technological change in many industries meant plant closures and unemployment in heretofore large-scale and well-paying industries (Task Force 1984).

After 1983, the problem of foreign penetration of the American market shifted. Many factors, such as an overvalued dollar and the fruits of underinvestment in research and development during the previous decade, led to a decline in American exports and, by a normal process, to a huge trade deficit. This time, the problems were not so much ones of worker dislocation and affronts to national dignity as a growing concern that the foreign financing of the trade deficit and the federal fiscal deficit could lead to large-scale foreign ownership and/or an oppressive debt load.

To many, the problems of the post-1979 period and the post-1983 period were different manifestations of the same phenomenon. In both cases, what was perceived to be a free and open market in America was set upon by foreign governments engaged in a new form of mercantilism, an idea that had supposedly fallen into disfavour after the middle of the 19th century.

Now, it seemed neomercantilist foreign governments had developed webs of subsidies and policies designed, first, to penetrate important parts of the domestic American market and then, second, to prevent American exporters from entering their own markets with their presumably competitive goods (see Vogel 1985). "Fair trade", in this scenario, meant that all countries had to abandon policies which distorted markets, or America had to develop an industrial policy that could match those of its competitors. Success, in either case, could be measured by the narrowing of trade imbalances with individual countries.[1] As we shall see, the response of the Reagan Administration was to try to eliminate barriers and restrictions, while hoping that tax policy and deregulation would be enough to restore corporate competitiveness. The response of the states was to explore export development policies as a part of an overall activist industrial policy thrust.

EXPLANATIONS AND IDEAS

There are a number of approaches that try to explain these events and to offer some ideas to American policy-makers about their possible resolution. Three will be explored here: the notion of the trading state; the globalization of markets centering on the so-called "triad" of East Asia, North America and Western Europe; and the problem of national competitiveness.

The Rise of the Trading State, by Richard Rosecrance, offers us an approach to the export problem that is grounded in history (Rosecrance 1985). Rosecrance suggests that in the milieu of international relations, there have been two major impulses: the first toward the accumulation of territory that results in a huge mass market and source of materials; the second, the accumulation of trading policies, intelligence and strategy that enables smaller nations to gain power in a more dynamic context. Czarist Russia and medieval Venice may be taken as polar examples.

The value of Rosecrance's ideas lies in the notion that international power may be pursued in more than one fashion. In effect, he suggests that the paralysis of the Cold War between two territorial powers, the U.S. and the U.S.S.R., has allowed others, such as Japan, the "four dragons" of East Asia and West Germany, to use trade policy and technical innovation to carve out significant niches for themselves in the world's power structures. Their ability

---

[1] Most versions of proposed U.S. trade legislation between 1986 and 1988 contained micro-trade provisions of this nature, as well as interesting explicit and implicit definitions of "fair trade".

to do so has led the world into a new time of turbulence. By forcing the pace in technological innovation and marketing, they have changed the economic "game". Nevertheless, if we apply the lessons of Edward Luttwak's recent book on strategy to the pseudo-warfare of competing industrial and export initiatives, we can expect that the stunning success of the trading state approach will soon be countered by its victims (Luttwack 1987).[2] Commentators, such as Lester Thurow, have offered their solutions, many of which are imitative of what they think the Japanese are doing (see Thurow 1980, Obey & Sarbanes 1986, Cohen & Zysman 1987). Even so, there is no doubt that the rapid shift to a technologically-intensive economy in much of the developed world has contributed significantly to both the erosion of traditional Communist economic methods as well as to the reformulation of the American economy in the 1980's.

A second approach to the export problem is suggested by *Triad Power*, a book by McKinsey associate Kenichi Ohmae (1985). The triad consists of the three major economic powers of Japan, the United States and the European Community, along with their associated states on each continent. Ohmae's thesis is that the triad's major markets are within itself, and that this bloc is not only economically dominant, but is creating a truly global economy. The industries of each power are beginning to penetrate the others' markets, products are becoming standardized, financial flows are global and inflation rates and other monetary standards are moving towards harmonization.

The problems afflicting America, from this viewpoint, are ones of adaptation to this international economy. Where American firms have been accustomed to keeping their domestic economy to themselves while penetrating others, that can no longer be the case. All penetrate all. As this process goes on, the turbulence in each part of the triad will rise and fall as adjustments are resisted and then accepted. The concerns raised in books like Susan and Murray Tolchin's on foreign ownership in America should, in the triad view of the world' be seen as normal concerns about adjusting to the integration process (Tolchin 1988).

After the 1988 Congressional elections, the notion of an American industrial policy, which had seemed to be put to rest by Reagan's 1984 victory, was resurrected under the guise of "competitiveness" (New York Times 1987). National competitiveness is derived from traditional notions of comparative

---

2 Luttwak's concerns are the paradoxes and logic in war strategy, but his ideas are applicable to all competitive organizations.

advantage. By allowing firms located in foreign countries to gain positions of lowest cost producer, or best product designer or best marketer, America is viewed as dissipating the strength it enjoyed after World War II. By focusing on policies designed to improve competitiveness of American firms in the international marketplace, this process can be reversed. Competitiveness therefore leads to the achievement of national security goals as well as to a higher standard of living.

Two studies exemplify the competitiveness literature. In 1983, President Reagan appointed The President's Commission on Industrial Competitiveness, which reported in January 1985. In its view:

> Today, imports and exports represent twice as large a portion of our gross national product (GNP) as they did just two decades ago. Almost one-fifth of our industrial production is exported, and fully 70 percent of the goods we produce compete with merchandise from abroad. Quite simply, no longer is there a truly domestic US economy (The President's Commission 1985a, p. 9).

and:

> Competitiveness is the degree to which a nation can, under free and fair market conditions, produce goods and services that meet the test of international markets while simultaneously maintaining or expanding the real incomes of its citizens (The President's Commission 1985a, p. 6).

The Commission made four broad recommendations that incorporated many more specific ones. The four were:
  (1) create, apply and protect technology;
  (2) reduce the cost of capital to American industry;
  (3) develop a more skilled, flexible and motivated workforce; and
  (4) make trade a national priority.
(The President's Commission 1985a, p. 2).

These recommendations focused on problems of technology and productivity, though the comments and definitions above also implied a concern that American trading partners might not be allowing free and fair markets, thus inhibiting whatever effects a competitiveness strategy might have. Bruce Scott and George C. Lodge, in their 1985 book, *US Competitiveness in the World Economy*, note:

> The significance of our traditional national advantages is thus greatly eroded and our competitive position depends increasingly on *man-made* advantages. Competitiveness is more and more a matter of strategies, and less and less a product of *natural* endowments...Our government has not been a passive spectator or neutral arbiter of market forces: instead it has steadily steered incentives away from work, saving, investment toward leisure, borrowing and consumption (Scott & Lodge 1985, p. 8).

To Rosecrance, the American trade problem is one of responding to an historical challenge between types of states. To Ohmae, the problem is one of adjustment to the forces of globalization. To the competitiveness advocates, the problem is one of redirecting national energies toward productivity and technology and arresting relative decline.

INDUSTRIAL POLICY AND TRADE

If comparative advantage today has been largely uncoupled from natural advantages and relies on policies and strategies for its elements at any given period of time, then it is to industrial policy literature that we must now turn.

The literature is too vast to really discuss in this chapter. What is important to note is that industrial policy tends to focus on a narrower range of behaviour than does the material presented in the previous section. Industrial policy is "micro". It implies the manipulation of sections of the economy, or specific elements, such as labour costs or capital costs. In the aggregate, these manipulations should add a degree of competitiveness to what existed in the first place. Some writers on the subject have tended to see industrial policy as a "third leg" of government economic policy, along with fiscal and monetary policy. This is probably too ambitious (Johnson 1984).

From an industrial policy point of view, there are at least four dimensions to the American trade problem. These are:
1. the selectivity of the import penetration problem;
2. the technology/development problem;

3. the problem of management failure;
4. the shift from national to global products.

The import penetration problem is not a general one. Instead, the impact of imports has largely been felt in sectors of the economy that are seen as traditional American strengths. These are concentrated around consumer durables such as automobiles and electronics. and intermediate goods and equipment, such as steel and construction machinery. Even if the problem of the trade deficit had not arisen, the need to maintain such industries in order to maintain national security would have resulted in an outcry (Hartland-Thunberg & Crawford 1982).

Thus, the selectivity of import penetration merges concerns about national security, in terms of the ability to produce needed goods, with industrial policy ideas. Even if imports would improve the economic welfare of Americans, they would lose, or appear to lose, the ability to produce many goods if a crisis were to arise (Wall Street Journal 1986).[3] The fact that this scenario could only occur in a World War I or II context is beside the point.

The second problem relates to the nature of the American economy in the future. Without a production system that is diverse, the potential avenues to express American creativity and technological superiority would be cut off. The literature on industrial policy is replete with assumptions that the American genius lies in innovation (Morici 1984).[4] Foreign producers, it is further assumed, have simply taken American innovations and turned them into mass products. Unless the country's manufacturers become more competitive, American technologists will simply find themselves producing ideas for foreign firms, or not producing ideas at all. Industrial policy must try to ensure that technology devised by Americans is effectively exploited by them as well, before foreign imitators can take the advantage.

A third approach taken by the proponents of an activist industrial policy is that of management failure (Magaziner & Reich 1983, Cohen & Zysman 1987). American managers have failed to adapt to changing conditions. They have focused on short-run profit pictures and on domestic competition that behaves in ways familiar to all American management. Meanwhile, foreign producers have concentrated on long-term objectives, global market share and on

---

[3] The tenor of these concerns can be easily seen in both a concise and complex fashion.
[4] Unlike many other, more inflammatory statements on this subject, Morici uses considerable data to make his point.

new ways of marketing and designing goods. American managers have lost domestic and global markets because they have been unwilling to concentrate on production, preferring instead to spend valuable resources and time on financial manipulation. As well, the American policy concern for maintaining a high degree of domestic competition has neglected the shift to global competition. The difficulty of meeting the global challenge is compounded by antitrust provisions that distract American producers into sometimes pointless domestic competitive stances.[5]

The fourth approach has been to recognize the emergence of a global market dominated by global products. Traditionally, American multinationals have been prone to see the world market as having distinct national tastes, so national plants and designs were featured (Sloan 1963). Emphasis was placed on overall financial and policy control from head office while leaving much of the marketing and design functions to local initiative. The genius of Japanese industry in the 1970's and 1980's was to capitalize on the convergence of market tastes in all the developed countries by producing consumer goods to a single standard (Ohmae 1985). As American producers adapted, they also began to move new production facilities offshore to take advantage of lower labour costs and other savings.

Producing global goods also helped to speed the "hollowing out" process of American firms. Production was detached from finance and marketing, so that a General Electric product, for instance, could be assembled in Singapore from parts produced in a dozen other countries and then marketed in the United States by an American company. The company might be doing very well out of the sales of the product, but manufacturing jobs in America would be reduced and the trade deficit aggravated by the global activity of this "hollow corporation" (Business Week 1986).

THE GLOBAL ECONOMY AND THE NATION-STATE

For over 40 years, the potential conflicts between the multinational corporation and the nation-state have been discussed by business analysts and

---

[5] The President's Commission on Industrial Competitiveness identified merger provisions and research and development funding as two areas where antitrust provisions hurt American competitiveness. See vol. II, pp. 85, 183.

political scientists. Recently, this potential has become heightened and the corporations appear to have gained the advantage, though possibly only temporarily.

The coupling of international finance to modern communications and computational technology has allowed global production to proliferate. At the same time, communication technology has helped to forge the urban areas of the triad into virtually one large market. French historian Fernand Braudel noted that it took over a century after 1500 for tobacco usage to spread from the Caribbean around the world (Braudel 1981). Today, the commercial introduction of a product can be made simultaneously in all the major world markets.

These developments have called into question the utility of national policy variations. Of what use is it to protect Russian central planning initiatives and structures when technological innovations can be introduced by the rest of the world in an unpredictable fashion with unpredictable timing with unpredictable results? Of what use are American policy measures to protect the diversity of the national production structure when both American producers and consumers elect to make and buy from abroad? The pace appears to be too fast for the world's slow-moving bureaucracies to react effectively. Yet, no one country can unilaterally move to slow down these processes because no one is large enough, or powerful enough, to effectively do so. As change continues in its neighbours, friends and enemies, it would increasingly see its own power eroded.

If it is not possible to control the pace or the vector of change that corporate competition has introduced into the global economy, the only alternative for the nation-state is to adapt to the new conditions and to force the pace so as to maintain or enhance its relative power. In the United States, this has been tried in two different ways at two different levels of government in the 1980's. Under the Reagan Administration, the federal government has tried to set basic conditions by lowering inflation and tax rates and then staying out of the way of American companies as they restructure to meet the challenges before them. This approach has had mixed success and failure. Some companies have prospered mightily, though there is a large trade deficit. The state governments have tried to force change in a more activist mode. They have generally moved to en-courage more local corporate development, especially in technologically-intensive industries, and have become quite active in the area of export development policy. Again, the record is mixed. Often the efforts are too new to evaluate, and it is clear that the resources expended, while growing, are still small and their effectiveness remains in doubt. These two approaches to export development are the subject of the next section.

THE EVOLUTION OF GOVERNMENT TRADE INITIATIVES

The Federal Experience

> The United States is the only nation in which it is necessary to justify exports; in every other country the importance of exports is self-evident and generally accepted...Not only are U.S. exports not accorded priority in domestic or foreign policy, they are actually regarded as subordinate to domestic production in importance (Hartland-Thunberg & Crawford 1982, p. 85).

This statement from a 1982 study of government support for exports generally sums up federal policy in this area. Over the past 25 years, only a few instances can be identified where the federal government took any active interest in the promotion of exports. These generally occurred as a result of growing trade deficits: export development was seen as a way of balancing accounts that were in difficulty because of an overvalued dollar. Even so, export development was seen as secondary to the main solution, which was to devalue the dollar and wait.

Besides devaluation, a popular device for export financing and promotion is the use of foreign aid credits. Yet the flows of foreign aid from the United States have consistently been tied to security needs rather than to the development of opportunities for exports (Shaw 1986, Hartland-Thurberg & Crawford 1982). It could be argued, with justice, that foreign aid should not be delivered with either of these motives in mind, but, in reality, this is rarely the case.

Federal financing and promotion of exports has, since 1934, been the responsibility of the Export-Import Bank (Eximbank). Since its inception, it has faced a number of situations where its abolition was proposed or where its promotional mandate was actually mixed with one of export restraint. For instance, in 1965, the Eximbank lent $24 million to a Moroccan potash agency to buy American equipment. This was later protested by Florida potash producers and a Senator from Florida in 1968 introduced a motion to require the

bank to prove that any and every loan it made would not adversely affect the
domestic economy in some way. The Bank's chairman protested that the Bank
would be "in the position of denying its facilities to one class of taxpayers,
namely, exporters of equipment, suppliers, or services in order to confer on
another class of taxpayers a proposed benefit, which, in most cases would be
wholly illusory" (Hillman 1982).

In 1971, faced with a deterioration in trade accounts, Congress acted to
encourage the Bank to adjust its credits and rates to meet foreign competition
(Hillman 1982). By 1976, the battle between public export financing agencies
was so severe that an international agreement was made to restrict the size and
scope of financing concessions, an agreement that is still in force today
(Hartland-Thunberg & Crawford 1982). Once again, in 1981-82, the Bank came
under fire as an agency that was distorting trade and its abolition was again
proposed. In 1983, the Bank was required to set aside a small proportion of its
lending authority for small businesses. It was also required to provide special
promotion programs for small business exporters. There is no question that
exporting is skewed towards large businesses, with only about 1000 exporters
providing seventy percent of American exports in 1978, yet this was hardly an
appropriate response to the deteriorating trade situation after 1982 (Office of the
President 1984).

The Year 1971 also saw the creation of the Domestic International
Sales Corporation (DISC) device. DISC was a method whereby American
companies could legally incorporate an entity that would sell the parent's
products abroad, but whose income would be protected from taxation (Hartland-
Thunberg & Crawford 1982). The DISC concept was a variation on income tax
protection accorded to companies producing in Puerto Rico for both export and
American consumption. The effect of a DISC was to lower the cost of exports
relative to domestic costs. Given the small number of export- intensive firms in
the United States, it is doubtful whether the DISC idea ever played as significant
a role as its proponents and potential competitors expected. Regulatory changes
and changes to harmonize DISC with GATT regulations made even potential
benefits very problematical.

In the end, the Foreign Sales Corporation Act of 1984 replaced the
DISC with a new method providing for tax relief for Foreign Sales Corporations
(FSC). An FSC must be incorporated in a country that shares tax information
with the United States and most of its affairs must be conducted outside of the
country. In return, the FSC gained tax relief on profits from its export sales on

behalf of its parent corporation. As well, an accumulated $13 billion of deferred taxes owed by DISCs were forgiven (Giffing 1984).

The Reagan Administration did not significantly respond to the trade situation of the 1980's except through its tax changes and currency exchange rate movements. The tax reform of 1981 was supposed to help make manufacturers more competitive and thereby encourage exports. The recession of 1981-82 and the strengthening domestic economy after that simply resulted in increased domestic demand and supply. A rising dollar on the exchange markets made it uneconomical to export and encouraged imports as well. A few moves were made to improve American competitiveness, but most activity on the trade front has focused on Congressional attempts to restrict imports, rather than to promote exports.

Two small efforts, though, are worthy of mention. In 1982, the President signed the Export Trading Company Act into being (Office of the President 1984). Export trading companies (ETC) have been in existence in Japan and Western Europe for many years. Some Japanese ETCs are major corporations in their own right. Mitsui, a Japanese ETC, was the sixth largest exporter of US goods in 1980. An ETC buys products for sale in other companies. Until the 1982 Act, joint exporting initiatives were subject to antitrust sanctions. The Act also allowed banks to take an interest in ETCs. By all accounts, the growth in size and numbers of American ETCs has been small, but the experiment became a precedent of sorts for a second initiative.

In 1984, the President signed the National Cooperative Research Act, which lowered the antitrust penalties for companies engaged in cooperative research projects (New York Times 1988). Cooperative research at the pre-competitive level in Europe and Japan was seen as having an effect on American technological leadership. Since nearly half (by value) of all American exports in 1984 were technology-intensive, both Congress and the President felt that these exports could only be increased if corporate research efforts were strengthened (Hatter 1985, Joint Economic Committee 1986). Within a year, 38 consortia had registered under the provisions of the Act (Wall Street Journal 1985).

Finally, it should be mentioned that the export promotion responsibilities of the Eximbank are now shared with other federal departments, most notably with the Department of Commerce. Even so, the federal effort is still relatively small, consisting of 194 offices at home and abroad (Hoffman 1988).

The State Experience

Before the 1980's, the states did very little to encourage exports. A few states maintained foreign offices primarily to encourage foreign investment, and these offices assisted with trade promotion as well. It was only as the state governments struggled through the recession of 1981-82 that they realized they were expected by their voters to use every means to increase employment. One response was to begin to deploy a wide range of export development programs. According to a report from the National Governors' Association (1986), the state role expanded and became "increasingly activist". An NGA survey noted two key factors which have made export development a priority for state governments:

1. The 1981-82 recession: 27 states responded that the recession was the key factor - it shook them up, and they realized they were not "recession-proof";

2. The post-recession economy: a withdrawal of federal financial support and pressure from declining industries produced more emphasis on promoting existing business through exports as opposed to inward investment promotion.

(National Governors Association 1986, p. 7)

Two examples of the beginnings of state activity are Wisconsin and California. In 1981, the State of Wisconsin formulated an export policy containing six initiatives. These included the creation of an advisory committee on international trade, the declaration of a "Wisconsin Export Week", the establishment of an honorary commercial attache program made up of foreign nationals with ties to Wisconsin, a program of annual visits by the Governor to small exporting companies to highlight their efforts, increased support for state trade missions and a state-supported export finance facility (Tesar & Tarleton 1983).

In California, a statute that became effective in January 1983 created the California State World Trade Commission (WTC). The WTC took over the function of the trade office in the state bureaucracy and gave it new profile by including as directors the Governor, the Lieutenant Governor and the Secretary of State. The WTC is a non-profit corporation with most of its directors coming from the private sector. It has four program areas: trade promotion, information and assistance, export finance, and trade policy advocacy (California Economic Development 1986).

In addition to the WTC, three bills were introduced in the California Legislature in 1983 to provide for export financing. One was passed and signed into law in September 1984 (Griffing 1984). As with all export financing programs, California's plan arose from the observation that, in part, small and medium-sized businesses were not exporting because they lacked financial support, and banks were usually uninterested in the smaller firms (Wall Street Journal 1987a). The Legislature also called for the creation of overseas offices and asked the federal government to compile better trade statistics.

The size of state efforts appears to vary considerably. It would seem that all 50 states have some activity, although many have very small programs. Their export development offices employ from one to forty professionals, employment being directly related to the extensiveness of the state's effort (NASDA 1984). Also, the focus of their programs varies. Some states choose to operate in conjunction with existing federal programs, while others are more independent. Nineteen states in 1984 received some type of federal funding for trade promotion, including those states with no budget of their own for export promotion. The National Association of State Development Agencies (NASDA) reported that almost $21 million was spent by 46 states in FY 1984 to encourage foreign investment in the US, some of which was dedicated to export promotion (NASDA 1984). According to NASDA, state investment promotion and export promotion budgets ranged from $7,000 (New Hampshire) to $2,500,000 (Illinois, New York). Most states had a budget of some sort, many over $150,000. Twenty-four states had some sort of travel budget, ranging from $6,400 (Montana) to $171,000 (Illinois). Fifteen states had an advertising budget, with a range of $2,000 (North Dakota) to $500,000 (New York). Advertising includes publications (NASDA 1984).

In discussing state initiatives, Dan Pilcher notes that more than 300 export promotion activities, such as trade fairs and shows, were sponsored by 34 states between 1980 and 1985 (Pilcher 1985). In 1987 alone, 47 states sponsored or organized trade missions (Hoffman 1988). By 1987, Forbes noted that "11 states are now spending more than $1 million per year to stimulate exports and the average budget has grown 66% since 1984 to $980,175" (Forbes 1987). According to NASDA, some 27 states ran 52 overseas trade and investment offices in 10 countries in 1984 (NASDA 1984). By 1987, the number had grown to over 80 offices in 40 countries (Hoffman 1988).

Results of this effort are not well known. According to the Wall Street Journal in 1984, "Taken as a whole, ... [state] government trade agencies seem

more a jumble of spare parts than a well-oiled machine" (Wall Street Journal
1984, p. 80). The article comments that programs are "falling flat" because they
are poorly organized. Many of the services offered involve too much paperwork
or make use of outdated information. Some states may even offer too many
program options. This lack of organization is not just restricted to the states.
In a 1987 article, the Wall Street Journal noted that, for the first time, foreign
trade export figures for individual states were available (Wall Street Journal
1987b). Before June of that year, neither the Federal Government nor individual
states had any idea how they were doing as separate units. The figures show the
top 10 exporters to be California, Texas, Michigan, New York, Louisiana,
Washington, Florida. Massachusetts, Illinois and Ohio.

       Program innovations by 50 states began chaotically. One presumes
that these programs have coalesced into a smaller number of more effective
activities and that experience has result in less paperwork and faster response
times.

EXPORT PROMOTION

       Export promotion programs are quite diverse, ranging from financing
assistance for trade missions and trade fair space to university intern programs.
In the end, the aim of all these programs is to lower the psychological and
financial costs to the exporter that come with the attempt to understand and
penetrate a foreign market. By and large, state programs are focused on the small
to medium-sized manufacturer or agricultural producer. The following section
identifies a dozen different programs and techniques commonly used by states to
assist exporters.

Seminars, Workshops and Conferences

       These activities are either organized by state officials or business
groups. They may be run in conjunction with a local federal office (SBA 1984).
The NASDA State Export Program Database for 1984 reports that 42 states had
held seminars or conferences with up to 86 per year being held in Florida and 50
per year in New York, Ohio and Oklahoma (NASDA 1984). Most often,
seminars are co-sponsored by businesses, the state and the federal government,
although NASDA notes that many states have "multiple conferences, and

sponsor a percentage of them on their own". The conferences and seminars focus on the "how to's" of exporting, as well as examining specific issues/functions and particular foreign markets.

Counselling and Advice

In 1984, 39 of the 50 states claimed they provided an on-site advisory service to businesses at the business location (NASDA 1984). This is a one-to-one approach, where counselling and marketing advice is provided on an individual business basis. Sometimes, this assistance is offered through unsolicited calls to businesses. where the state initiates the offer, either at random or as a focused service for targeted businesses. Experienced local exporters are often used in the counselling sessions.

Trade Missions

These "missions" to foreign markets give local business persons a chance to meet potential importers/buyers and sales representatives in their own countries. They are led, typically, by state officials, up to and including Governors.

Trade Fairs

Industrial trade fairs are sponsored at sites all around the world. Most focus on one or more industrial sectors. State officials may represent exporters at these fairs, or the business persons themselves may attend with financial support from the state. As most are held overseas, state financial support is frequently needed.

Trade Lead Referral Service

This service provides current and potential exporters with information abut foreign importers expressing interest in certain products. These leads are particularly important to small and medium-sized businesses interested in exporting but who are new or inexperienced and do not yet have "connections". The leads are represented in several forms. They may be sent in a newsletter, or may be part of a computerized service, such as the NETWORK service provided by the World Trade Centres affiliated around the globe. Many states use the federal International Trade Administration's "Trade Opportunities Program (TOP)", which is a computerized trade deal matching service. The potential exporter is matched with the services available to him/her (NASDA 1984).

State-University Cooperation

Universities in some states offer assistance as part of the state's export promotion activities. Schools may do market research, business counselling, or provide language assistance to small and medium-sized firms looking to export. Some schools actually have started special export development programs designed to introduce and enhance export "know-how". In using university resources to help their export programs, 21 states, such as New York and South Carolina, offer intern programs (NASDA 1984). These intern programs involve assigning university students to businesses to help prepare market studies.

Exporter Awards

These are state-sponsored, achievement-oriented awards. States such as New York, Ohio and Florida provide such awards help raise the profile of successful exporters and to encourage others to imitate the recipients.

Honorary Attaches

These are unpaid state representatives living abroad. Their job is to assist in the promotion of the state's export efforts. Wisconsin, for example, uses "foreign nationals who have graduated from Wisconsin universities" and appoints them as "honorary commercial attaches". Their primary job is to find export trade leads for state exporters (NASDA 1984, Pilcher 1985).

Ambassador program

This is similar to the above except that it makes use of local business persons who regularly travel overseas regularly to assist in export promotion. Thirteen states, according to NASDA, were using this idea in 1984 (NASDA

1984). It is also used in other jurisdictions, such as the state of New South Wales, Australia.

Language Banks

A type of "volunteer translation service" may be offered through local residents. The resident is "matched" with a foreign-speaking visitor who arrives in the state in order to encourage better communication and, hopefully, export sales.

Publications

As part of their export promotion activities, some states publish newsletters and magazines which are partially or entirely devoted to international trade. The frequency of these publications varies from state to state. New York, for instance, publishes a number of informative papers, including an export service directory, exporter/importer directory, and a "how to" handbook on exporting (NASDA 1984).

Catalogue Presentations

Products are "advertised" in a catalogue, in sales brochures or on videos. These catalogues, brochures, and other "graphic aids" are distributed and shown around the world.

Export Trading Companies

In 1982, when Congress Passed the Export Trading Company Act, it instructed the Department of Commerce to assist states and municipalities to set up ETCs based on the successful Japanese models. By 1985, nine states were developing ETCs or had passed legislation allowing their creation. Antitrust laws were amended to allow competitors to work together in trading companies such as Virginia's VEXTRAC to pursue foreign sales (Pilcher 1985, Sylvester 1988).

EXPORT FINANCING

Export financing by state governments is designed as an addition or complement to federal financing, particularly that of the federal Eximbank. Export financing efforts in the states are directed towards assisting small and medium-sized businesses to enter the export market, or to increase their competitiveness abroad. The most common forms of state export financing are loan guarantees and a type of insurance for exporters in case an importer defaults on a transaction. Direct loans are infrequently used. The guarantees are designed to encourage banks to make loans to small and medium-sized exporters who would otherwise often have immense difficulty in acquiring such assistance. In some states, financing for working capital, for inventory, or for the firm's export development (i.e., money for trade show attendance) may also be provided. Where states offer export credit insurance, it is typically provided in cooperation with the Foreign Credit Insurance Association (FCIA) which works with the Eximbank. The Small Business Administration notes that these state financing programs have usually been supported through the sale of bonds (SBA 1984).

According to NASDA's 1984 survey, 12 states had some form of export financing legislation enacted; five states had proposed but not officially enacted some sort of authorizing legislation; two states were prohibited from inaugurating such a program by the state's constitution (Alabama, Florida); 10 states had neither proposed nor considered financing programs (e.g., Hawaii, New Hampshire); and 15 reported considering a program (NASDA 1984). As of 1987, 23 states had adopted such legislation (Sylvester 1988).

As an example of state export financing, Minnesota created the Minnesota Export Finance Authority (MEFA) in 1983.[6] The legislation mandated MEFA to "aid and facilitate the financing of exports by small and medium-sized businesses". The principal reason for MEFA's creation was the reluctance of large banks to get involved with financing small and medium-sized firms' exports because the profit margin is too small. Smaller banks are put off by the perceived risk factor as well as their lack of expertise in the international export financing market. Often, smaller companies do not have enough working capital to fill a product order for export, so MEFA helps out by providing working capital loan guarantees for up to 90% of the loan and interest. The Authority guarantees loans from $25,000 to $250,000 over a maximum 12-

---

[6] Taken from Minnesota promotional materials.

month period. Those eligible for assistance are businesses which have been refused by the banks but which meet MEFA criteria. The order for the goods must be confirmed by letter. A fee of 1-3% is charged, based on both the company's credit rating and the duration of the guarantee. This aid is provided on a first-come/first-served basis.

MEFA's export credit insurance umbrella policy is designed to protect exporters from the problem of non-payment by foreign importers "for commercial or political reasons". This type of insurance policy is found in other states as well. Manufacturing, service and trading firms are eligible, provided they had sales of $2 million or less over the past two fiscal years. Also, they cannot have been insured by the Foreign Credit Insurance Association in the past two years. The credit terms give 180 days over coverage from the arrival of the goods at the import point. Some products, such as agricultural or "consumer durables" get a 360-day term. Credit insurance can be used as collateral for a loan. There is a minimum premium of $100 which is non- refundable.

FOREIGN TRADE ZONES

"Free" or foreign trade zones are a special case in American export promotion. They have been used for decades by countries all over the world. A foreign trade zone (FTZ) is defined as an enclosed and policed area legally outside a country's customs territory. It is designed to promote exports by providing a duty-free area to store and re-work imported components, though this has not really been the case in American experience. American FTZs include facilities for loading, unloading, handling, storing, manipulating, manufacturing and exhibiting goods, as well as for re-shipping them by land, water or air.

The Foreign Trade Zone Act was enacted by the Roosevelt Administration in 1934 (Commonwealth of Puerto Rico 1985). The first FTZ was then opened in New York City (see Business Facilities 1987). Today there are 247 FTZs and special purpose sub-zones scattered across the United States and Puerto Rico (Wall Street Journal 1987c). One hundred and eighteen FTZs are active and the rest consist of single plants or complexes that use the designation to reduce manufacturing costs (Business Facilities 1987). In 1975, only 27 FTZs were active (Wall Street Journal 1987c).

The volume of activity in FTZs has mushroomed along with the number of zones. In the financial year 1971, the zones had $213 million worth of activity growing to $975 million in 1978, $5.5 billion in 1981 and $39.2 billion in 1988 (compiled from Wall Street Journal 1987c, Commonwealth of Puerto Rico 1985). This growth in activity has spurred new interest in creating zones and some 50 applications were under consideration in 1989, with more applications awaiting processing.

Zones are run as public utilities by state and local governments and specially-chartered corporations, but their creation rests with a federal board (Commonwealth of Puerto Rico 1985). The board may approve any zone or sub-zone which it deems necessary to adequately serve "the convenience of commerce". The District Director of the Customs Service then acts as the representative of the board to ensure that the local FTZ is run in accordance with board regulations and customs laws. The salaries of the officers assigned to the FTZ are reimbursed by the local FTZ administration.

The American trade deficit has led to a controversy concerning the activities within FTZs (Wall Street Journal 1987c). Many manufacturers, especially auto assemblers, have taken advantage of the FTZ structure to import foreign parts for inclusion into assembly line processes for products then sent into the US market. Others produce finished goods from imported parts when the duty on the finished good is less than that on the parts or raw materials. For instance, the duty on pipe made from foreign steel is less than that on the steel itself, making the FTZ a logical place to fabricate imported steel into pipe for the US market.

Opponents to the present FTZ arrangements argue that the zones, far from encouraging exports, simply allow imports to come in through the back door. Proponents argue that it is better to get the additional fabricating and assembly jobs in the FTZ than to have the whole operation undertaken in foreign countries.

CONCLUSION

For decades American exports have been seen by Americans as a desirable, but not critical adjunct to production for the domestic market. Alfred P. Sloan, Jr., writing in the early 1960's in *My Years at General Motors*, exemplified this attitude when he noted in an offhand manner that the peak export year for the North American operations of the corporation was 1928

(Sloan 1963). Since that time, exports have trailed domestic production and overseas investment.

The combined effect of the oil shocks of the 1970's and the recession and trade deficits of the 1980's changed all that. America was faced with the penetration of European and Asian firms and products on a scale that resembled that which had occurred in reverse fashion in the 1940's and 1950's. The ability to export became a proxy for long-term competitiveness.

The Reaganite philosophy of letting the private sector settle its own affairs was acceptable as national policy but state legislatures and administrations found themselves pressured otherwise by voters. Their almost universal move to encourage exports and export-related jobs is one policy reaction to this pressure.

There is little doubt that exports help to create employment. Dan Pilcher quotes Eleanor Robert Lewis, an assistant general counsel at the US Department of Commerce, as saying that exports of $1 billion create 25,000 jobs, most in small/medium-sized firms (Pilcher 1985). This is equivalent to one job for every $40,000 in exports. The US Department of Commerce has released other, somewhat conflicting data; it says that for every $1 million in exports, 23 direct and 12 indirect jobs are generated. One billion dollars in exports would thus create 23,000 direct and 12,000 indirect jobs (South Carolina 1985).

The state programs are diverse and pragmatic. They appear to have borrowed or reinvented techniques and developed by sub-national jurisdictions in Canada, Australia, West Germany and elsewhere, but their experience is so limited so far that evaluation of their performance is not possible.

Inevitably, the desire to promote exports has led to a more active stance on the part of Governors with respect to foreign economic policy. In turn, this had led to a reaction that the United States is developing 50-plus foreign policies (Pilcher 1985, Hoffman 1988). There is no doubt that state activity is complicating American foreign policy, as seen in the pressures on the so-called unitary tax issue and on the control of technological exports. California has been especially contentious on both scores. Yet one cannot expect to see states enter the export development field without expressing opinions on national policy.

REFERENCES

Braudel, Fernand (1981). *The Structures of Everyday Life*, New York: Harper and Row.

Business Facilities (1987). March, pp. 51-59.

Business Week (1986). "The Hollow Corporation", 3 March.

California Economic Development Corporation, Pacific Rim Task Force (1986). California and the Pacific Rim Sacramento, Cal.: California Economic Development Corporation, Appendix IV, p. 2.

Cohen, Stephen S. and John Zysman (1987). *Manufacturing Matters*, New York: Basic Books.

Commonwealth of Puerto Rico, Economic Development Administration (1985). "Foreign Trade Zones and Federal Insular Bonded Warehouses", San Juan: EDA, p. 1.

Forbes (1987). "States Look Abroad", April 20, p. 13.

Griffing, John (1984). "The Other Deficit: A Review of International Trade in California and the U.S.", Sacramento, Cal.: Senate Office of Research, November.

Hartland-Thunberg, Penelope and Morris Crawford (1982). *Government Support for Exports*, Lexington, Mass.: Lexington Books.

Hatter, Victoria L. (1985). *U.S. High Technology Trade and Competitiveness*, Washington, D.C.: U.S. Department of Commerce, February, Staff Report, International Trade Administration.

Hillman, Jordan Jay (1982). *The Export-Import Bank at Work*, Westport, Connecticut: Quantum Books.

Hoffman, Ellen (1988). "Overseas Sales Pitch", *National Journal*, 16 January, p. 132.

Johnson, Chalmers Ed. (1984). *The Industrial Policy Debate*, San Francisco: IPC Press.

Joint Economic Committee, Congress of the United States (1986). *Technology and Trade: Indicators of U.S. Industrial Innovation*, Washington, D.C.: U.S. Government Printing Office, 14 July.

Luttwak, Edward N. (1987). *Strategy: The Logic of War and Peace*, Cambridge: Harvard University Press.

Magaziner, Ira C. and Robert B. Reich (1983). *Minding America's Business*, New York: Vintage Books.

Morici, Peter (1984). *The Global Competitive Struggle: Challenges to the United States and Canada,* Washington, D.C.: National Planning Association.

NASDA - National Association of State Development Agencies (1984). "NASDA State Export program Database", Washington, D.C.: NASDA, August, p. 1.

National Governors Association (1986). Committee on Economic Development and Technological Innovation, "Revitalizing State Economies", (prepared by Marianne Clarke) Washington, D.C." National Governors Association, February.

New York Times (1987). "The Clamour for Competitiveness", 14 January.

New York Times (1988). "A New Spirit of Cooperation", 14 January.

Obey, David and Paul Sarbanes, Eds. (1986). *The Changing American Economy,* New York: Basil Blackwell.

Ohmae, Kenichi (1985). *Triad of Power,* New York: Free Press.

Office of the President (1984). *The State of Small Business,* Washington, D.C.: U.S. Government Printing Office.

Pilcher, Dan (1985). "State Roles in Foreign Trade", *State Legislatures* 11(4) April, p. 19.

Rosecrance, Richard (1985). *The Rise of the Trading State,* New York: Basic Books.

SBA - U.S. Small Business Administration, Office of Advocacy (1984). *State Export Promotion Activities,* Washington, D.C.: USGPO, October, p. 2.

Scott, Bruce R. and George C. Lodge, Eds. (1985). *U.S. Competitiveness in the World Economy,* Boston: Harvard Business School Press.

Shaw, Harry J. (1986). "Coping with the Foreign-Aid Pinch", *Wall Street Journal,* 15 July.

Sloan, Alfred P. Jr. (1963). *My Years with General Motors,* Garden City, N.Y.: Doubleday.

South Carolina General Assembly. Legislative Audit Council (1985). *Review and Assessment of the State's Economic Development Activities,* Columbia, S.C.: General Assembly, p. 108.

Sylvester, Kathleen (1988). "Exporting Made Easy (Or How States and Cities are Selling Products Overseas)", *Governing* 1(4), January, pp. 41-42.

Task Force for a Long-Term Economic Strategy for Michigan (1984). *The Path to Prosperity,* Lansing: Cabinet Council on Jobs and Economic Development, November, Chapter 11.

Tesar, George and Jesse S. Tarleton (1983). "Stimulation of Manufacturing Firms to Export as Part of National Export Policy" in Michael R. Czinkota, Ed. *Export Promotion: The Public and Private Sector Interaction,* New York: Praeger, pp. 33-35.

The President's Commission on Industrial Competitiveness (1985a). *Global Competition: The New Reality,* vol. I, Washington: U.S. Government Printing Office.

Thurow, Lester (1980). *The Zero-Sum Society,* New York: Basic Books.

Tolchin, Martin and Susan (1988). *Buying into America,* New York: Times Books.

Vogel, Ezra (1985). *Comeback,* New York: Simon and Schuster.

Wall Street Journal (1984). "Exporting Chaos", May 20, p. 80.

Wall Street Journal (1985). "Quiet War Rages on Technology's Front Line", 24 December.

Wall Street Journal (1986). "U.S. Economy Grows Ever More Vulnerable to Foreign Influences", 27 October.

Wall Street Journal (1987a). "States Launch Efforts to Make Small Firms Better Exporters", 2 February.

Wall Street Journal (1987b). "State Foreign Trade Figures Finally Becoming Clearer", 7 July, p. 31.

Wall Street Journal (1987c). "Foreign Trade Zones and Many Companies Stir Up Criticism", September 30, p. 1.

CHAPTER THREE

Export Promotion Organizations in Developing Countries: Their Role, Scope and Function

F.H. Rolf Seringhaus[*]

SUMMARY

The export promotion activites of public organizations in the developing world assist nations to develop a broader-based supply system and draws them more fully into the worldwide trading system.

This chapter describes the institutional aspects of export promotion in developing countries. The function, services and programs of export promotion organizations are described and an overall framework is presented, based on a large-scale survey.

INTRODUCTION

Export promotion in developing countries is broadly regarded as an important part in their process of export development and greater participation in the global trading system. Two powerful reasons underly the increasing importance of export promotion of developing countries. First, imports and exports account for close to one-half of the gross domestic product in these countries. Second, they can ill afford to neglect the development and expansion of non-traditional exports in light of external constraints such as debt servicing and volatile commodity prices. The strengthening of international

---

[*]   Wilfrid Laurier University, Waterloo.

competitiveness is increasingly part of national development plans and is a policy objective aimed for through export promotion organizations.

This chapter provides an empirical analysis of export promotion organizations (EPO) in developing countries. First, the rationale of export promotion is presented, then countries' experience with export development is considered, this is followed by a discussion of the survey results on the scope, role and activities of EPOs. The last part of the chapter addresses implications of the findings.

THE RELATIONSHIP OF EXPORT DEVELOPMENT AND PROMOTION

Development and expansion of non-traditional exports has gained broad acceptance as both a guiding philosophy and a concept through which economic development and growth in the developing world can be realized. A key vehicle for helping to implement this concept is export promotion. Today, most developing nations have some formal organization or institutional structure concerned with the promotion of exports. As shown later in the chapter, while these export promotion organizations vary in scope, role and function, the essential point to note here is their very existence and the recognition that they hold the potential for a positive contribution to economic development. Expansion and diversification of exports benefits the balance of payments and foreign exchange earnings, and reduces dependence on traditional exports (such as raw materials). Exports can also lead to forward and backward linkages and with this to a more dynamic and competitive business community and thus increasingly important participation in global trade (Dymsza 1983). Such is the theory underlying what has broadly been labeled as export development. This has also been referred to as an outward orientation (World Bank 1987). The other side of this coin, namely an inward orientation mainly in the form of an import substitution policy emphasis often works counter to both export and economic development. Figure 3.1 contrasts the processes of these two orientations.

The debate over economic growth and exports has often been carried on from the economists' perspective using macro economic analysis as the main methodology. It will be useful to review some of these results to set the backdrop to the discussion of the role of export promotion. It has been suggested that an outward, export orientation provides advantages over an inward,

Figure 3.1: Disaster or success?

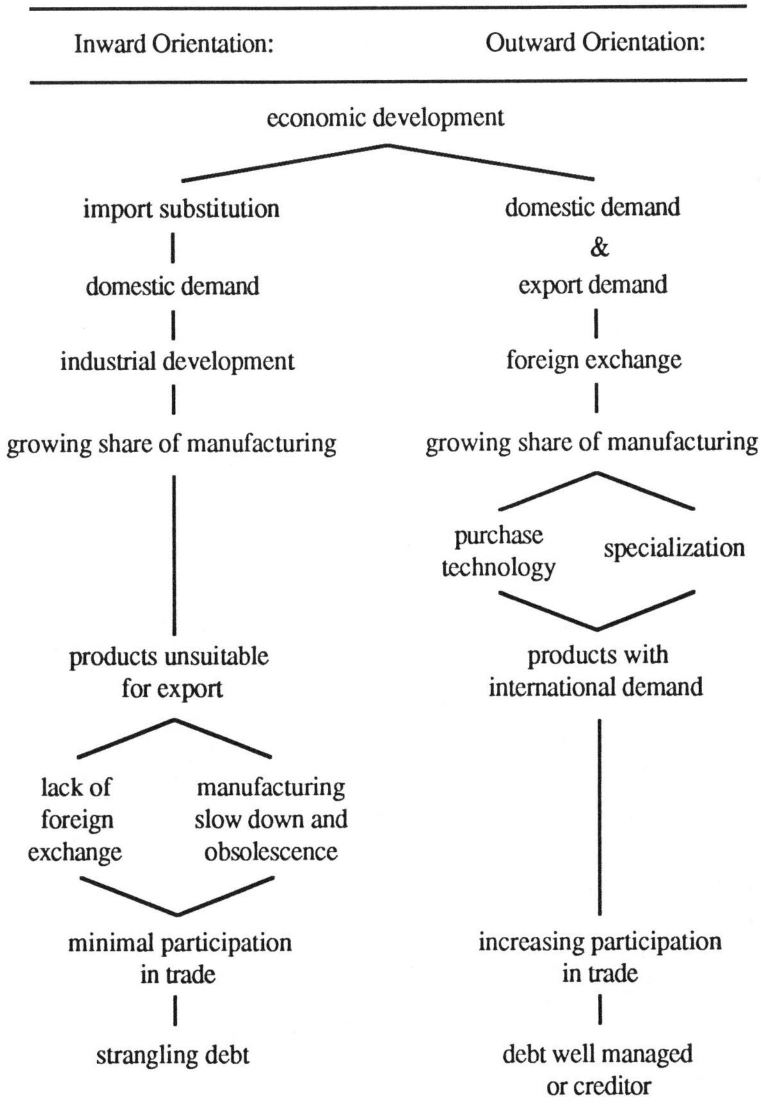

Inward Orientation:	Outward Orientation:

economic development

import substitution	domestic demand
	&
domestic demand	export demand
industrial development	foreign exchange
growing share of manufacturing	growing share of manufacturing

purchase technology   specialization

| products unsuitable for export | products with international demand |

lack of foreign exchange   manufacturing slow down and obsolescence

minimal participation in trade	increasing participation in trade
strangling debt	debt well managed or creditor

Source: Prepared by author.

import substitution orientation because resources are allocated according to comparative advantage, capacity utilization is increased, economies of scale are achieved, and improvements in technology are stimulated by competition in foreign markets (Balassa 1979). A recent study (Ram 1985) of 73 less developed countries concludes that export performance seems important for economic growth. The question whether export performance is responsive to governmental export promotion efforts then becomes of immediate interest. An analysis of 12 developing countries and their industry-specific exports and penetration of foreign markets suggests that export-oriented economic policy appears to be effective in stimulating the expansion and diversification of exports (Donges & Riedel 1977). Country-specific studies, such as those of Brazil (Hesse 1972) and Korea (Jung & Lee 1986) looked at particular policies and programs including export promotion activities and demonstrate the beneficial and positive influence they can have on exports. It becomes increasingly apparent, however, that exporting can best be understood in a behavioural context, that is: What know-how and expertise is needed to conduct international trade? Schwartz (1988) lends support to this view and argues that behavioural analysis is essential in understanding economic activities, such as exporting, involved in the development process. The available methodology of economics has little relevance at the level of practical application and models of entrepreneurial response and business behaviour require an understanding of perception, judgement and motivation at both the private sector (i.e. companies) and public sector (i.e. government officials in export promotion organizations). In a seminal study, de la Torre (1971) showed that understanding of the relationship between marketing characteristics and export behaviour are critically important. In particular, marketing knowledge and skills are necessary conditions for exploiting export markets. Marketing factors then are instrumental when considering export promotion policies for manufactures from developing countries. One can argue that the thrust of export promotion activities, then, should emphasize marketing and export management.

Awareness of the need to approach export development and promotion systematically has resulted in the development of frameworks and models of export promotion systems and strategies at the national as well as organizational levels (Root 1971, 1974, Dymsza 1983). These attempts seek to develop an integrated and generalised approach to export promotion that could serve as a blueprint for EPOs in developing countries. To date, such efforts have been largely normative because of the absence of empirical data, thus often ignoring the practical behavioural and political dimensions involved in interaction of business and government in the developing world. Consequently, well-intended recommendations are often not seen through to implementation since the model may not fit the particular situation of the country. Export promotion and export development are closely linked and several economic studies suggest the positive influence promotion programs can have. It is equally apparent that managerial behaviour plays a vital role in the process and that export promotion organization policies need to reflect this. Efforts to present a general integrated model of an effective EPO, however, have not been successful to date, mainly because of the diversity of conditions and circumstances in developing countries. Next, we will briefly review some countries' export development progress.

COUNTRIES' EXPERIENCE WITH EXPORT DEVELOPMENT

Developing countries as a group have not followed, nor been able to implement, such normative frameworks uniformly. To be sure, there are success stories where one-time or present-day developing countries have risen to impressive levels of economic development through export development and promotion. The most notable of these are Japan and the so-called four tigers in South-East Asia: Hong-Kong, Singapore, South Korea and Taiwan.

As a group, developing countries have experienced some noteworthy changes in their export situation. Since the 1960's they have expanded their share of global manufactured exports at the expense of developed market economies. Over the period from 1965 to 1985 growth in output and exports in developing countries was nearly double the rate of industrial countries, namely 7.4 percent vs. 3.8 percent for output and 12.2 percent vs. 6.8 percent for exports (World Bank 1987). As Figure 3.2 shows, developing countries have more than doubled their global market share of manufactured exports while their share of production grew only moderately over the two decades. Thus, it can be said that developing countries as a group have become more effective competitors in the international trade arena.

How have the developing countries achieved this impressive performance? Most of the organized export promotion efforts in developing countries began in the 1970's and 1980's. This was largely prompted by two main influences. First, the rapidly expanding global trade accompanied by broad trade liberalizing efforts under GATT negotiations, and second, by the establishment of the International Trade Centre (ITC) in 1964 to function as a catalyst for exporters in developing countries to increase their participation in global trade. Among the earliest developing countries to set up export promo-

Figure 3.2: Production and exports of manufactured products

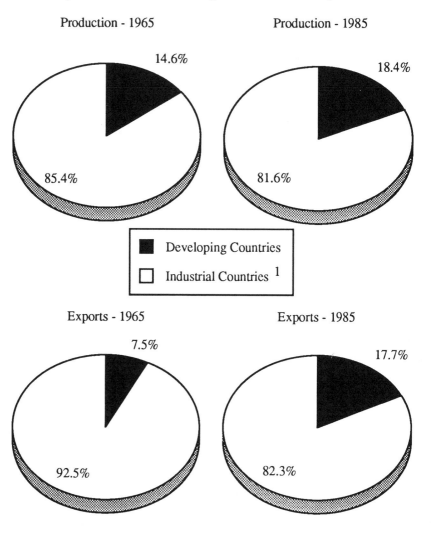

1 - Industrial market economies

Source: World Development Report 1987, New York,
          Oxford University Press, 1987, Table 3.1, p. 47.

tion efforts were Mexico (1937), Thailand (1952), Brazil (1953) and Korea
(1962). To deal with this question we turn now to a brief review of the structure
of developing countries' manufactured exports which shows that these countries,

as a group, have diversified from traditional labour-intensive products (such as textiles) or products based on natural resources to chemicals and engineered products (such as non-electrical machinery and transport equipment). Thus, while their manufactured exports have become more sophisticated, fears are being expressed that microelectronics and robotics may reduce the traditional labour-cost advantage which helped expand the developing countries' role in world trade of manufactured products (World Bank 1987). The increase in the volume and sophistication of manufactured exports suggest something about a country's industrial development. A country capable of increasing manufacturing value added will show such development through growth in real Gross National Product (GNP) and Gross Domestic Product (GDP). It is accepted that the basic forces of economic development – technological change, specialization and trade – all combine to increase output as well as the share of manufacturing in GDP (World Bank 1987).

The experience of many individual countries has been quite different. For example, a typical pattern shows an increasing share of manufacturing in GDP – thus indicating industrial development – only to be followed by a decrease in that share. A contributing factor to such a development is government, namely various public policies impacting the economic climate and trade conditions in a country. An example is the early adoption of import substitution policies in developing countries. The initial burst of industrial growth resulting from manufacturing to fill the domestic demand created by displaced imports (which directed resources away from export production) was not sustained. The main reason for this was that production often required imported intermediate and capital goods which could no longer be purchased due to a drastic reduction in, or absence of, foreign exchange-generating exports. Countries unable to make the transition from import substitution to export expansion to generate needed foreign exchange were unable to sustain economic development and growth. Those that did, such as the four tigers referred to earlier, have developed industrially to become an integral part of the global trading network (World Bank 1987).

There is some question of whether import substitution is necessary for the subsequent required expansion of exports (Balassa 1979). The evidence is not conclusive. For example, Hong Kong exports expanded rapidly without prior import substitution. Korea, Singapore and Taiwan, on the other hand, experienced a relatively short phase of import substitution involving certain goods (non-durable consumer goods and imports). Other technical goods were not involved in the import substitution process since this would adversely affect economies of scale and costs for the user industries and hence render their exports less competitive (Belassa 1979). Several Latin American countries (Argentina, Brazil, Colombia, Mexico) had more extensive import substitution phases before turning to export promotion efforts. Indeed, when the balance of payment situation began to constrain economic development, export promotion activities were undertaken (in the second half of 1960's) and intensified in the early 1970's.[1] It appears clear that a country's industrial and commercial situation needs to be carefully assessed in relation to global market opportunities and competitive requirements, and that normative prescriptions of an ideal development process may be inappropriate.

Now we turn to the characteristics of EPOs and discuss the survey results by reviewing first, their organization and scope, second, their functions and activities and third, interaction between EPOs and the business community.

CHARACTERISTICS OF EPOS

The analysis presented in this chapter is based on data collected through a mail survey undertaken by the International Trade Centre of UNCTAD/GATT[2] (ITC 1986a, 1988).

The discussion is divided into three main parts. First, we focus on the organization and scope of EPOs. To appreciate the role EPOs play in their respective environment, it is important to understand the different organizational forms under which they exist, and the role they are permitted to play in export policy. Second, discussion of the functions and activities carried on by EPOs provides insight into the actual, practical side of their role in the export development process. Third, the interaction of EPOs and the business community is examined. This is a critically important aspect of the export promotion process because it suggests how the actual implementation of an EPO's mandate is carried out.

---

[1] A parallel development of creating additional production capacity became necessary, changing the focus from export promotion to export development.

[2] A mail survey using a semi-structured questionnaire was sent to all known export promotion organizations in developed and developing countries. The raw data was obtained from ITC, then coded and computerized. Some 70 valid responses from developing countries were used in this analysis.

Organization and Scope of EPOs

Organizational Form of EPOs: The legal status and position of an EPO within government suggests something about the importance accorded to export development and promotion.   Figure 3.3 summarizes the organizational forms found among EPOs. EPOs tied to government, and thus to the bureaucracy, as is the case with 39 percent of EPOs, are also constrained by it. While on one hand, government may find it easier to create such an organization within the purview of its budget, on the other hand the organization's autonomy is curtailed. Autonomous EPOs, the most popular form (51%), while often tethered to government, appear to offer the best arrangement to carry out the export promotion task. Few EPOs are either independent, semi-private, private or some other legal form.

Figure 3.3: Organizational form of export promotion organization

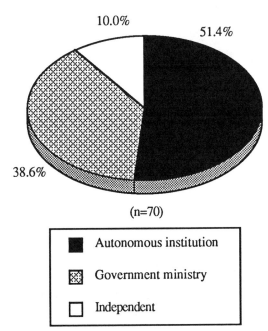

Source: Prepared by author.

As far as funding sources are concerned, many EPOs draw on several sources, as shown in Figure 3.4. National budgets are an important source for funding EPOs in 4 out of 5 cases, indeed for over 50 percent of institutions surveyed it is the only source. Some 10 percent of EPOs, however, are funded entirely from sources other than national budgets. In general, charges for services, contributions from business or the use of levies constitute relatively minor sources of funds.

Figure 3.4: Funding sources of EPOs

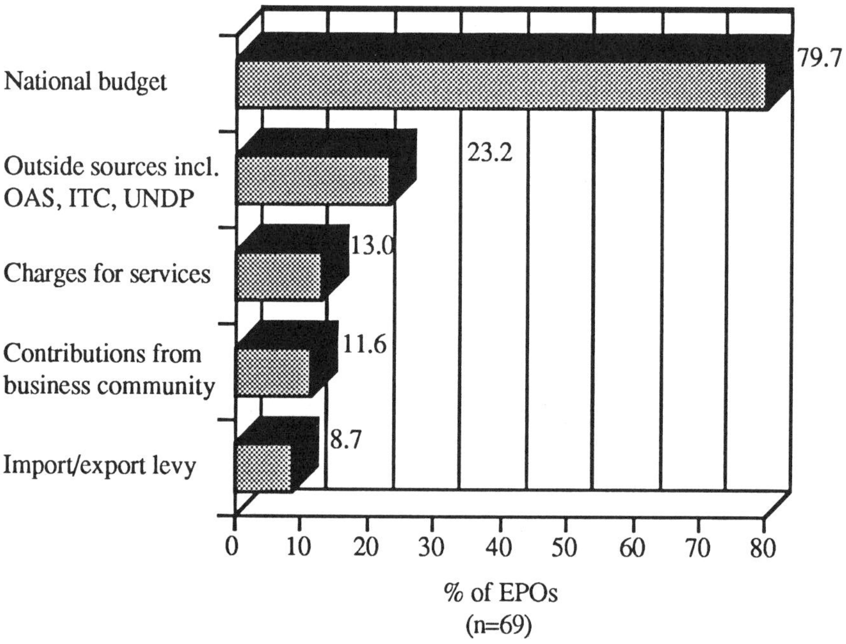

% of EPOs
(n=69)

Source: Prepared by author.

The governing body of an EPO serves as the interface between the organization and the business community. Boards are the most often used governing body (39.1%). Councils (15.9%) and Committees (8.7%) are not dissimilar from boards except that they may be involved more at the policy level rather than with strategic and operational guidance. Over one-third (36.6%) of the EPOs do not have a distinct governing body, which raises the issue of direction and orientation, both of which are of importance in the operation of an EPO. A board typically comprises seven public sector and six private sector representatives. The board's involvement in the management of an EPO varies from a general periodic review of the EPOs' plans to participation in day-to-day operations.

As noted earlier, EPOs are sometimes *de facto* a part of government and thus may not have a board at all. The problem with such a situation – which may also obtain in the case of a public-sector only board – is that the interface with the business community is wanting and the latter's interests are not represented. Indeed, as one observer notes, an independent EPO is preferable as otherwise export promotion programs result from bureaucratic values and rivalries and not from a concern with export problems in the business community (Root 1971). As we see later, the role of an EPO is that of a facilitator of export development and thus, to a large extent is dependent on the cooperation of the business community. Board membership from business, then, can make an important contribution to the proper functioning of an EPO.

While EPOs are instrumental to export development, their goal should not be maximizing incremental export sales because they cannot be held responsible to directly negotiate export sales on behalf of companies, nor are they accountable for creating export supply capacity in the business community (Root 1974). In view of the fact that EPOs are set up to address the issue of how government can overcome obstacles to exporting at both the national and company level (Root 1971), an appropriate goal for an EPO then is to stimulate and facilitate export activities.

No clear statement of EPO goals or objective is explicitly subscribed to by the organizations covered in this survey. EPOs, whether public or private, are deemed to have as their main purpose helping the business community to enter and expand export markets. Their services, therefore, should be primarily developed for, and devoted to, that objective. One attempt to define the key objective of an EPO states that it should "design and implement activities conducive to export promotion, the development of new export mechanisms for local products, and to secure an increased and continued presence of these products in foreign markets" (ITC 1986b).

One aspect of the scope EPOs have been granted is apparent from their product responsibilities. Some 57.1 percent report global responsibilities for all products, that is traditional and non-traditional products. About one-third (31.4%), however, are responsible only for non- traditional products, the remainder (11.4%) share the export promotion task for both product categories with other institutions. A brief explanation of the product characteristics is in order. Traditional products in developing countries generally account for the majority of their production as well as exports. Where countries have a narrow export base, or where there is no useful or logical distinction made between exportable products, EPOs tend to have broad responsibilities for all products. In situations where traditional products have historically provided a large share of exports, well functioning marketing boards or similar institutions generally continue to handle these exports. Thus, the EPO is given responsibility for the emerging but often small non-traditional product sector to help diversify export products (ITC 1986b).

The Role of EPOs in Export Policy: Export policy is a broad label under which numerous, diverse foreign trade-related matters may be combined. In terms of Root's (1978) definition of foreign economic policy, export promotion is defined as an instrument of commercial policy. The applicability of this definition for developing countries is questionable for two reasons. First, trade development and infrastructure development are often an integral part of a national development policy of a developing country. Second, export development is often the main thrust underlying general economic activity. Thus, export policy necessarily encompasses a range of facets which, in the developed world, are often separate and compartmentalized. The extent to which EPOs are involved in this broad process of export policy suggests what degree of importance the government of a developing country attaches to export development, that is the demand side as well as the export supply side. Table 3.1 shows the degree of EPO participation in export policy.

Nearly all EPOs play a role in policy recommendation for exporting and about one-third participate fully in the process to provide such input to government. Formulation of more clearly defined policies, however, points to export development strategy as the prime domain of EPOs' policy formulation: 90 percent have either total or partial involvement. The next highest level of EPO participation occurs in the formulation of foreign trade programs (81.4%), followed by export incentives (71.4%). It is evident that governments do not view EPOs as major participants in the formulation of national development plans. More than one-half have no involvement and somewhat less than one-half are involved only to some extent.

Having seen this mixed state of affairs at the policy formulation stage, it is of interest to consider EPOs involvement in the implementation of policy. While EPOs are, by and large, not involved in the implementation of export financing schemes (such as export credit and insurance), about one-half of them participate in the administration of export incentives. Their main concern rests with export development activities and almost two-thirds are fully involved in their implementation. This observation shows some consistency with the emphasis EPOs indicated with respect to the formulation of export policy.

Table 3.1: EPO participation in export policy

	% of EPOs with extent of participation: (n = 70)		
	None	Some	Full
Policy recommendation	7.1	62.9	30.0
Policy formulation areas:			
• National development plan	52.9	40.0	7.1
• Foreign trade program	18.6	54.3	27.1
• Export development strategy	10.0	37.1	52.8
• Export incentives	28.6	38.6	33.9
Policy implementation areas:			
• Export development activities	5.7	32.9	61.4
• Export incentives administration	48.6	37.1	14.3
• Direct export credit granting	84.3	10.0	5.7
• Export credit insurance	81.4	12.9	5.7
Other policy areas:			
• National/foreign investment promotion	51.4	37.1	11.4
• Control of national/ foreign investment	94.3	4.3	1.4
• International trade negotiations	28.6	55.7	15.7

Source: Prepared by author.

Earlier we saw that the economic policy process is often relatively unpartitioned, however, it is evident that the financial side of export development, as indeed any function related to the promotion or control of

investment, lies generally outside of EPOs influence. In the realm of
international trade negotiations EPOs are also seen as only peripherally involved.
This is not altogether unreasonable because such activity requires different
expertise and involvement over protracted periods. It is equally logical, however,
that influence on trade policy, can and perhaps should contribute to the agenda a
developing country brings to such trade negotiations[3] (Economist 1987).

Having seen that the policy emphasis of EPOs is on export
development, the next section will discuss the profile of their functions and
activities in this area.

PROFILE OF EPO FUNCTIONS AND ACTIVITIES

Four areas in which EPOs concentrate their activities will be discussed.
First, product and market development, second, export management assistance,
third, activities abroad, and fourth, support to other institutions.

Because of the relative newness of non-traditional products in the
economic activity of developing countries, they often lack the knowledge of
what role such products should play in their export development and of the
characteristics and nature of suitable foreign markets. It was seen in the previous
section that EPO policy emphasis was on export development. Given the need
for clear objectives with respect to a country's product portfolio and focus on
prospective markets, EPOs' challenge is to concentrate their efforts on the
identification of export supply, information on the requirements of the export
community, and the analysis of export market opportunities.

It is evident that export development is viewed in an integrated manner,
that is export supply and export demand both require attention. A very high
proportion of EPOs report undertaking supply-related activities (Figure 3.5). It
is also shown that such efforts appear to proceed from generally broad-based
export supply studies to specific studies of product profiles, which identify or
target particular business enterprises as export suppliers. It should be

---

[3] The current Uruguay Round of GATT negotiations shows the importance of
trade negotiations to developing countries. Improved market access by developing
countries to industrialized markets may require giving up their trade preferences and
become equal negotiating partners in return for developed countries' reducing market
access barriers. Developing countries thus would have to improve their bargaining
power and become better negotiators.

remembered that any export supply activity needs to be tied in with the prospects of foreign market demand for the products and services identified for export. The extent to which export supply and export demand activities are coordinated and interactive, as well as the competence with which both are conducted, will undoubtedly influence the effectiveness of the EPO and with it the success of a country's export market involvement.

Figure 3.5: EPO activities – product and market development

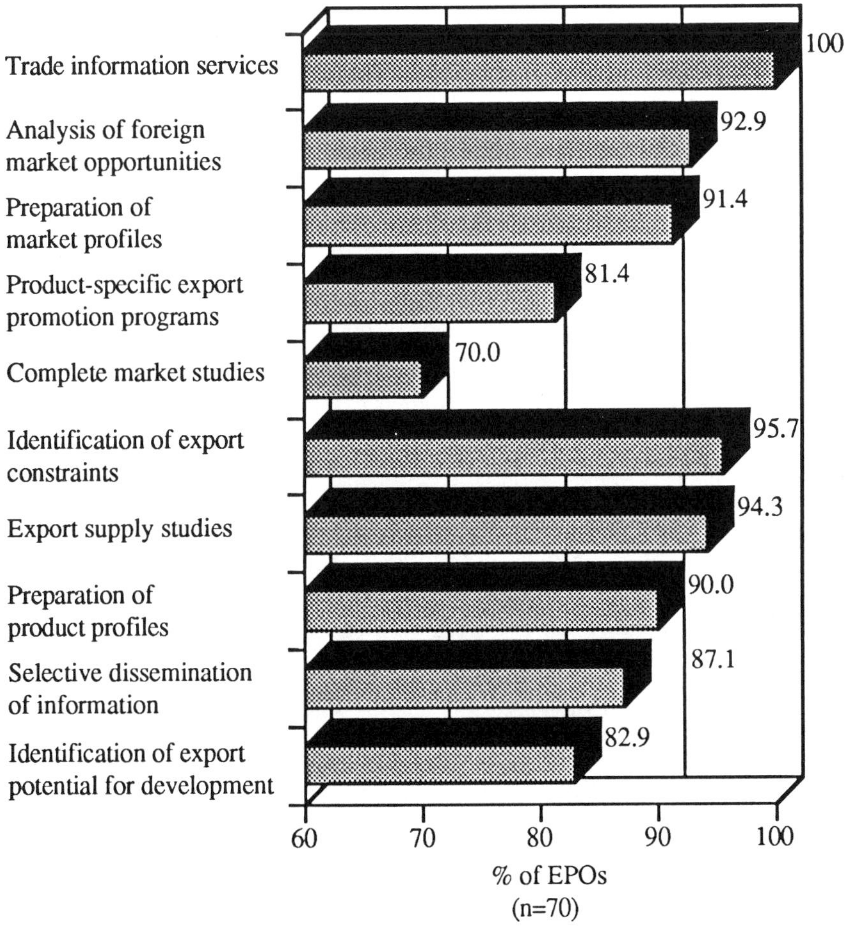

% of EPOs
(n=70)

Source: Prepared by author.

The extent to which EPOs undertake export demand activities is consistent with the need for an integrated approach to export development. Although no indication is given of how effectively EPOs carry on these activities, it certainly is noteworthy that complete market studies are undertaken by fewer EPOs than any other activities. Such studies are generally the source from which more specific target markets and product profiles are generated. The purpose of the latter is to render broad opportunities more specific in order to match existing or planned export supply.

A further caution about the reported high levels of specific EPO activities relates to consistency. It is not indicated how regular or systematic such efforts are, not to speak of the level of expertise and competence available and devoted to such activities.

Figure 3.6 provides an overview of different kinds of export management assistance EPOs provide. In general these activities are practical and of immediate benefit to the exporter. The two most often mentioned types of assistance EPOs offer are marketing assistance and procedural help for exporting. In contrast with some of the other items, marketing can be interpreted as having a sales and promotion emphasis. Export of services and quality control help are the least often mentioned assistance. It is not surprising that most developing countries do not appear to have the capability to export services. However, a matter as crucial as product quality, would warrant a great deal more emphasis in view of its direct influence on acceptance and success of products in international markets.

The extent to which this group of EPOs is engaged in specific assistance can also be interpreted as a reflection of the need for particular help in the business community. Weak areas then are in marketing know-how, the ability to handle the procedural aspects of exporting, handling publicity and training. Adaptation of existing products to suit foreign markets and financing of exports, although mentioned less often, figure as areas of assistance with a majority of EPOs.

Figure 3.6: EPO activities – export management assistance

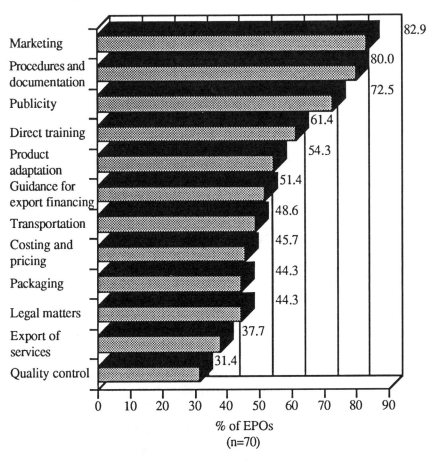

% of EPOs
(n=70)

Source: Prepared by author.

One of the traditional areas of EPO activity in developed countries is their leading role in helping companies with contacts in foreign markets. Trade fairs, trade missions and other forms of buyer-seller interaction thus also feature as the main activities developing country EPOs provide to their business community. As Figure 3.7 shows, nearly all of the EPOs offer participation in foreign trade fairs and missions abroad.

Figure 3.7: EPO activities abroad

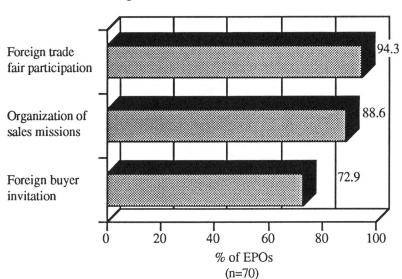

Source: Prepared by author.

The foreign market activity of an EPO is influenced by its organizational form and the way in which it is connected with government. When EPOs have their own trade representatives abroad, such staff is usually exclusively devoted to trade and export promotion. Where an EPO is structurally part of a ministry, foreign office representatives tend to carry a variety of other duties as well. In two-thirds of the organizations reporting on foreign offices, the latter have a direct dependency with the EPO, while one-third are dependent on a ministry in government. The actual workings of trade representatives abroad provides a clearer picture. Nine out of ten EPOs (89.1%) communicate directly with the trade representative abroad and nearly as many (83.6%) issue direct work instructions to them. The remainder communicate indirectly through government channels.

EPOs also engage in other activities which, however, are not so readily identified with their main functions discussed earlier. Figure 3.8 shows ten support services most often provided. A distinct focus on small and medium-size business evidently reflects particular needs of the business community. Training institutions draw on EPOs for participation, as do governments in matters of economic development. Joint export mechanisms, such as consortia, stand to benefit from the expertise EPOs have developed. Motivational programs, while not of direct export impact, are a vital part in raising export consciousness and thus creating an awareness of the role exports play in economic development.

Figure 3.8: EPO activities: support to other institutions

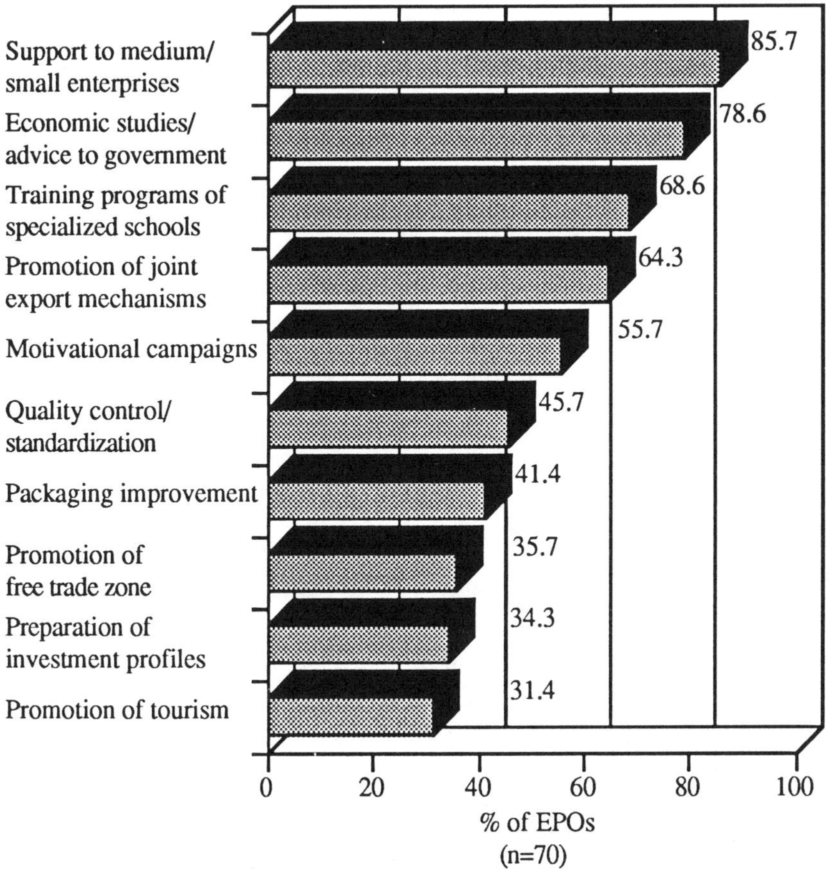

Source: Prepared by author.

Next, we turn to the implementation of the activities, namely, how EPOs interact in the business community.

INTERACTION OF EPO AND BUSINESS COMMUNITY

Perhaps the most critical area in the realm of export development and promotion is the interaction between EPOs and exporters and potential exporters. The survey asked EPOs about both how the contact between them and the business community came about and what benefits emerged from it. The views of the business community are indirect and are mirrored through perceptions on part of the EPO. Nevertheless, the attempt at describing the EPO/business contact and its result contribute to a better understanding of the role of EPOs. Figure 3.9 shows that direct visits and contacts are by far the most frequent means of interaction (74.5%). Other organizations and associations, in other words, third party-generated contacts, while still important are used much less frequently (32.7%).

These data suggest that, by and large, EPOs endeavour to foster direct interaction with the business community. These results, however, do not allow interpretation of the efficiency of EPOs efforts to establish contacts with business. For example, how are companies singled out for EPO-initiated contacts? What level of awareness of EPOs and their programs exists in the business community? How is the EPO perceived and how willing are companies to become involved with it?

Research addressing such questions has only recently been undertaken in developed countries. Initial conclusions suggest that governments in such countries, despite all available sophistication in communication and promotion techniques, still have considerable challenges before them to make the business community not only aware of EPOs and their role but also to motivate companies to look upon export promotion support as a potential resource (Cullwick & Mellallieu 1981, Walters 1983, Gronhaug & Loretzen 1983, Reid 1984, Seringhaus 1986a & b, 1986/87, 1987). No such research or evidence is available for developing countries.

The issue of benefits arising from the EPO/business interaction is an important one since it suggests who may be benefiting and in what way. Table 3.2 provides a summary of benefits, albeit through the eyes of the EPO.

EPOs benefit primarily by being able to improve export policy and program planning as a result of a better understanding of the needs of exporters. The business community, on the other hand, stands to gain through improved export marketing, better knowledge of export opportunities, and all round improved service from the EPO. In two areas, namely information exchange and

Figure 3.9: EPO-business community interaction

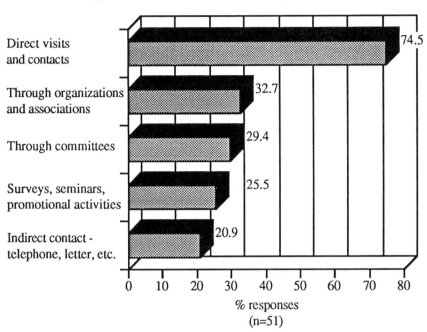

% responses
(n=51)

Source: Prepared by author.

Table 3.2: Benefits from contacts

| Type of benefit | Primary benefit at: | | responses[a] (n = 51) |
	EPO level	Business level	
Policy, program planning and design	✔		29.8%
Knowledge of exporter needs	✔		27.7
Improved export marketing		✔	19.1
Knowledge of business opportunities		✔	14.9
Improved service to exporters		✔	16.3
Information exchange	✔	✔	23.4
Handling export problems	✔	✔	12.8

[a]   Multiple responses
Source: Prepared by author.

dealing with export problems, both EPO and companies benefit. Information relevancy is achieved best when both parties shape requirements supply. Exporting problems can arise at EPO or company level, however, the shaping of solutions is an interactive process.

The survey data does not give concrete evidence of benefits arising from the EPO/company contacts, but rather suggests where the primary locus of such benefit lies. The effectiveness of EPO/company contacts was rated by EPOs. Some 26.8 percent gave a rating of very good, 22.0 percent good, and 51.2 percent fair or poor. No inference as to the effectiveness of specific contacts is possible, nor any assessment of the impact of EPO/company interaction.

CONCLUSIONS AND IMPLICATIONS

This chapter has developed a picture of EPOs in developing countries based on a recent survey. Hitherto, the literature on export development and export promotion has been characterized by studies with primarily a macro-economic focus, or by conceptual and normative discussion of these topics. This empirical analysis of how EPOs are set up, what their functions are and how these are discharged, provides convincing evidence that: (1) some of the normative ideas about export promotion can be put into practice and, (2) export promotion approaches are broadly adopted and fairly well organized throughout the developing world. Figure 3.10 summarizes the main findings of the survey to show where the involvement of EPOs in export development is concentrated. What is particularly noteworthy is the role EPOs play in the export supply side of export development.

As pointed out earlier, the results leave many questions unanswered. There is, of course, the overriding issue of whether or not export development, and export promotion's part in it, will be able to generate industries that remain viable in the long-term, in the context of international trading relationships. Can developing countries expect to speed up the domestic accumulation of skill and capital by adopting an export orientation? Of course, the political dimension must not be forgotten, in particular concern over the compatibility of political ideology and an outward trade orientation (Schmitz, 1984).

Convincing evidence exists of the positive impact of an outward-focused, pro-export attitude in both the public and private sector. South Korea,

Figure 3.10: Export promotion organization functions and modes

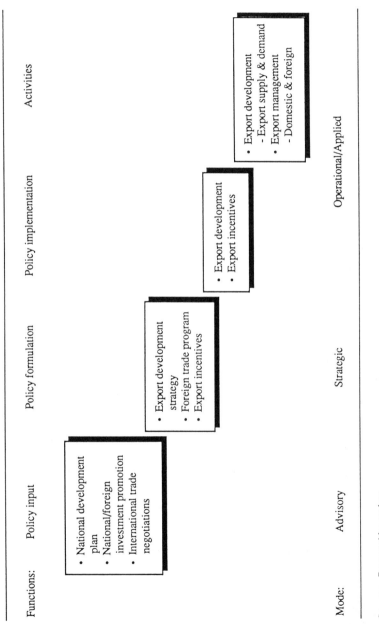

Functions: Policy input   Policy formulation   Policy implementation   Activities

• National development   • Export development   • Export development   • Export development
  plan   strategy   • Export incentives   - Export supply & demand
• National/foreign   • Foreign trade program   • Export management
  investment promotion   • Export incentives   - Domestic & foreign
• International trade
  negotiations

Mode: Advisory   Strategic   Operational/Applied

Source: Prepared by author.

Hong Kong, Singapore, Taiwan and Thailand are cases in point. Apart from the export development and promotion infrastructure, however, the importance of an outward orientation cannot be overemphasized. There is evidence that countries without such an orientation are only marginal participants in global trade and have great difficulty in their economic development (for example, Sri Lanka, Argentina, India to mention a few).

Clearly, export promotion is only one element in the export development process. It has the potential of contributing in a critically important area, namely in motivating the business community and helping in the learning process so vital in the global competitive environment. As discussed earlier, understanding the needs of the business community and recognizing the importance of the behavioural aspects of EPOs can make the latter the facilitator in the process of building expertise and knowledge for export involvement. It was also noted that the data from this survey do not permit inferences about the effectiveness of EPO activities. However, yardsticks for measurement of EPO functions are essential in order to assess whether or not the efforts mounted are the most beneficial to stimulate exports. Measurement is also critical for understanding the effectiveness of EPOs in the developed world.

To return to the profile suggested in Figure 3.10, it is necessary to recognize that circumstances across developing countries vary a great deal, thus this framework should be viewed with some caution. Indeed it may be hazardous to attempt the development of generally applicable strategies or approaches for this group of countries. It would be equally inappropriate to prescribe approaches successfully employed in the developed world for use in developing countries. More research among EPOs in the latter group of countries is needed, possibly looking for characteristics and suitable models of export support linked with the degree of outward orientation and progress along the economic/export development continuum.

ACKNOWLEDGEMENT

Permission to use data from a survey of trade promotion organizations by the International Trade Centre UNCTAD/GATT, Geneva, is gratefully acknowledged.

REFERENCES

Balassa, Bela (1979). "Export Incentives and Export Performance in Developing Countries: A Comparative Analysis", in Barend A. de Vries, *Export Promotion Policies*, World Bank Staff Working Papers, No. 313, Washington, D.C., The World Bank, pp. 20-28.

Cullwick, T.D.C. and J.P. Mellallieu (1981). "Business Attitudes to Government Export Services and Export Marketing Behaviour", *New Zealand Journal of Business*, Vol. 3, pp. 33-54.

De La Torre, Jose (1971). "Exports of Manufactured Goods from Developing Countries: Marketing Factors and The Role of Foreign Enterprise", *Journal of International Business Studies*, Vol. 2, No. 1, Spring, pp. 26-39.

Donges, Juergen B. and James Riedel (1977). "The Expansion of Manufactured Exports in Developing Countries: An Empirical Assessment of Supply and Demand Issues", *Weltwirtschaftliches Archiv*, Band 113, Heft 1, pp. 58-85.

Dymsza, William A. (1983). "A National Export Strategy for Latin American Countries", in Michael R. Czinkota, Ed., *U.S.-Latin American Trade Relations*, Praeger Publishers, New York, pp. 5-25.

Economist (1987). "A Survey of the World Economy", Sept. 26, pp. 6-56.

Gronhaug, Kjell and Tore Lorentzen (1983). "Exploring the Impact of Governmental Export Subsidies", *European Journal of Marketing*, Vol. 17, No. 2, pp. 5-12.

Hesse, Helmut (1972). "Promotion of Manufactured exports as Development Strategy of Semi-Industrialized Countries: The Brazilian Case", *Weltwirtschaftliches Archiv*, Band 108, Heft 2, pp. 236-255.

ITC (1986a). *Selected Export Promotion Organizations: Structures, Functions and Activities*, International Trade Centre UNCTAD/GATT, Geneva, Sept. 25.

__ (1986b). *Trade Promotion Institutions: Monograph on the Role and Organization of Trade Promotion*, International Trade Centre UNCTAD/ GATT, Geneva.

__ (1988). *Profiles of Trade Promotion Organizations*, International Trade Centre UNCTAD/GATT, Geneva.

Jung, Woo S. and Gyu Lee (1986). "The Effectiveness of Export Promotion Policies: The Case of Korea", *Wiltwirtschaftliches Archiv*, Band 122, Heft 2, pp. 341-357.

Ram, Rati (1985). "Exports and Economic Growth: Some Additional Evidence", *Economic Development and Cultural Change*, Vol. 33, pp. 415-425.

Reid, Stanley Douglas (1984). "Information Acquisition and Entry Decisions in Small Firms", *Journal of Business Research*, Vol. 12, No. 2, pp. 141-157.

Root, Franklin R. (1971). "A Conceptual Model for Export Promotion Strategy at the National Level", *Foreign Trade Review*, July-Sept., pp. 184-194.

_____ (1974). "Conceptual Foundations for the Strategy of a Government Export Promotion Agency", *Foreign Trade Review*, January-March, pp. 326-338.

_____ (1978). *International Trade and Investment*, 4th Edition, South-Western Publishing Co., Cincinnati.

Schmitz, Hubert (1984). "Industrialization Strategies in Less Developed Countries: Some Lessons of Historical Experience", *Journal of Development Studies*, Vol. 21, No. 1, October, pp. 1-21.

Schwartz, Hugh (1988). "The Potential Role of Behavioral Analysis in the Promotion of Private Enterprise in Developing Countries", *Columbia Journal of World Business*, Spring, pp. 53-56.

Seringhaus, F.H. Rolf (1986a). "Empirical Investigation of Awareness, Use and Impact of Export Marketing Support by Government in Manufacturing Firms", in K. Moeller and M. Paltschik, Eds., *Contemporary Research in Marketing*, Vol. 1, European Marketing Academy, Helsinki, p. 249-267.

_____ (1986b). "Market Entry and the Impact of Export Marketing Assistance: A Conceptual Approach to Causal Modelling", *The Finnish Journal of Business Economics*, Vol. 35, No. 4, pp. 275-285.

_____ (1986/87). "The Role of Information Assistance in Small Firms' Export Involvement", *International Small Business Journal*, Vol. 5, No. 2, Winter, pp. 26-36.

_____ (1987). "Export Promotion: The Role and Impact of Government Services", *Irish Marketing Review*, Vol. 2, pp. 106-116.

Walters, Peter G.P. (1983). "Export Information Sources – A Study of Their Usage and Utility", *International Marketing Review*, Vol. 1, Winter. pp. 34-43.

World Bank (1987). *World Development Report 1987*, Oxford University Press, New York.

PART II

Challenges in Export Development: Some Regional Perspectives

INTRODUCTION

Part II contains various regional perspectives on export promotion and public organizations drawn from countries in Latin America and Europe. Dominguez and Sequeira examine how export promotion organizations can assist exporters in Costa Rica in Chapter four. An extensive discussion of export policy shows that, by and large, the country's orientation is an outward one but that a survey of exporters reveals many marketing problems. Companies look to the export promotion organization more than any other source, for help in this and other areas. The conclusions from the research are of relevance for other outward-looking developing countries.

In Chapter five, Brooks and Frances report on the barriers faced by companies that export non-traditional products in four Latin American countries. Foreign market access is a major problem for these companies but so too is home country commercial and transport infrastructure, government policies and regulations, all of which seriously impede export performance. This demonstrates that export promotion will not help in the absence of supportive infrastructure and trade policy.

Camino argues in Chapter six that Spain's integration into the E.E.C. has increased export promotion consciousness and activity in that country. Spain's export promotion organization is undertaking ambitious and focused efforts to support exporters. Camino also provides a comparison between the export promotion program in Spain and six other E.E.C. member nations.

Sbrana and Siena-Tangheroni describe the Italian export promotion system and how it serves smaller exporters in Chapter seven. Three findings from this research stand out. First, the level of knowledge among companies about available support from public and private organizations is low; second, exporters appear to have more specific needs for support than are provided by available programs; and third, there is an overlap in the services provided, creating confusion and inefficiency.

CHAPTER FOUR

Nontraditional Exports in Costa Rica: An Exploration of Public Policy Issues

Luis V. Dominguez and Carlos G. Sequeira[*]

SUMMARY

As LDC's turn from inward focused to export oriented development, nontraditional exports have taken on added significance. This chapter examines LDC export marketing problems and practices from a policy point of view. Costa Rican exporters regard marketing problems as their most serious concerns. However, exporters' means of gathering information about target markets, and their own choice of marketing strategies, raise serious concerns. Moreover, distinct approaches to export marketing are not evolving as firms become more experienced. It is suggested that export promotion organizations must become more involved in "marketing" marketing, if export-led development strategies are to succeed.

INTRODUCTION

This chapter examines the perceived importance of marketing problems of Costa Rican exporters relative to documentary, financial, and logistical problems that have been the primary concern of export promotion programs in many LDCs. Having established the importance of marketing problems to

---

[*] University of Miami and INCAE (Central American Institute of Business Management), Costa Rica respectively.

exporters, this study examines the extent of utilization of different sources and types of marketing information. It then suggests how export promotion organizations might tailor their assistance programs to fill those gaps. Although the findings of a single-country study cannot be indiscriminately generalized, Costa Rica's experience as a successful exporter may be an excellent indicator of challenges faced by other LDC's. This is particularly so for many other small LDCs hoping to increase their exports to developed markets.

IMPORTANCE OF EXPORT MARKETING IN LDCS

The marketing literature on economic development has been almost entirely devoted to studying marketing systems and marketing behaviour within LDCs. Such an internal focus is justified by the importance of domestic infrastructure development. It was particularly suited to inward-focused, import substitution development strategies. As many LDCs have increased their reliance on outward-oriented, export-led development, formulation and testing of export marketing programs have become matters of utmost priority.

Many LDCs have responded to deteriorating terms of trade and mounting balance of payments problems – and to the success of Pacific Rim nations – by fostering a nontraditional export sector. However, a number of studies have suggested that the experience of Pacific Rim nations with export-led growth may not be easily repeatable (Evans and Alizadeh 1984). In fact, Caribbean nations' total exports to the United States declined every year from 1981 to 1986 despite institution of special incentives by the U.S. and the governments in the area. Two countries in the Caribbean, Costa Rica and the Dominican Republic, have clearly outperformed the rest.

With few notable exceptions, development policy has tended to overlook or to underestimate the potential contributions of marketing. Under import substitution, domestically focused policy created sellers' market conditions which tacitly restricted competition and discouraged customer oriented firm behaviour (Balassa 1984) that is traditionally associated with the adoption of modern market (Dominguez and Vanmarcke 1987). Marketing was seen as unnecessary or possibly detrimental (Kaynak 1982).

The shift to export promotion raises new issues for policy planners who must now wonder how LDC firms, many of them relatively inexperienced exporters, will succeed in highly competitive foreign markets without the benefit of domestic industry protection. Referring to the Costa Rican experience, Artavia, Colburn and Saballos (1987), characterize the magnitude of needed adjustments as inflicting a "management shock" on would-be exporters. An earlier study by Bulmer-Thomas (1979) warns that Central America's efforts to develop a nontraditional export sector would require more than fiscal and financial incentives. Direct technical assistance in the areas of production, management, and marketing would be necessary.

Nevertheless, export-led development policy for the most part has focused on what elsewhere in this volume are defined as "indirect" or supply-sided incentives – on establishing exchange rate regimes that encourage exports and on financial and fiscal incentives to exporters. Much of the attention, as in the case of Peru, has been on whether such indirect fiscal and financial incentives, in the aggregate, pay for themselves in marginal exports (Schydlowsky 1986). Without denying the importance of aggregate results, truly effective export assistance programs must be solidly grounded in an appreciation of the problems experienced by LDC exporters as well as of the determinants of firm-level export success. Such an understanding should be a cornerstone of export-led development programs.

However, there is considerable controversy and scepticism about the effectiveness of what in this volume are labelled direct or demand-side export assistance programs. Empirical assessments have yielded a wide range of results from effective to ineffective, with the majority showing relatively little impact. Three studies from the developing world are specially revealing as to the reasons why there is so wide a range of utilization and perceived effectiveness of export assistance programs. Christensen, Da Rocha and Gertner (1987) compared Brazilian firms which continued to export over a six-year span with those which had ceased. They found that firms which continued to export had made less use of fiscal and financial incentives and had expressed less desire for incentives or technical assistance. On the other hand, a study by Brezzo and Perkal (1983) suggested from case studies of four Uruguayan industries that direct technical assistance programs were more effective when they focused on specific product quality and marketing improvements than was indirect assistance in the form of fiscal incentives. Two studies, one Turkish (Bodur & Cavusgil 1985) and the other Brazilian (Christensen, Da Rocha & Gerner 1987) found a relationship between export success and use of a variety of information sources on the target export market.

One may therefore hypothesize that direct incentives are effective only when they are tailored to the specific needs of selected categories of exporters, e.g., those in certain industries, or at specific stages of internationalization, or targeting developed nations. Seringhaus (1986) concluded from a review of the extant literature on export promotion programs that the low effectiveness of export promotion programs that is reported in some studies may be attributed to conceptual/methodological flaws. Some studies have employed highly general measures of government assistance. As a result, the overall assessment of effectiveness is low either because the respondent is unaware of all the available programs or because only some are relevant to the exporter's needs. Frequently, studies have failed to discriminate among separate exporter groups, i.e., exporters and nonexporters, or to realize that programs may have to be tailored to the stage of internationalization of the firm. The measurement scales themselves differ widely among studies. Seringhaus (1986) calls for multiple measures of response and for behavioural measures directly relevant to the objective of the program in question. For example, if the goal of an export promotion program is to obtain higher export prices, then incremental export revenues might be broken into volume and price contributions to assess program effectiveness.

COSTA RICAN EXPORT POLICY

At its inception in 1961, the Central American Common Market (CACM) was to provide a framework for industrial expansion in the region by opening each country's borders to intra-regional trade. Incentives offered by import duties and import bans led many companies to establish production facilities in the region. The failure of CACM to provide sustained growth has been blamed on revolutions in El Salvador and Nicaragua and on the Honduras-Salvador border dispute. In fact, a convincing case has been made that economic stagnation predated those events (Bulmer-Thomas 1979).

As early as 1971 INTAL, the Central American Institute for Economic Integraton had proposed a framework for stimulating development of nontraditional exports as an alternative to import substitution in the region (INTAL 1971). It envisioned a host of direct ad indirect incentives for nontraditional exports. Indirect incentives centred chiefly around: duty exemption for imported raw materials and equipment earmarked for export activity; tax exemptions on sales and profits derived from nontraditional exports;

export credit insurance; accelerated depreciation schedules; reduced interest rates; relaxed conditions for export-oriented credit, and favourable repayment terms; and direct subsidies for exports. Costa Rica's indirect incentives have included tax rebates tied to extra- regional exports of nontraditional goods, substantial income tax reductions to firms wholly dedicated to exporting, and duty exemptions on imports of machinery and raw materials for export production (CENPRO 1983; Artavia, Colburn and Saballos 1987). A number of these incentives are in agreement with GATT policies (for a discussion of export promotion permissible under GATT see Seringhaus and Rosson 1990); others, particularly the more overt export subsidies, have been a source of controversy. Costa Rica's nontraditional exporters have been eligible for tax credit certificates (CATs) equivalent to 15-20 percent of the FOB value of exports outside CACM. In addition, CAT beneficiaries were eligible for cash-redeemable certificates (CIEXs) valued at to 4-10 percent of their increase in exports over the preceding year (IMF 1988, UNCTAD 1982). GATT as well as developed nations individually have taken a rather critical view of such export incentives as potentially unfair trade practices. In the United States, certain categories of Costa Rican flowers, for example, have been subjected to countervailing duties because of alleged export subsidies. An agreement has been negotiated with GATT during 1988-89 which allows Costa Rica to retain CAT in exchange for a commitment to increased import liberalization.

Indirect incentives proposed by INTAL included creation of infrastructure such as free trade zones and improved air and maritime port facilities. However, the most important element was the creation of a host of technical assistance organizations whose mission was to enhance the competitiveness of regional products. Of all those that were contemplated, private and public-sector export assistance organizations have proven the most visible and active. The U.S. Agency for International Development has lent considerable support to such initiatives through throughout the region. In Costa Rica, CENPRO and the Costa Rican Chamber of Industries have actively supported export initiatives and provided a host of export assistance programs. In an attempt to redirect export priorities, CENPRO was instituted as a public sector agency for channeling all export incentives to the private sector.

Perhaps as a result of all this concerted activity, Costa Rica has significantly diversified its export base and increased its nontraditional exports outside CACM; nontraditional exports to the United States rose from $160 million in 1980 to over $350 million in 1987 (U.S. Department of Commerce 1988).

Thus Costa Rica presents an interesting setting for research on the effectiveness of export promotion programs. If marketing considerations are important to exporters, and if there remain important gaps in marketing strategies of exporters and in export promotion programs in a country that is achieving a moderate degree of success with nontraditional exports, then it might be suggested that LDCs should devote significant resources to marketing assistance programs for nontraditional exporters.

METHODOLOGY

Research Questions

It is widely believed that many LDC's nontraditional exports are being priced below full cost. Variable cost pricing hardly seems to offer an incentive to expand productive capacity or invest in developing necessary export marketing skills. Much exporting could be a transitory phenomenon of firms that have not truly committed to internationalization but which instead are biding their time until home markets in LDCs are once again able to absorb idle capacity. It is therefore plausible that the entry of new or existing firms into the export market may temporarily mask other firms' stagnant or possibly even receding export activity or, more importantly, oversimplify the hurdles to successful exporting. Effective programs can ensure an enduring commitment to exporting only if they address real needs of entrepreneurs.

Exporting has been characterized as a stepwise process of learning, deepening involvement, and increasing investment in export markets (Jackson 1981, Johansson & Vahlne 1976, Lee & Brasch 1978, Ursic & Czinkota 1984). Firms that have reached far into this process are depicted as: (a) interested in diversifying their product-market base so as not to be overly dependent on a single customer or market, or on a single product (Piercy 1981a);[1] more interested in increasing their participation in the distribution process in export markets (Cavusgil 1984); and more likely to research foreign markets (Reid &

---

[1] Cavusgil's (1984) study, however, does not tend to support this finding.

Mayer 1980).[2] Less successful exporters seem to approach exports as a more or less necessary evil caused by domestic market saturation or contraction (Lee & Brasch 1978, Piercy 1981b).

It would be hazardous, however, to indiscriminately extend such generalizations to LDC exporters. Most research has focused on exports from developed nations or newly-developed countries; much of it concerns small and medium-sized firms that did not have commanding shares of their home markets. Problems and determinants of success are likely to differ. LDC exporters usually lack the extensive support that is available to developed market exporters through their government trade offices; product image is a potentially serious problem and may work against those marketing products under their own (rather than a distributor's or customer's) identity; lack of currency convertibility makes it difficult to travel to foreign trade fairs or to visit customers; and channel selection and control policies may be infeasible for small exporters hoping to target specific market niches.

Such a humble role in export markets is psychologically rather distant from the positions of market dominance and control that LDC firms are often able to exercise in their home markets. Furthermore, the whole premise that successful LDC exporters "market" their products might be called into question. It may be hypothesized that, on the contrary, successful exporters limit themselves to being producers who turn marketing responsibility for their products to developed-market specialists in the target country.

The first question, therefore, is whether exporters regard marketing issues as important obstacles to exporting. That is, in comparison to documentary, financial, and logistical issues, are marketing problems more or less important to Costa Rican exporters? The research proposition is stated thus:

Proposition 1:
   Marketing problems are more important and represent more serious issues to LDC exporters than are documentary, financial, and logistical ones.

A second issue concerns whether private and public sector export promotion programs are addressing important concerns of exporters. Recent

---

   [2]   Lee and Brasch's study (1978) found the contrary. However, their study is flawed by design problems.

research (Seringhaus 1987) suggests a significant correlation between exporters' perceived problems and their methods of decision making, including information search; in particular, it found that exporters' search for and acquisition of appropriate market data were significantly constrained by resource availability. It has also been suggested that a firm's decision to venture into international markets is not easily subjected to formal research. Information about foreign markets must encompass more than hard data; understanding a country's cultural values and behaviour is an experiential process not easily confinable to numerical data (Lee & Brasch 1978). In contrast, Reid (1981) has shown that market entry decisions are characterized by considerable information gathering, although much of it may be gathered by informal methods. Such methods may include visits to prospects; contacts with customers and intermediaries, or contacts with friends, relatives and expatriates overseas.

Thus, we would expect LDC exporters to be most prone to engage in the least costly methods of information gathering, relying most heavily on free or subsidized market research services offered by export promotion agencies. We would further expect substantially lower use of formal (primary and secondary) research methods than of informal research. Finally, since marketing problems are perceived to be more important than documentary, financial and logistical ones, they would be the most heavily research. Three further research propositions emanate from this discussion.

Proposition 2:
    LDC exporters most heavily rely on informal methods of information gathering.

Proposition 3:
    LDC exporters more heavily research marketing issues than documentary, financially and logistical ones.

Proposition 4:
    LDC exporters employ export agencies more heavily than other methods of information gathering.

Discussion of results will centre on whether resources and institutions aimed at supporting nontraditional exporters are being effectively directed at key obstacles and decision problems perceived by nontraditional exporters.

Survey Design

Sixty firms were interviewed from a list of 333 nontraditional exporters compiled by the Costa Rican Chamber of Industries, a private-sector trade association. Their list, derived from official customs records, is widely regarded as a virtual census. All 333 firms were classified according to five categories of export volume outside CACM. Forty-eight respondents were selected from each stratum according to a stratified random sampling design with proportional representation at each stratum.

It had been originally intended that an additional 12 firms that were not actively exporting during 1985 would be employed as a control group. However, by 1986, eight of those were already exporting outside CACM. The remaining four nonexporters were excluded from further analysis. Three others were excluded on the ground that they were wholly owned, dedicated-purpose offshore plants of foreign companies not actively marketing their own products. All subsequent discussion refers to the remaining 53 firms.

The President of each company was mailed a personal letter jointly signed by the Dean of INCAE (Central American Institute of Business Administration) and the President of the Chamber of Industries of Costa Rica. This was followed by a telephone call to set up an interview. If after three attempts a personal interview could not be arranged, another firm from the same stratum was randomly selected and the process was again repeated. Seventy-five firms had to be contacted in order to fulfil all cell quotas, for a realized 80 percent response rate. Approximately 55 percent of all interviews were conducted with the President or General Manager, 15 percent with the highest ranking officer in charge of marketing or exporting, and 19 percent with the head of finance; the remaining interviewees assisted the President or General Manager in various administrative functions.

RESULTS

Perception of Obstacles and Problems

It may be argued that nontraditional exporters are engaged in commodity selling, exerting only limited marketing effort. Research proposition No. 1 suggests that exporters would prefer to market more aggressively but are thwarted by lack of needed information about and understanding of foreign markets and marketing practices. They perceive lack of information as an important problem and would like to overcome it.

If the latter assumption is incorrect, exporters' chief preoccupation should be with the process of international transactions, suggesting that documentary, financial and logistical issues should be their greatest concern. Documentary/financial/logistical issues[3] can be more readily resolved and usually a company's real preoccupation is with finding means of segmenting, positioning, distributing and promoting products for target markets.

To test Proposition No. 1, respondents were asked their perceptions of the extent to which selected issues presented serious obstacles to the firm's export efforts. Each item was rated on a three-point scale ranging from (1) not an obstacle, to (2) and obstacle, but not too important, to (3) a serious obstacle. Table 4.1 classifies obstacles and problems into marketing or documentary/financial/logistical and ranks them according to the percentage of respondents who regarded them as "serious". It is readily apparent that marketing issues are regarded by most respondents as generally the most serious. Affirmation of Proposition No. 1 requires that marketing considerations be ranked above nonmarketing ones. The Wilcoxon matched-pairs signed-ranks test rejected the null hypothesis ($p<.02$) in favour of the alternate hypothesis that marketing considerations ranked above documentary/financial/legal ones.

Higher ratings given to marketing issues do not in any way deny the importance of other problems. For example, respondents voiced a high level of concern with difficulties in securing air or maritime transportation. High transport costs can rob a country of its competitiveness in selected product markets such as apparel; unreliable transport service and delays can bankrupt exporters of perishables such as fresh fruits or flowers; and unreliable delivery of other goods may force importers to keep much higher safety stocks, detracting from an exporter's competitiveness or its ability to command higher prices.

It is of course reasonable that private- and public-sector efforts emphasize documentary, financial, and logistical infrastructure development from the outset. The resulting macro framework dramatically influences the benefits,

---

[3] Infrequently scheduled or unreliable maritime and air transportation are frequent complaints of Central American exporters. Such logistical issues may arguably be regarded as marketing problems. On the other hand, they may also be treated as supply and production-related issues. Given the likelihood that logistical issues would be a high concern of exporters, the authors decided to err on the conservative side, treating them as nonmarketing issues.

Table 4.1: Selected obstacles to exporting
(% of respondents rating issue as serious)

Issue:	Marketing	Documentary/ financial/ logistical issues
Setting the proper price for our product	38*	
Finding importers, agents or distributors able and willing to market our products	37	
Arranging air transport		35
Financing of exports		30
Securing information about competitors' products, prices and distribution	26	
Determining consumer preferences and habits	25	
Identifying services required by users and intermediaries	20	
Satisfying Costa Rican government documentary requirements for export permits		20
Arranging maritime transport		17
Adapting the product to customer preferences	17	
Satisfying documentary requirements in order to qualify for Costa Rican government export incentives		16
Completing documentary requirements for investing in Costa Rica		14
Trustworthiness of information supplied by clients and intermediaries	12	
Shipping costs	6	
Obtaining information on customs and other documentary requirements for importing into foreign markets		6

*   To be read: 38 percent of respondents believed that setting a proper price for
    export markets was a serious obstacle.
Source: Prepared by authors.

costs, and risks faced by entrepreneurs, the speed with which decisions can be
made and, perhaps just as importantly, entrepreneurs' perceptions of the
desirability of investing and exporting. In fact, it may be argued that the
ultimate significance of such problems lies in how they limit the range of
marketing options available to LDC exporters. However, a single-minded

concern with infrastructure development may repeat, albeit in a different context, errors of earlier decades, when financial and production issues were overemphasized to the detriment of demand, customer needs, and marketing entrepreneurship considerations. It has been suggested that the most serious problems lie in the internal environment of the firm (Cavusgil & Nevin 1981, Cavusgil 1984, Reid 1981), in no small part in its ability and commitment to understanding customer needs, competitive behaviour and channel practices.

Exporters' Market Information Needs and Activities

The marketing management literature repeatedly stresses the importance of analytic, information-based over intuitive decision-making. For LDC exporters, foreign market penetration represents a quantum leap in complexity. A firm grasp of competitive, customer, and channel environments is required for differentiated marketing. Yet the literature also warns that acquiring an appreciation of a nation's values and behaviour is almost intrinsically an experiential process; hard data alone are not sufficient for export marketing. For LDC exporters, the challenges are considerable, not the least of which is the lack of financial and human resources with which to undertake market investigations.

Even if exporters continue to perceive the same problems, they might learn to cope with information problems. Moreover, there exist different types of marketing information sources and methods. Both the use of marketing information and evaluation of the effectiveness of technical assistance programs must be viewed in the context of the range of exporter information needs and use of information sources. Evaluation of the effectiveness of export promotion programs must address this multidimensionality (Seringhaus 1986). Accordingly, respondents were shown a brief description of each of the following methods of information gathering and were asked whether they had been employed for any of several prespecified purposes:

1.   Secondary data sources
2.   Primary data gathering
3.   Information from final users and intermediaries
4.   Exploratory visits to foreign markets
5.   Other approaches as indicated by the respondent.

In virtually every case, "other" sources meant informal contacts with associates, relatives, and friends overseas; in fact, an exporter's suppliers are frequently used as sources of market information and for securing sales contacts (e.g., Edmunds 1984, Sequeira & Saballos 1987). Hence 3, 4 and 5 may be regarded as informal and 1 and 2 as the formal data-gathering procedures.

Respondents' mentions of application of each of the five methods were evaluated over ten specific export decision areas:

1. Product adaptation
2. Price setting
3. Channel selection
4. Competitive assessment
5. Customer need determination
6. Customer service needs
7. Financing of export transactions
8. Costa Rican export documentation
9. Documentation for importing into foreign country
10. Documentation for receiving Costa Rican export incentives.

Items 1 to 6 comprise marketing-oriented issues while 7 to 10 address documentary, financial and logistical matters.

Table 4.2 shows the relative frequency of mentions of use of formal and informal research. The results clearly support Proposition No. 2 in the sense that informal methods were much more heavily employed than formal methods. Proposition No. 3, in contrast, could not be sustained on the basis of overall mention of marketing and documentary, financial, and logistical issues. Marketing issues were not significantly more heavily researched. However, when use of research methods is compared according to topic important differences arise in the use of formal and informal research methods. Marketing information was predominantly obtained from informal sources, whereas documentary, financial, and logistical issues were primarily drawn from formal sources.

The last proposition (No. 4) concerns the use of export promotion organizations for any aspect of export marketing. If a respondent stated that a given methods, e.g., secondary data analysis, had been employed, he/she was then shown a list of potential information sources and was asked to state which specific source of information had been used. Table 4.3 summarizes the results classified by source. The results clearly indicate meagre use of export promotion agencies for marketing decision purposes. Such agencies are being utilized as sources of information on supply-sided incentives.

Table 4.2: Formal and informal information gathering by exporters

Issue Area	Informal	Formal	Total (%)
Marketing	311	43	354 (59%)
Legal/Documentary/			
Financial/Logistical	119	130	249 (41%)
Total	430	173	603 (100%)

Chi-square: 114.68, df=1; p<.001
Source: Prepared by authors.

Table 4.3: Exporters' reliance on export promotion agencies
compared to other sources

Issue area	Export promotion agency	Library	Client/ intermediary	Personal contacts
Marketing	4%*	0%	35%	61%
Product adaptation	9**	0	26	65
Channels	7	0	30	63
Pricing	0	0	32	68
Competitor analysis	3	0	48	48
Consumer needs	2	0	31	67
Legal/documentary/				
financial/logistical	52	6	18	24

*   To be read: 4 percent of reported marketing-related information inquiries
were conducted by means of export promotion agencies.
**   To be read: 9 percent of reported product adaptation inquiries were conducted
by means of export promotion agencies.
Source: Prepared by authors.

It may be argued that Costa Rican exporters are behaving as rational
decision-makers. Strapped for resources with which to undertake formal
marketing research, they are gathering information from inexpensive sources,
using early customers and intermediaries as mentors and information filters, and

relying on first-hand experience to gain insights and possibly verify suspect data. In those regards, Costa Rica's experience mirrors that of successful, newly industrialized countries such as Korea in their early stages (see Westphall, Rhee & Pursell 1981). On the other hand, exporters are highly dependent on an individual client in the export market, a major point of difference with the Korean exporters (Westphall, Rhee & Pursell 1981), and on their own culturally-bound incapacity to acquire and to judge possibly ambiguous and contradictory market signals. In view of scant differences in behaviour according to experience, export success, or even operating scales of firms, it appears that export assistance programs ought to focus on making more pertinent, market-related information available to exporters; there is a generalized need for more varied and extensive information on potential target markets, competitors, and marketing options that may enhance bargaining position with the channel and facilitate customer/market diversification. This need is not currently being successfully fulfilled by existing institutions.

DISCUSSION AND CONCLUSIONS

The experience of Costa Rican exporters has important implications for other nations who wish to pursue vigorous promotion of nontraditional exports. Costa Rica is widely acknowledged as Central America's pioneer in export promotion, as well as for its good business climate. Its efforts at creating a supportive institutional framework have been followed by others in the region. Nevertheless, such infrastructure development is a necessary but not sufficient condition for success. Unless institutional reform is paralleled by program that can realistically assist exporters with their marketing problems, a danger exists that expectations of significant export expansion will not be realized.

Two great difficulties stand in the way of such parallel development. These are planners' natural bias toward aggregate problem formulation and solution schemes, and the nature of LDC firms themselves. The former has to do with problem identification while the latter pertains to strategy development.

Firstly, policy planners, because of their mission and perhaps their training, tend to view problems from an aggregate perspective. There is therefore a preference for actions and schemes that deal with problems on a broad basis. This bias shortchanges marketing, albeit in a more subtle way than the literature has perhaps identified. In yesteryear, it had meant a total neglect of marketing considerations that has been eloquently illustrated in the marketing literature by examples of failed industrial schemes that neglected to take into consideration market needs and characteristics. Today, we live in a more sophisticated world in which planners may realize to a degree some of the marketing implications of their policy choices. For example, trade officials in many LDCs are keenly aware that cumbersome and slow customs procedures can diminish or destroy the useful life and market value of perishables exports; hence steps are taken with varying success to solve institutional problems that have definite implications for managers.

Rather, the problem is more complex. Planners' bias for broadly scoped issues and solutions may conspire against a clear understanding and appreciation of the nature of exporters' purely micromarketing problems. It may simply be assumed that exporters will become more skilled and resourceful as well as technically and economically more self-sufficient as time goes on; or that no intervention from public or private sector sources need be undertaken for purely micromarketing problems such as pricing or marketing channel selection, as firms will learn necessary skills. There is a significant danger that export activity of individual firms will simply plateau.

Planners' biases would not be so significant a hurdle were it not for a second complicating factor. Even if they fully appreciated the necessity of positive intervention in support of exporters, the choice of an action plan would not be immediately clear. The undertaking of analytic, information-intensive export marketing programs is beyond the capability of most individual LDC exporters. Not only are the resource requirements beyond the capacity of most firms, but a tradition of protected oligopolies within LDCs leaves exporters inadequately prepared to face serious competition and discriminating consumers. This study has shown that Costa Rican exporters are well aware of the problems they face.

Although the purpose of this chapter has been to determine the nature of nontraditional exporters' problems rather than to attempt a comprehensive policy for Costa Rica or elsewhere, specific directions can be suggested.

The study has suggested that channel, competitor, and customer need-related issues are of the greatest concern to nontraditional exporters. However, the sources of information being employed and most likely to be open to exporters are tainted by the information providers' self-interest or by limited and potentially culturally biased insights of exporters' relatives and acquaintances and short overseas business trips. Costa Rica's export promotion agencies, whether private or public sector, are not currently filling those gaps, although they are serving other functions. The importance of this gap cannot be minimized.

Many studies have reported that export assistance agencies are notably underutilized (e.g., Kedia & Chokar 1986, Ford 1986). Two reasons are readily suggested: there is a need to promote agencies' services, i.e., to "market" marketing; and the agencies are not emphasizing the kinds of services most needed by entrepreneurs. If market research studies are generally beyond the capability of individual firms, omnibus studies conducted in collaboration with trade associations may be possible. Development of networks of contacts and sources of information overseas is of the utmost importance, yet this task is often hampered by the great diversity of industries and products with which export assistance agencies are faced. It may be necessary to select industries for special efforts as well as to earmark specific consular and agency offices overseas for expertise on certain products, e.g., agricultural products in Miami, fisheries in New Orleans, and textiles in New York.

Successful Costa Rican exporters tend to be ambitious and committed, but their export marketing strategies, by and large, are not distinct. Their continuing reliance on few customers, a limited product line, and limited use of marketing information suggests that in the final analysis, sustained export expansion will require new marketing strategies that will be rather more complex than those presently utilized. Exporters' problems and needs are not likely to disappear. There is a generalized need for marketing assistance to a wide spectrum of companies.

Clearly, the findings of this study need to be examined in a broader context. More research is needed to arrive at an understanding of the issues facing LDC firms exporters across a wide spectrum of nations representing different stages of export development. It is hoped that this chapter will encourage scholars elsewhere in the Third World to replicate our design and compare results and implications.

ACKNOWLEDGEMENTS

This study was supported by grants from INCAE, Instituto Centroamericano de Administración de Empresas (Central American management Institute) and by the International Banking and Business Institute of the

University of Miami. The authors wish to thank Ms. Alice Howard, who directed the survey of Costa Rican farms.

REFERENCES

Artavia, Robert, Forrest D. Colburn and Iván Saballos (1987). "De Sustitución de Imprtanciones a Promoción de Exportaciones: Lecciones de Costa Rica," *Revista INCAE*, Vol. 1, No. 1, pp. 44-52.

Balassa, Bela (1984). "The Process of Industrial Development and Alternative Development Strategies," Essays in International Finance, No. 141, 4-11, as reprinted in *Leading Issues in Economic Development*, Gerald T. Meier, Ed., Oxford: Oxford University Press.

Brezzo, Roberto and Isaak Perkal (1983). "The Role of Marketing Incentives in Export Promotion: The Uruguayan Case," *Export Promotion*, Michael R. Czinkota et al., Eds., New York: Praeger, 227-40.

Bulmer-Thomas, V. (1979). "Import Substitution vs. Export Promotion in the Central American Common Market," *Journal of Economic Studies*, 6 (2), 182-203.

Cavusgil, S. Tamer (1984). "Differences Among Exporting Firms Based on Their Degree of Internationalization," *Journal of Business Research*, 12, 194-208.

_____ and John Nevin (1981). "Internal Determinants of Export Marketing Behaviour," *Journal of Marketing Research*, 18 (February), 114-119.

CENPRO (1983). "Ley Costarricense de Incentivos a las Exportaciones," Mimeographed document, Centro para la Promoción de las Exportaciones e Inversiones, San José, Costa Rica.

Christensen, Carl H., Angela Da Rocha and Rosane Kerbel Gertner (1987). "An Empirical Investigation of the Factors Influencing Exporting Success of Brazilian Firms," *Journal of International Business Studies*, 28 (Fall), 61-78.

Dominguez, Luis V. and Cristina Vanmarcke (1987). "Market Structure and Marketing Behaviour in LDCs: The Case of Venezuela," *Journal of Macromarketing*, 7 (Fall).

Edmunds, John (1984). "Pórtico S.A." Case, Centre for Documentation and Exchange of Cases, INCAE, Alajuela, Costa Rica.

Evans, David and Parvin Alizadeh (1984). "Trade, Industrialization and the Visible Hand," *Journal of Development Studies*, 21 (October), 22-46.

Ford, David (1986). "Export Development From the Third World: A Structure for the Analysis of Buyer-Seller Relationships," Staff Paper, National Centre for the Export-Import Studies, Georgetown University, Washington, D.C.

IMF (1988). *Exchange Arrangements and Exchange Restrictions 1988.* Washington, D.C.: International Monetary Fund.

INTAL (1971). *El Desarrollo Integradeo de Centroamérica en las Presente Década.* San José: Instituto para la Integración de América Latina.

Jackson, Graham I. (1981). "Exporting--From the Importer's Viewpoint," *European Journal of Marketing* 15 (October), 3-125.

Johansson, Jan and Jan-Erik Vahlne (1976). "The Internationalization Process of the Firm--A Model of Knowledge Development and Increasing Foreign Market Commitment," *Journal of International Business Studies*, 8 (Spring-Summer), 23-32.

Kaynak, Erdener (1982). *Marketing in the Third World*, New York: Praeger.

Kedia, Ben L. and Jagdeed S. Chokar (1986). "An Empirical Investigation of Export Promotion Programs," *Columbia Journal of World Business*, 21 Winter, 13-20.

Lee, Woo-Young and John J. Brasch (1978). "The Adoption of Export as an Innovative Strategy," *Journal of International Business Studies*, 9 (Spring-Summer), 85-93.

Piercy, Nigel (1981a). "British Export Market Selection and Pricing," *Industrial Marketing Management*, 10 (October), 287-97.

_____ (1981b). "Company Internationalization: Active and Reactive Exporting," *European Journal of Marketing*, 15 (Spring), 107-16.

Reid, Stan D. (1981). "Managerial and Firm Influences on Export Behavior," *Journal of the Academy of Marketing Science*, 11 (Summer), 323-332.

_____ and Charles C. Mayer (1980). "Export Behaviour and Decision Maker Characteristics: An Empirical Investigation," *Marketing 1980: Marketing Excellence in the 1980's*, ed. by V. Jones, University of Calgary, 298-307.

Schydlowsky, Daniel M. (1986). "The Macroeconomic Effect of Nontraditional Exports in Peru," *Economic Development and Cultural Change*, 34, 490-508.

Sequeira, Carlos and Iván Saballos (1987). "HILASAL" (A), (B) and (C) Case, Centre for Documentation and Exchange of Cases, INCAE, Alajuela, Costa Rica.

Seringhaus, F.H. Rolf, (1986). "The Impact of Government Export Marketing Assistance," *International Marketing Review*, 4 (Summer), 55-66.

_____ (1987). "Do Experienced Exporters have Market Entry Problems?", *Finnish Journal of Business Economics*, 4 (1987), 376-388.

Seringhaus, F.H. Rolf and Philip J. Rosson (1990). *Government Export Promotion: A Global Perspective*, London: Routledge.

UNCTAD (1982). *Incentives for Industrial Exports*, New York: United Nations Conference on Trade and Development.

United Stated Department of Commerce (1987). *1986 U.S. Foreign Trade Highlights*, Washington, D.C.

Ursic, Michael L. and Michael R. Czinkota (1984). "An Experience Curve Explanation of Export Expansion," *Journal of Business Research*, 12, 159-68.

Westphall, Lee E., Yung W. Rhee, Garry Pursell (1981). "Korean Industrial Competence: Where It Came From," World Bank Staff Paper No. 469, The World Bank, Washington, D.C.

CHAPTER FIVE

Barriers to Exporting: An Exploratory Study of Latin American Companies

Mary R. Brooks and Antonio Frances*

SUMMARY

Until recently, many Latin American countries sought industrial development through import substitution policies. Increasing globalization of world markets has resulted in the need to participate in global trade with diversified exports. Recognizing that non-traditional exports can contribute to industrial development, many Latin American countries have created institutions and programs to encourage private sector export activity. Substantial barriers to export development remain. This chapter addresses the issue of barriers and considers approaches aimed at overcoming them in Costa Rica, Venezuela, Peru and Chile.

INTRODUCTION

Many Latin American countries have, until recent years, gained industrial development through import substitution policies and the promotion of traditional export products. With the increasing globalization of world markets, it has been recognized that export diversity is needed to counter many countries' dependence on a few resource-based traditional export products.

---

* Dalhousie University, Halifax and Instituto de Estudios Superiores de Administracion, Caracas, respectively.

This recognition that growth in non-traditional exports can serve as an engine for industrial development has meant that many countries have developed a variety of institutions and programs to encourage and facilitate private sector export activity. But these programs have not been completely successful and barriers to exporting remain.

The objective of this chapter is to identify such barriers so that meaningful planning for private sector support of export promotion in Latin American countries is facilitated. Such barriers to exporting may stem from inadequate governmental policies and regulations, lack of a suitable export infrastructure, or difficulties concerning access to foreign markets. The individual manager's assessment of export barriers may not be fully realistic in some cases, but nevertheless it will determine the firm's export behaviour and ultimately be reflected in his/her country's export performance.

In this chapter the barriers to exporting perceived by managers of manufacturing firms in a sample of Latin American countries are explored with the aim of determining the means by which some of these barriers may be overcome through business self-help as opposed to conventional governmental means.

FRAMEWORK

Dymsza (1983) reports that an essential element in the development of a national export strategy is the identification of the obstacles facing industrial development in a country. He identifies the obvious primary obstacle as an import substitution policy but goes on to itemize a number of other barriers including unrealistic exchange rates, inadequate export infrastructure and international marketing capability and cumbersome export procedures. He suggests using these, in conjunction with an evaluation of the country's strengths and weaknesses, as a base upon which the development of suitable export goals and an export strategy for a particular country can be built.

This study is compatible with Dymsza's normative approach – the identification of obstacles as the base for the development of a public policy focused on export promotion, but with one essential difference. As this study's objective is to uncover the means by which the private sector can support the promotion of exports, in particular non-traditional exports, the approach is a microeconomic one. The study explores barriers to exporting from a firm or company perspective and is an assessment of needs as well as an identification of barriers.

OVERVIEW OF THE RELEVANT LITERATURE

The literature relevant to this study focuses on three related areas: (1) macroeconomic tools of export promotion in Latin America and their related microeconomic effects; (2) export behaviour at the firm level; and (3) perceived barriers to exporting, also at the microeconomic or firm level.

In a recent article, Luis R. Luis (1982) presented the traditional tools of macroeconomic policy used by the Latin American countries in their efforts to "obtain a more dynamic export behavior", particularly for non-traditional exports. He concluded that exchange-rate policy is the single most important export promotion tool, as efforts consistent with short-term management of the economy through exchange-rate policy may not be compatible with national long-term objectives of export promotion. Despite the importance of exchange-rate policy in public sector export promotion, he indicates that it is a difficult tool to use in the face of persistent monetary and fiscal disequilibrium, and concludes that most Latin American countries will continue to promote exports through other means, e.g. fiscal, credit and institutional instruments. But exchange rate policy influences export financing programs and the availability of some methods of payment, and the impact of these factors on the firm cannot be ignored.

As the focus of this study is not on macroeconomic policy but on barriers, real and perceived, faced by individual companies, it is research conducted at the company level that is of greatest interest. Researchers at the Instituto Centroamericano de Administracion de Empresas (INCAE) at Alajuela in Costa Rica have undertaken a significant research effort aimed at examining the export promotion activities of the public sector with regard to non-traditional exports by examining the activities of existing exporting companies, specifically those exporting to developed countries.[1] The INCAE research focuses on the problems of non-traditional exporters, generalizing that traditional exporters view the world from a commodity perspective. The study's preliminary report concludes that marketing issues are the greatest export barriers, being more

---

[1] See Chapter Four in this book.

important than financial, legal or infrastructure difficulties. This may be true for non-traditional exporters in Costa Rica exporting to developed countries, but should not be generalized to the situation facing Latin American exporters of non-traditional products in general. It is expected that the importance of different barriers will vary with the situation in each country, and that different programs will be in place to overcome these barriers. Incentives to promote an initial decision to export are also likely to vary by country.

Throughout the late 1970s and early 1980s there appeared a large body of literature focusing on the characteristics of the export decision or on factors which inhibit or stimulate developed country firms to export. (Goodnow & Hanz, 1972; Rabino, 1980; and Tesar & Tarleton, 1981 are some examples; two excellent collections of research efforts in this field are Czinkota & Tesar, 1982 and Rosson & Reid, 1987). The barriers identified by a number of these studies included elements such as national policies and export promotion programs, currency factors, export financing and so on.

Bauerschmidt, Sullivan and Gillespie (1985) noted that this period was overtaken by one which looked to internal firm factors as export barriers and indicated that

> "in spite of the apparent shift in research focus from exogenous to endogenous factors, a large body of literature that details the problems associated with the decision to export suggests that barriers inhibit the internationalization of business firms."

They place significant reliance on the work of Dichtl, Leibold, Koglmayr & Muller (1984) who propose that neutralization of the "threshold fear" that inhibits exporters is partly contingent on identifying those environmental problems confronting both interested and active exporters. Again, this directs study efforts towards the identification of "problems", real and perceived, as the first step in resolving the "threshold fear", the risk, for both the potential and existing exporter. After all, problem identification is always the first step in any successful program development.

These developed country studies, however, may provide little detailed contribution to problem identification in Third World countries. Few conclusions can be drawn from these developed country studies in a cross-national sense as they themselves present quite divergent empirical results even within one country.[2] Given the multi-country nature of this research, an empirical study was viewed as unsuitable.

In spite of the dearth of Latin American research activity in the field of export behaviour, one study was undertaken by de Souza, Schmidt and Colaiacovo (1983) using the case study method to evaluate the export decision by nine Brazilian firms. It was found that tax and credit incentives offered by government act on the export decision as a secondary stimulus, rather than a primary one, and that both rational and behavioural factors play an important role in the export decision process. The findings of this research were further supported by a study by Christensen, Rocha & Gertner (1987) who evaluated continued export success; their study of Brazilian firms, which compared those still exporting with those who had discontinued exporting activity, found that government export incentives may prompt companies to export prematurely thus leading to failure. Both of these studies of export behaviour concentrate on government support to exporting rather than on private sector initiatives possible, the intent of this study.

The classical study regarding barriers to exporting in Latin America is probably Morawitz (1981). He addressed both macroeconomic and firm level issues and found foreign exchange policy and governmental red-tape to be paramount as determinants of the international competitiveness of the Colombian clothing industry.

In 1982, Juan Luis Colaiacovo reported on export development in Latin America, identifying three sets of export problems: export supply problems (essentially firm-specific difficulties such as managerial capacity), export demand problems (such as lack of knowledge of market opportunities, tariffs, distributions difficulties, and so on) and problems of transport and communication infrastructure. He concluded that infrastructure difficulties are still an important factor in Latin American export activity, that problems with the efficient operation of available infrastructure remain, and that Latin American exporters face a greater number of barriers than their developed country counterparts.

Frances, in a 1985 study of 75 Venezuelan exporting manufacturers, found the main perceived barriers, in order of importance, to be official red-tape,

---

[2] A study of exporting success conducted in Canada concluded that there are "surprising few consistencies" in the reasons for export success and that research needs to explore the situational context of export companies and their overall business strategy using an approach of paradigmatic pluralism (Kamath et al 1987).

lack of suitable maritime transportation, limited availability of certain raw material inputs as well as imported intermediate goods, restricted access to foreign markets, unsuitable infrastructure and support services, and unsatisfactory financial facilities.

It is the intent of this chapter to explore potential barriers in four Latin American countries to determine if common issues arise and what such commonalities may hold in the way of private sector opportunities and solutions.

METHODOLOGY

In order to learn how business people's perceptions regarding barriers to exporting compared throughout Latin America, an exploratory study was devised. Four middle-sized countries – Costa Rica, Venezuela, Peru and Chile – were selected.

In each country, an academic facilitator organized a one-day workshop inviting 15-18 businessmen to participate. To facilitate comparison a standard list of likely barriers was developed to guide discussion. This list did not purport to be exhaustive and was not meant to be confining. The participants were free to point out any additional barriers they perceived and to collapse any categories they viewed as indistinguishable.

The sample of companies represented in each country was small (Table 5.1), and cannot claim to be an unbiased cross-section of actual and would-be exporters in their country. They can be trusted, however, to voice any widespread perceptions regarding export barriers in that country, although barriers affecting particular industries or groups not represented could go undetected.

The next section of the chapter presents the views of the participants, but the conclusions are those of the authors.

BARRIERS TO EXPORTING

As illustrated in Table 5.2, barriers to exporting were viewed by the authors to be of two types: (1) those barriers associated with the logistics of making an export sales and meeting the conditions of that sale (e.g., the factors affecting the firm's ability to conclude the export deal); and (2) the export "mentality" of the firm as reflected by its corporate policies and its marketing plans. This second organizational/strategic set of factors also included the firm's perception of its trading environment, including the role of government policy, government agreements and of course cultural factors.

Table 5.1: Participants

Type of company	Venezuela	Peru	Chile	Costa Rica
Exporter – traditional products	-	2	3	-
Exporter – non traditional products	6	10	12	13
Non-exporters	1	0	-	-
Total companies	7	12	13	14

Source: Prepared by authors.

Packaging and labeling requirements

Although Costa Rica's exporters did not think that packaging or labeling affected export development in their firms, the others viewed packaging and labeling as important factors in marketing and also in preventing pilferage in transit. Problems with these requirements were often of a technical nature. One Venezuelan exporter had difficulty with unit labeling. The Peruvians indicated difficulties with canning technology. More importantly, the problems experienced by the Peruvians and the Chileans reflected infrastructure and marketing difficulties rather than product-based technical problems.

In Peru, exporters faced two infrastructure problems: a shortage of cardboard boxes of acceptable quality and the lack of a government agency to certify packaging quality, closing the doors to some markets which require such certification.

The Chileans complained of the high price of cardboard boxes owing to a monopolistic producer. However, it was the buyer's specification of packaging and labeling standards that created the greatest barriers for Chilean producers. It was reported that more and more U.S. buyers require products to be labeled in their final form for retail sale, including scanner codes and other minutia. Chileans sometimes find themselves in a dilemma: buyers do not want the "Made in Chile" designation on the label although U.S. and European law requires it. There was a general consensus that there is a need for information provision as well as technology transfer in the packaging area.

Table 5.2: Barriers to exporting

Logistical	Organizational/strategic
Packaging and labelling requirements	Special customs requirements
Export documentation	Free trade zones (legislation, regulation, operation)
Export financing (private and public)	Market information (particular markets, availability, usefulness, awareness)
Methods of payment (documentary credits, etc.)	Cultural, language differences
Transport services (modes, routes, operators)	Product design and specification requirements
Transport infrastructure (ports, airports, warehousing facilities)	Product competitiveness
Export insurance (type, availability)	Market entry method and expansion (direct, agent/distributors, indirect)
	Government policy

Note: There is no significance to the order in which these are presented; the order for discussion was selected by the workshop participants from an expanded version of this menu. Several categories were collapsed during the discussions and subsequent analysis.

Source: Prepared by authors.

Export documentation

Only Chile indicated no difficulties in this area, while Venezuelan exporters faced the most problems. In Venezuela, two types of predicaments were encountered. First, the bureaucratic red tape is complex and daunting for those just starting to export, although seasoned exporters were conditioned to it. The second is potentially the more damaging: most export documentation must be done in Caracas thereby limiting the development of the export potential of the balance of the country.

Costa Rica's situation is similar to Venezuela's regarding red tape, and this is aggravated by the wide dispersion of institutions involved and high level of intervention of the Costa Rican government in business affairs in general.

Peruvian exporters also faced bureaucratic difficulties. The requirement to provide buyers with certificates of quality by the Societe Generale de Surveillance bestows greater power on local Societe officials than is desirable as the certification service is viewed to be poor and quite costly. Without these certificates, customs clearance cannot be made and export incentive payments are withheld.

The authors conclude that problems in the export documentation area provide opportunities for private sector solutions. There is room, particularly in Venezuela, for "how-to" courses on export documentation, or for private export management companies to provide export documentation services. Banks could also assist by absorbing some of the documentation services, particularly in inland Venezuela, if sanctioned by change arriving to pay for exports was often used to pay down public debt and not immediately remitted to the exporter, causing a cash flow crisis and requiring the exporter to go to the parallel banking system (and provide sufficient collateral) to get working capital at above normal interest rates. The exporters reported that countertrade has not provided a suitable solution as the government requires that the exporter sell 30 percent more than purchased in such transactions and this deters many the government to assist exporters in meeting the documentation requirements for incentive payments. Smoothing the paper trail would be one means of promoting the export of non-traditional products, the producers of which now view the bureaucratic paper chase with trepidation.

Export financing and methods of payment

Problems in export financing could be generally traced to the economic well-being of the country and priority placed by the government on export promotion programs. At one extreme is the situation facing Peru while at the other is that faced by Chile.

Peru's problems are tied to the severe financial situation faced by the country as a whole and, despite some programs to promote non-traditional exports, this is made worse by a general import substitution policy and a multi-tier foreign exchange system. At the time of the workshop, there were a number of official foreign exchange rates and the one used depended upon the government's foreign exchange priority rating. While one exchange rate applied to preferred imports, another to exports and still others to tourism and debt repayments, the most pressing problem for Peruvian exporters existed in remission of earnings. Such severe financial infrastructure obstacles overwhelm all other financing problems.[3]

In much less difficulty is Venezuela. Here the focal point of export financing concern was competitive bid tendering. It was reported that bidding companies are not able to offer firm financial arrangements as government financing is available only after a firm contract is signed. Banks cannot guarantee the financing without government approval. Clearly, a whole market is lost to Venezuelan businessmen who might be interested in participating in the non-traditional export of project development.

In contrast, Costa Rican exporters indicated that their country has ample liquidity and special credit lines for export finance both in public and private institutions. Participants, however, considered that access to credit was difficult, the cost too high, and the approval process too slow. Export credit was formerly available at subsidized rates and with simple and quick processing. Now the cost has risen in real terms to a level above international rates and the exporters were dissatisfied.

Chileans are closer to exporters from developed countries in their views of export financing issues. Many Chilean companies recounted that they are now seen as valuable and trust-worthy trading partners and are able to offer open account payment terms. The question for them has become one of identifying payment options and efforts are now underway to try and improve export credit terms. Chile, like many developed countries, is now facing the dilemma of government participation, even competition, in export credit schemes. However, Chileans declared that they continue to have some difficulties in the area of credit assessment and export financing. The former is an informational deficiency

---

[3] Since the date of the workshop, the situation has worsened; the multi-tier exchange rate exploded in early September 1988 with massive devaluation of the Inti and inflation out of control. The economy is on a survival footing.

while the latter problem is based on commercial practice. Commercial banks in Chile, like many of their developed country counterparts, require collateral for export credit which inhibits smaller firms from contemplating the export alternative. The Chilean government plans to provide a guarantee fund for non-traditional small exporters to overcome this hurdle. There remains one last difficulty to be resolved: the pre- and post-shipment credit so critical to the development of further high-value export activities is not readily available.

The authors conclude that, in the financing area, there is a "critical mass" necessary in the area of banking infrastructure provision before private sector efforts can be fruitful. The problems facing Peruvians will not be responsive to private sector activities in the area of exporter education or credit assessment provision until the country's foreign exchange difficulties are less dominant. This is in direct contrast to the benefits which might accrue to Chileans from private sector efforts as the requisite financial infrastructure is firmly established.

Insurance

The availability and cost of export credit insurance were declared as barriers to exporting in Latin America. Businessmen complained of the lack of rejection and political risk insurance in Venezuela and Peru and the unavailability of buyer insolvency insurance in Chile. It was felt that the absence of these services was rooted in information availability and that better use of commercial bank networks would enable the banks, where legally allowed, to contemplate providing the insurance coverage.

As for transportation insurance, Venezuelans, Costa Ricans and Peruvians all had problems in this area. It was reported that this type of insurance is too expensive in Peru and only covers derailment on the inland leg of the journey. Comprehensive fire and theft policies are not available and so all sales must be made f.o.b. or c & f. Furthermore, there is a credibility problem with insurance in Peru as all re-insurance is by the government. Some Costa Rican exporters mentioned the need to develop an efficient system of transportation insurance for fresh agricultural products. The Venezuelans saw the cost of marine transportation insurance premiums as excessive but noted that handling damage and pilferage levels at the port are high. Insurance problems of both types generally deserve greater attention.

Transport services and infrastructure

All four of the countries faced problems in transport infrastructure and service provision, although the degree varied. Many of these problems stemmed from public policy decisions or differences in the regulation of transport services between countries. For example, for Peruvians, the problems of transborder trucking facing Peruvian exporters were exacerbated by poor quality domestic inland road networks and labour union regulations about stuffing/destuffing containers or trucks at ports and borders. (This complaint is commonly heard in Canada where regulations in the trucking industry are quite different from those required of U.S. operators.) The impact of public policy on transport services was a cause for concern in Venezuela; exporters complained of the poor quality service of the national shipping lines.

In Costa Rica, the most serious problem was the high port charges coupled with low cargo-handling productivity. This problem is also present in Peru and Venezuela. Deficiencies regarding air cargo facilities and discriminatory rates for ocean transport were also mentioned by Costa Rican exporters.

In most cases, efforts are underway to resolve these barriers. In Venezuela, a Council of Transportation Users (CONUTRA) has been formed to strengthen the negotiating power of shippers when dealing with steamship lines. In Peru, private businessmen have led the development of a new containerport south of Lima at Punta Pejerrey (Pisco), served by the CGS Steamship Line as a means of bypassing union problems and pilferage at the port outside of Lima. (However, this does not address the lack of infrastructure available for Peru's bulk mineral exports.) Finally in Chile, after a concerted effort to eliminate the problems at ports and harbours through new legislation, there remains the problem of inland transportation infrastructure which is poor. For this reason, the government is encouraging the private sector to invest in port development in the south of the country to better serve that part of the country than is currently possible through Valparaiso.[4]

---

[4] According to further enquiries, this solution is not moving forward at an acceptable pace.

Special customs requirements

These barriers were seen by participants to be of two types: (1) those imposed by overseas governments and (2) those imposed domestically.

As for the former, complaints about the political interference of importing countries were common. There was a general consensus that it is easier for the exporter to deal with precise documentation or product specification requirements than to deal with an ever-changing regulatory environment. For example, Venezuelan exports to the U.S. have undergone extensive customs inspections as U.S. officials escalate their efforts to curb the illegal Colombian drug trade.

For Chile, where an open door for exports is the general rule, no particular problems were evident in the latter category. Only two of the Costa Rican participants considered that customs procedures constituted an obstacle to exporting. In Venezuela, customs clearance is being done at the factory and the major complaints centre on customs facilities on the overland route to Brazil. Peru's system suffers corruption with "kickbacks" expected and customs inspectors often sampling valuable goods resulting in a shortfall in delivered quantity. There the number of inspections required to export defeats all but the most persistent of companies.

The authors concluded that the businessmen were very much concerned with long-term market stability, abhorring government intervention for political purpose.

Trade agreements

Although many readers might view trade agreements only in a positive light, they do have a negative aspect. Trade agreements may open markets to companies in participating nations, but they can also discriminate against third party traders. For example, the gradual loss for North American companies of some European markets to European Community Members is a well-documented result of the Treaty of Rome.

The Latin American businessmen concluded that their country's participation in some type of multinational trading agreement is not always advantageous. For example, the Venezuelans viewed the ANDEAN Pact as a hindrance rather than a help and felt they could do better without. Chilean exporters agreed with the Venezuelans, not regretting the departure of their country from the ANDEAN Pact. Peruvian exporters felt that bilateral agreements reducing tariffs for certain products were usually negotiated on a government-to-government basis without regard to private interests and that this did not always result in an environment supportive of their export activities.

Market information

Market information can be an important barrier for exporters, particularly in the early stages of exporting. For Venezuelans, the local availability of information on international markets was considered to be limited and foreign trips viewed as very expensive. Government information systems were seen to be of little help and the businessmen reported that Venezuelan embassy personnel, with their largely political outlook, seldom give any real help to exporters. Costa Rican exporters agreed; they are used to protected and subsidized local markets and are unfamiliar with quality standards and marketing systems prevailing in the international marketplace. In Peru seasoned exporters felt they had well-established channels of information but agreed that this can be an important barrier for new exporters, particularly as the information available from the Instituto de Comercio Exterior[5] has deteriorated. In Chile, market information was also viewed an important barrier and an industrial development focus on product imitation has resulted in buyers providing detailed specifications, short-circuiting Chilean efforts at market development. Expectations of PROCHILE (the government export promotion agency) as a source of information were high and performance was considered disappointing by some.

The authors conclude that, even if government agencies can be of help providing market information, the bulk of the task must necessarily lie with the exporters themselves. There is clearly room for improvement through education, as many companies are at a loss regarding how to proceed in their first attempts to enter foreign markets. There is a definitive need to improve the information environment in all the participating Latin American countries as government agencies tend to fall behind exporters' needs. Privately-run information centres could provide the basic information needed by prospective exporters. Such information might include international publications and access to world trade

---

[5] ICE is a full-fledged ministry which recently subsumed FOREX, the export promotion agency, and took over external responsibilities of the Vice Ministry of Commerce.

information systems. World Trade Centres, like those existing in the U.S. and Canada, provide such services and similar centres could be promoted in Latin America.[6]

Cultural, language differences

Exporters agreed that culture and language are not important barriers to international commerce. The only exceptions to this were Peruvian companies who expressed their need to know more about foreign business practices. It should be pointed out that Peru is the most restrictive of the four countries in its policies regarding the foreign travel of local businessmen.

The Latin American businessmen concluded that an international trade culture appears to be emerging, one whose language is English. Chilean exporters indicated that requirements regarding prices, quality, delivery and so on are becoming homogeneous and felt that by-and-large the same demands are to be met in every market, but particularly those in the developed countries. They believe that the problem lies in changing the internal culture of the organization to an "export mentality."

Product design and specifications

A dearth of original industrial design was noted in virtually all Latin American manufactured exports. This situation relegates Latin American companies to be market followers rather than market innovators. A lack of design skills and traditions as well as largely imitative industrial development is to be blamed for this. Following buyers' designs can be a necessary first step in industrial development, but design awareness and abilities need to be nurtured in order to secure long-term markets. This is another area where information collection and dissemination by trade centres or associations can help foster non-traditional exporting.

For Latin American exporters, both the perception and the reality of their product's poor quality can be a serious barrier. Such an image results in either lower prices paid for products of similar quality to those from countries with a good image or an inability to use product branding. Chilean exporters

---

[6] At this time, the only World Trade Centre in all of Latin America is in Rio de Janeiro in Brazil and that trade centre does not provide trade information services.

frequently felt forced to use the client's brand name with the attendant buyer dependency and lower profit margins. As a second example, this image barrier often means that Peruvian agricultural goods must be sold on consignment, pending quality inspection and approval.

However, efforts by the individual exporter may not be enough if a company's reputation for poor quality spills over onto all or most of a country's export products. Quality certification by government agencies is a possible alternative but one abhorred by most exporters. It can become a new source of bureaucratic red tape and even kickbacks, further hindering the development of non-traditional exports. Exporter associations, either country-wide or by industry, could play both informational and self-policing roles. Awarding "export-quality" certificates, "seals" of approval and acting as liaisons with buyers' associations as well as governmental agencies (such as the U.S. Food and Drug Administration) are some of the activities which could be undertaken by these associations to overcome some of these barriers. Furthermore, adequate information on market requirements assists companies in their quest to meet international standards.

Methods of market entry and expansion

In the project context, method of entry was treated as market channel choice, as virtually none of the participating companies had undertaken foreign direct investment. Problems were similar and the importance of choosing the right channel(s) stressed.

Chilean exporters emphasized the importance of using well-informed local agents as a source of information on foreign markets. Participating Chilean exporters of manufactured goods lacked familiarity with export markets and relied, for the most part, on foreign buyers and distributors. Venezuelan exporters used a more direct approach, involving some trial and error, with a broader outlook in their choice of channels, including the establishment of sales subsidiaries in the U.S. Similarly, Chilean fruit exporters had reached a stage of export development allowing them to take virtual control of distribution in many markets.

Exporters tended to take greater control of market channels as they mature and increase their market commitment. This process appears to be both market- and product-specific, and little help is expected from government agencies. Therefore a measure of education, information gathering and dissemination can be extremely useful, and economies of scale in these activities possible. Trading companies, where they exist and possess well developed information systems, can also be helpful.

Product competitiveness

In this area government economic policy can be all important. Except for Chilean exporters, companies mostly complained. For Costa Rican exporters, the two most important factors influencing the competitiveness of their products are government policies (and their effect on the exchange rate) and the managerial capacity of exporters. They found the rate of devaluation of the Costa Rican currency out of alignment with the level of inflation. They also found management attitudes and expectations regarding export activity to be rather unrealistic and in need of adjustment to the current conditions faced in foreign markets.

Venezuelan and Peruvian exporters benefitted from their government's export incentive programs but complained about prevailing foreign exchange policies. In both of these cases, exporters had to surrender their foreign currency earnings to the central bank at the official exchange rate, roughly half the free market rate, and at the same time they could only get necessary foreign inputs and spare parts by paying for them at the free market rate. From 1983 to 1985, Venezuelan exporters were able to sell part of their foreign currency earnings at the free market rate and enjoyed a non-traditional export mini-boom. Following a 90 percent currency devaluation in December 1986, exporters were forced to surrender their foreign earnings at the official rate. At the same time tariffs on some foreign inputs were increased.

The central complaint of both Peruvian and Venezuelan exporters was a lack of continuity and reliability in economic policy, particularly regarding foreign exchange. Such a situation discourages them from undertaking medium and long-term commercial commitments and impedes investment in plant expansion for export. This problem seems to have been successfully resolved in Chile; after a period of instability, exchange rates are now periodically adjusted based on domestic and international inflation rates.

Beyond macroeconomic policy, Venezuelan exporters considered themselves to be competitive in industries where plants using advanced technology were installed during the oil-boom years. However the small size of the domestic market caused concern as it does not allow for full economies of scale in many industries. This is important because inconsistency in public policy curbs investment in export-related activities.

Chilean exporters stressed that product competitiveness is very much dependent on comparative advantage. Open-economy and deregulation policies have allowed plant modernization and encouraged the development of managerial and administrative skills, affording Chilean companies a competitive edge in recent years.

The authors concluded that competitiveness is strongly influenced by government policy. Governments foster or dampen competition both domestically and internationally. Individual companies may succeed in spite of ill-conceived official policies, but broad export development can not be expected in a climate of uncertainty.

Government policy

In addition to the consensus that domestic government policy influences product competitiveness and the trading environment as discussed above, the exporters from all participating countries also agreed that foreign government policy may serve as an important export barrier. Although protectionism by foreign governments was perceived to be the main barrier, it was recognized little can be done about it by the private sector except to complain to your own government.

A whole range of domestic economic and social policies impinge on export performance, from social security to foreign exchange rates. Governments obviously have priorities other than export promotion but exporters can certainly lobby for more favourable policies. Unfortunately different and opposite interests are to be found within the private sector, particularly between domestic and export-oriented companies but also between new and established exporters, small and large ones or between producers and traders. To the extent that such differences can be negotiated within the private sector and a more united front presented to government, more clout can be wielded to promote favourable policies. However, what exporters need most from their governments is stability of public policies. If this can be achieved, the private sector can develop its own solutions to many of the problems of non-traditional export promotion.

DISCUSSION

Part of the difficulty of addressing the promotion of nontraditional exports lies in defining a non-traditional export. As an example: How much value-added processing must take place before the traditional export is changed enough to be considered a non-traditional one? By adding value, the evolution of a traditional agricultural export, like bananas, into one decreed by observers as non-traditional, for example prepared banana fritters, is often a matter of time. In the case of industrial diversification, products which are non-traditional may also become traditional over time. Therefore, the promotion of non-traditional exports can be served by strategies which encourage industrial diversification and exporting in general.

Although the initial objective of this exploratory study was to identify private sector opportunities and strategies for the promotion of non-traditional exports, political influence is hard to divorce from the barriers discussed. When many barriers are thrown up in the face of exporters, as seen in Peru, it is difficult to achieve export diversification. Until the basic problems of currency exchange, transport infrastructure and customs inspection are dealt with by the public sector, private sector options will have questionable influence. In other words, for developing countries there is a "critical mass" of export infrastructure and a threshold of public sector export awareness to be achieved before private sector initiatives will be successful. Successful public sector export promotion requires an overall policy commitment to the strategy of export promotion (as opposed to import substitution). Initiatives must be coordinated. Isolated programs, like Peru's CERTEX program, will not be successful without that level of commitment.

To reiterate, in order to identify private sector opportunities and possible strategies to promote exporting, barriers (real and perceived) must be evaluated and needs identified. This study identified three "needs": information provision, exporter education and organizational support for exporting.

Information provision

Deficiencies exist in two areas: financial information and market information. Financial information gaps exist in Latin America primarily in the area of credit assessment of prospective buyers and this deficiency provides an opportunity for commercial banks to expand the services of their international information networks.

In the area of market information there is greater room for private sector initiatives. New exporters can be found searching again and again for basic information which could be provided by private agencies. This includes country-specific information on business practices, government regulations and customs procedures, as well as publications and other sources of market information on distribution channels, business associations and the like. Market information agencies run by the public sector exist throughout Latin American but appear to be largely ineffectual. They are often out of touch with the needs of exporters and seem to be hard put to provide relevant, current and timely information. This is due to bureaucratic rigidity and, in the Venezuelan and Peruvian cases at least, a lack of adequate staffing and administrative continuity. Providing information free of charge, may also contribute, paradoxically, to their current bad image.

To run such a service involves some costs but there are obvious economies of scale in establishing national or local nonprofit agencies to provide such information on the principal markets for each country's exports. The service does not need to be free of charge. Potential and existing exporters will be willing to pay for information saving them time, effort and travel expenses. Information agencies could be promoted and run by exporters' associations, trade associations or "World Trade Centre" type organizations. Market research is usually needed to get specific information by product and is often available in-house by large exporting companies, but out of reach for smaller companies. Export trading companies and market research service companies can provide them in a cost- effective way, as illustrated by the experience of Venezuelan exporters.

This is not to say there is not a role to be played by public sector agencies in providing information on foreign markets. A country's network of embassies and consular offices provides a unique international infrastructure for *in situ* information gathering complementing any market information services to be provided by private non-profit agencies. Although some Latin American exporters have complained of the political rather than commercial orientation of these overseas offices, this network may be a useful starting point in the information gathering process.

Exporter education

The specific detail of education requirements will need to be more clearly defined but, in general terms, the participants did identify several deficient areas: export documentation fundamentals, customs procedures and practices, transport requirements, financial requirements and practices, and countertrade practices to name a few. English language training was also mentioned.

In all cases, exporter education should serve two purposes: (1) to encourage non-exporters or new exporters to make exporting a business commitment for the long-term, and (2) to move the exporters of non-traditional products along the continuum of export development so that, in time, their products are viewed as "traditional" exports.[7]

Tremendous opportunities exist for the private sector to provide exporter education. Non-profit Chambers of Commerce and industrial associations, or local World Trade Centre type organizations can provide short courses on specific topics. There is also a role for trade and business schools to provide more managerial and technical education. However, the details of such education provision needs to be further examined and developed, particularly as the needs of various export groups are quite different (Sekely, Capella & Collins 1987).

Organizational support for exporting

The question of an appropriate change agent for implementing improvements in information provision and exporter education is central to the success of export promotion in Latin America. Although Luis (1982) indicates that many Latin American countries have established export or trade institutions aimed at providing technical services to exporters, the workshop discussions indicated that further research is needed to evaluate the effectiveness of these institutions as barriers to export remain in areas that should have been addressed by existing public and private sector institutions. Such mixed feelings about the effectiveness of such institutions warrants their further examination.

---

[7] Although this would not necessarily be welcome in the practical sense as many Latin American exporters would then lose access to government incentive programs targeted to "non-traditional" exports.

CONCLUSIONS

Clearly, programs which address these identified needs do not counter all the barriers identified in the course of this exploratory study. There are opportunities for individual entrepreneurial efforts in the areas of credit assessment, insurance, transport and private service agencies to assist exporters in developing and diversifying their overseas activities. There is also the challenge to existing associations, organizations and educational institutions to take a more proactive approach to information provision and exporter education. But how this is to be undertaken is also an avenue for further work.

It is important to keep in mind the limits of such business self-help. If a particular government maintains a policy orientation towards import substitution or focuses its capital spending on internal industrial growth, private sector efforts may be less effective. As well, this effectiveness will be diminished by instability or inconsistency in government policies. There is also the problem of too great a dependence on government incentives to promote export interest and market information. Business can help business with the assistance of government (or in spite of government) but first the needs of business must be identified. This study has done that for four Latin American countries.

ACKNOWLEDGEMENT

The authors wish to thank the Canadian International Development Agency for funding its work under its Management for Change Program as part of the Canada-Latin America CFDMAS-CLADEA Project.

REFERENCES

Bauerschmidt, Alan, Daniel Sullivan and Kate Gillespie (1985). "Common Factors Underlying Barriers to Export: Studies in the U.S. Paper Industry" in *Journal of International Business Studies*, vol. 16, no. 3, pp. 111-123.
Christensen Carl H., Angela da Rocha and Rosane Kerbel Gertner (1987). "An Empirical Investigation of the Factors Influencing Exporting Success of

Brazilian Firms", *Journal of International Business Studies*, Fall, pp. 61-77.

Colaiacovo, Juan Luis (1982). "Export Development in Latin America", in Michael R. Czinkota and George Tesar, Eds. *Export Policy: a Global Assessment*, New York: Praeger Press, pp. 102-111.

Czinkota, Michael R. and Wesley J. Johnston (1983). "Exporting: Does Sales Volume Make a Difference?" in *Journal of International Business Studies*, vol. 14, no. 1, pp. 147-153.

Czinkota, Michael R. and George Tesar, Eds. (1982). *Export Management: An International Context*, New York: Praeger Press.

de Souza, Linda-Mar, Angela Schmidt and Juan L. Colaiacovo (1983). "Pre-Export Behaviour: An Analysis of the Variables Influencing the Decision Process" in Michael R. Czinkota, Ed. *Export Promotion: The Public and Private Sector Interaction*, New York: Praeger Press, pp. 227-240.

Dichtl, E., M. Leibold, G. Koglmayr and S. Muller (1984). "The Export Decision of Small and Medium-sized Firms: A Review" in *Management International Review*, vol. 24, no. 2, pp. 49-60.

Dymsza, William A. (1983). "A National Export Strategy for Latin American Countries: in Michael R. Czinkota, ed., *U.S. – Latin American Trade Relations: Issues and Concerns*, New York: Praeger Press, pp. 5-25.

Frances, Antonio (1987). *La Empresa Manufactura Venezolana y las Exportaciones No Tradicionales*, Papel de Trabajo PTI-1987-11 Caracas: Instituto de Estudios Superiores de Administracion.

Goodnow, J. and J.E. Hanz (1972). "Environmental Determinants of Overseas Market Entry Strategies" in *Journal of International Business Studies*, Spring, pp. 33-60.

Kamath, Shyam, Philip J. Rosson, Donald Patton and M. Brooks (1987). "Research on Success in Exporting: Past, Present, and Future", in Philip J. Rosson and Stanley D. Reid, Eds. *Managing Export Entry and Expansion*, New York: Praeger Press, pp. 398-421.

Luis, Luis R. (1982). "Macroeconomic Management and Export Promotion in Latin America" in Michael R. Czinkota and George Tesar, Eds. *Export Promotion: A Global Assessment*, New York: Praeger Press, pp. 35-42.

Morawitz (1981). *Why the Emperor's New Clothes Are Not Made in Colombia*, New York: Oxford University Press.

Rabino, S. (1980). "An Examination of Barriers to Exporting Encountered by Small Manufacturing Companies", in *Management International Review*, vol. 20, no. 1, pp. 67-73.

Rosson, Philip J. and Stanley D. Reid, Eds. (1987). *Managing Export Entry and Expansion*, New York: Praeger Press.

Sekely, William S., Louis Capella and J. Markham Collins (1987). "Determining Information Needs of Exporters: A Segmentation Approach", *Issues in International Business*, vol. 4, no. 1, Spring, pp. 1-6.

CHAPTER SIX

Export Promotion Policies in Spain and Other E.E.C. Countries: Systems and Performance

David Camino[*]

SUMMARY

Export promotion has been a long standing policy tool supporting the private sector in its foreign trade activity. The export support systems in selected E.E.C. countries are contrasted and in this context, Spain's recently established export promotion organization ICEX is discussed. Considerable similarity in export support measures is noted across the countries reviewed, however, public funding shows wide variation. Spain's ICEX embarked on an ambitious program in terms of budget expansion and highly focused programs and services. While export involvement and development is contingent upon many factors, an econometric approach used to predict the development of exports suggest the beneficial impact of export promotion expenditures.

INTRODUCTION

The aim of this chapter is to bring some insights into the role export promotion systems play in improving the performance of exporters in Spain and other countries in the European Economic Community (E.E.C.).

Our knowledge and understanding of the impact of export promotion policies on exports is still at an early stage, and the costs of such programs as

---

[*] Universidad Autonoma, Madrid.

well as the benefits generated by them are still being questioned. Furthermore, some countries have expressed growing concern that export promotion organizations, through their involvement in the private sector, pose a new form of unfair competition in international markets. Nevertheless, nearly all industrial countries have some kind of export-related public policy usually implemented through a government department or public agency.

Such public export promotion organizations were created to help companies cope with barriers and to increase their exports. Some of the agencies such as the French Centre Francais du Commerce Exterieur (C.F.C.E.) or Italian Instituto Italiano Per El Commercio Estero (I.C.E.) have long experience in assisting exporters, while others as the Spanish Instituto Espanol de Comercio Exterior (I.C.E.X.) are more recent. The instruments used by them to support their exports are basically similar. The main differences appear to lie in the efficiency and cost of these systems.

The Spanish export promotion system has evolved rapidly by expanding services and available funds to meet exporters' demand for support and assistance, and aims to increase the export promotion budget up to the equivalent of one per cent of f.o.b. export value by 1992. The performance of the export support system in terms of its trade impact is only tentative, however, projections to 1992 look promising.

The chapter will first set the export promotion scene by reviewing export policies and promotion systems in selected E.E.C. countries. This is followed by a discussion of the Spanish export promotion organization. Then future developments of export promotion and export performance for Spain are considered. Finally, conclusions are presented.

EXPORT POLICIES AND PUBLIC PROMOTION SYSTEMS IN THE E.E.C.

It is well known how the level and change in exports (or imports) will affect a country's national income. Countries are linked together by trade and a change in one country's national income will have repercussions on the income of its trading partners. Markets, however, may not always be fully competitive and tariffs, quotas and the numerous other forms of protectionism or trade distortion often act as barriers for exporters. Firms may be compelled to enter a foreign market by way of direct investment instead of exporting their products to the foreign country.

Besides public policy there are other factors which influence a country's export performance. These include size of domestic market, geographical situation, availability of resources and so on. Often, these factors can be changed over a period of time if a country's trade policy is outward oriented. For these reasons government plays a direct and influential role in international trade. Thus, states become more and more directly engaged, not least through their own procurement activities, in international trade, and with enhancing the role of exports.

In Figure 6.1 we see how important exports are in selected industrialized countries, but also the considerable range in export dependence. European countries, especially small open economies such as Belgium or the Netherlands, have traded with one another for centuries, while countries with large domestic markets such as the United States, have almost neglected foreign markets as a source of income through exports.

In recent years many governments have realized the importance of export promotion in order to enhance the success of local companies willing to sell their goods abroad. Traditional trade policies were often viewed as inadequate and most industrial countries, especially those in Western Europe, felt that special public organizations devoted to assist and support exporters were required.

Trade policy to promote exports can be broadly classified into three main categories:

1. Fiscal: including reduced tax rates, reimbursement of value added tax (VAT), tariff exemptions for some imports, etc.
2. Financial: mainly export credits and credit insurance
3. Promotion: through information, market research, exhibition centres and trade fairs, publicity, etc.

Public export promotion organizations are concerned with the latter category. The other two, when not regulated through international institutions such as GATT or UNCTAD, are usually agreed between the governmental bodies in different forums (OECD Consensus for Credit, Bern Union for Credit Insurance, VAT returns in the E.E.C., etc.).

Figure 6.1:   Export dependence of selected countries

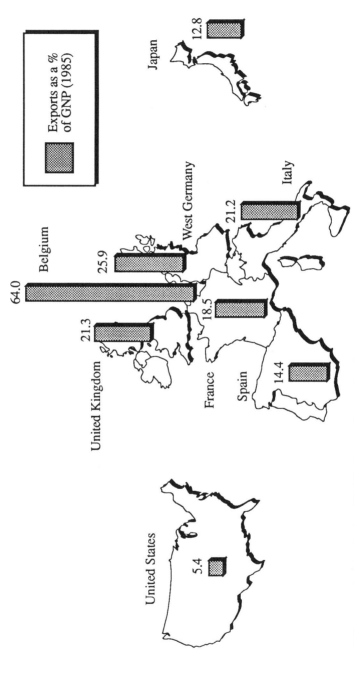

Source: A Comparative Analysis of Public Export Promotion Support in Spain
and EEC Countries - Ministry of Industry and Energy (1985).

The purpose of these agreements is to avoid unfair competition between exporters and leave the promotion alternative as the basic tool available to countries to increase their exports, without provoking confrontation with trading partners or international institutions.

In recent years many governments have become aware of the need for new trade policy initiatives to help exporters in their efforts to increase sales abroad. Thus, two new policy aspects have emerged:

1. The creation or reorganization of public agencies dedicated to export promotion.
2. The development and use of new tools aimed at making exports more profitable for domestic companies.

For this study we have selected six E.E.C. countries to emphasize the variety of export promotion approaches. Some, like Belgium, France, Italy and the United Kingdom, have public organizations with a longstanding tradition in promoting exports, either under a ministry or department of commerce or independent agencies. Spain's ICEX is one of the most recent organizations and was created in 1982. Germany differs from the other countries discussed here in that its export promotion task has been largely left to the private sector (chambers of commerce and trade organizations), with some minor assistance provided by different federal institutions.

The agencies devoted to export promotion in these countries are briefly reviewed:

- France: The Centre Francais de Commerce Exterieur (C.F.C.E.) founded in 1943, is the public organization engaged in promoting French exports, under the Ministry of Economy and Foreign Trade.
- Belgium and Luxembourg: Both countries promote their exports through the Office Belge du Commerce Exterieur (OBCE), set up in 1948.
- United Kingdom: The Department of Trade and Industry is the parent Ministry of the British Overseas Trade Board (BOTB), which is the main organization concerned with export support in the UK.
- Germany: As mentioned above there is no central governmental agency specialized in promoting exports in Germany. Instead the Ministry of Economy set up several organizations at the federal level providing informational assistance to exporters.

- Italy: The Istituto Italiano para il Comercio Estero (I.C.E.) is a public entity founded in 1926 to support Italian exports under the Ministry of Foreign Trade.
- Spain: The Instituto Español de Comercio Exterior (ICEX) was set up in April 1982 under the name of Instituto Nacional de Fomento a la Exportacion (I.N.F.E.) as a public entity dependent of the Ministry of Economy and Finance to promote exports.

These agencies usually are in close touch with the commercial staff of their embassies whom they often use to collect market data. The organizations, however, mainly act as information centres to exporters. Their major forms of assistance can be grouped under

1. Information and documentation
2. Advice and assistance
3. Promotion activities (Fairs, trade missions, etc.).

A comprehensive list of services provided within each of the three groups by the different organizations is provided in Tables 6.1, 6.2, and 6.3.

These six countries have set up services of information, assessment and promotion addressed to similar user targets. There is also considerable similarity in the promotional tools across the countries.

In terms of information, all the agencies have developed computerised systems designed to collect and distribute export intelligence, both on a sectoral and geographical basis. Data is collected through commercial officers at overseas embassies and from worldwide publications. Such data includes trade opportunities, tenders, enquiries for products or services and marketing intelligence, which is then classified, stored and distributed to subscribers by computer or mail. Such documentation and statistics are also available through a public reference library to any exporter seeking information about foreign markets.

Advice and assistance are readily available to exporters in most of the agencies, either directly or through commissioned consultants. Assistance usually takes the form of country-specific marketing research or advice on prevalent conditions as to customs, transport, agents, payment conditions, and so on. Sometimes financial help is provided to a firm or group of companies to undertake market research overseas by themselves. Technical help to obtain and

Table 6.1: Information and documentation

		France	Belgium	U.K.	F. R. G.	Italy	Spain
Export promotion public organizations		C.F.C.E	O.B.C.E.	B.O.T.B. through Directorates of Ministry of Commerce	Federal Ministry of Economy	I.C.E.	I.C.E.X.
Publications: Non-selective information	Special:	Monographic studies on countries	Study groups by sectors	Export Intelligence Service (EIS)	Studies on foreign markets	*Esportare* (fortnightly)	Guides on countries
		Reports of basic information			Studies by sector	*Informazione per il Mercato* (daily)	Market studies
		Reports of products-countries			Yellow Guide: magazine about foreign trade	*Notiziario Ortofrutticolo* (monthly)	INFE brochures
	Regular:	*Moniteur de Commerce Int.* (weekly)	In Belgium *Les informations du Commerce Exterieure* (bi-monthly)	*World Economic Comments* (quarterly)	News about Foreign Commerce (NFA) (bi-monthly)		*Expansion Comercial* (monthly)
		Agriculture Bulletin	Abroad *Belgique, informations*	Monographic studies			

Table 6.1: Information and documentation (cont'd)

	France	Belgium	U.K.	F. R. G.	Italy	Spain
	Fiscal & law papers	*economique et commerciales* (quarterly)	Market advisory service Studies by sector			
Selective information (computerized service)	TELEMAQUE Information directly sent to companies about: Public markets, developing plan, large projects and local entities	FORIMPA Information directly sent to companies about: Commercial opportunities FLASHFIN Projects internationally financed FLASH promotion services with OBCE	EIS Information directly sent to companies about: Demand for products or services Demands of possible foreign agents or companies Import regulations in foreign markets International tenders Large projects	N.A.	GESVIS Through data processing centre of ICE they transmit all available information about: • Chambers of commerce • Industrial associations • Ministries • Offices of ICE abroad DKBIE Sector information	BISE Directly to companies: • Commercial opportunities • International tenders (TED) • OFERES, SYCE • Transmission to peripheral network of INFE • Situation of export offers

Table 6.1: Information and documentation (cont'd)

	France	Belgium	U.K.	F. R. G.	Italy	Spain
Document centre	• Library • Centre of documentation on foreign countries • Centre of documentation agriculture and food	• Library with computer data file	• Library of statistics and reports about foreign markets (SMIL) • Product data store	• Federal Offices	• Library: Data base of information	• Library documents about foreign markets (BIBLOS, ESTACOM) EEC information (CELEX, SCAD)

Source: A Comparative Analysis of Public Export Promotion Assistance in Spain and EEC Countries; Ministry of Industry and Energy (1985); and author's compilation.

Table 6.2: Assistance to exporters

	France	Belgium	U.K.	F. R. G.	Italy	Spain
Orientation and assistance	• Sectoral specialist: - industrial product - agro-food products	• Welcome and orientation department	• Market advisory service	Federal offices	• Technical information service	• Basic information service
	• Standards and regulations (AFNOR, NOREX*)	• Regional action dept.	• Technical assistance to exporters		• Commercial information service	• Expert information service (contracts, transport, standards).
		• Sectorial assistance	• Projects in foreign markets			• Scholarships and training courses.

* NOREX is not associated with C.F.C.E.

Source: A Comparative Analysis of Public Export Promotion Assistance in Spain and EEC Countries; Ministry of Industry and Energy (1985); and author's compilation.

Table 6.3: Promotion actions with government assistance

	France	Belgium	U.K.	F. R. G.	Italy	Spain
Within the country	• Special fairs • Welcome of industry, missions and foreign buyers	• Invitations to missions and foreign buyers • Welcome to foreign buyers	• Export marketing research scheme • Export representative service • Market prospects service	• There are no specific programs of export promotion • Attendance and financing to national fairs	• There are no specific programs of export promotion • Financial help to export associations	• Fairs in Spain
Abroad: international fairs and exhibitions	• Official attendance • Attendance in groups • Single attendance	• Official attendance • Attendance in groups • Single attendance	• Official attendance • Collective introduction of products or services in fairs or similar • *All British Exhibition:*	• Official attendance • Attendance in groups	• Official attendance • Attendance in groups	• Official attendance • Attendance in groups • Single and private attendance
Commercial, economic and technical exhibitions	• Tests of products • Commercial missions	• Meetings and symposia • Commercial	• Symposium and seminars • Meetings		• Exhibition of products • Commercial	• Inverse commercial missions

Table 6.3: Promotion actions with government assistance (cont'd)

	France	Belgium	U.K.	F. R. G.	Italy	Spain
of collective character	• Technical symposia • Commercial promotion in department stores	weeks • Economic missions • Inverse missions	• Inverse missions		missions • Commercial promotions in department stores	• Technical seminars • Mini-exhibit
Assistance to single companies	• Market research missions • COFACE prospecting mission • Tests of products	• Market research missions • Specific actions	• Market research missions • Publicity service (COI)		• Market research missions • Publicity service	• VIAPRO (market prospecting travel) • Market opening programs and promotion abroad • Multisector. promotion agreements
Support of companies carrying out large projects abroad	• ANVAR risk covering program	• Foreign Commerce Fund	• The Aid & Trade Provision • The overseas project fund	• The GTZ supports exporters assoc. for big projects in LOC	• Long term sectorial plans	• FAOT (offers funding assistance).

Table 6.3: Promotion actions with government assistance (cont'd)

	France	Belgium	U. K.	F. R. G.	Italy	Spain
Assistance to export associations	• (ACECO)* Barter Assoc.			• Subsidies to associations to reduce export cost	• Tax and credit subsidies	• Association Program A.N.E.X.
Support of sectorial plans	• (ACTIM)* Technical Cooperation				• Medium and long term projects	• Two or more years sector projects. • Promotional centers
Investments	• CODEX, co-finance system Special cash credits COFISE finance.	• Credits, that become subsid. after 6-7 years of insufficient exports.	• Market entry guarantee scheme: Low interest credits, up to 50% of costs		• Preferential 5 years credit at up to 8% of budget costs	• Foreign investment program (COFIDES) • Promotion projects for smaller firms

* ACECO and ACTIM are not associated with C.F.C.E.

Source: A Comparative Analysis of Public Export Promotion Assistance in Spain and EEC Countries; Ministry of Industry and Energy (1985); and author's compilation.

interpret foreign technical requirements concerning their products (standards, design, safety legislation or codes, etc.) is also available from the agencies.

Promotion activities usually include some kind of financial assistance to exporters in any of the following schemes:

1. International trade fairs or exhibitions. Assistance is usually provided for a collective presentation of national goods or for the rental of space or booth facilities by firms or groups.

2. In- and outward trade missions sponsored by a trade association or chambers of commerce are furnished with financial support for travel expenses. Help is available also for overseas market research, seminars, technical presentations, etc..

3. Export trade associations of small and medium size companies are encouraged through different schemes that supply temporary technical and financial assistance to establish basic export services (telex, translations, professional advice, etc.) for new exporters.

The overall cost of these export development programs is difficult to estimate primarily because of a general lack of information about the expenses involved in export support, and methodological difficulties in determining how funds are allocated by the respective public or private sector organization.

Comparisons involving the budgets and expenditures of the different agencies allocating funds for public export promotion are difficult due to differing approaches of countries. Thus while in Germany, Japan and the United States the main role of export promotion is in the hands of the private sector, in many of the E.E.C. countries there is a tradition of providing public support to the private sector.

When we consider the countries in which public resources are allocated by government to central export promotion agencies, the size of promotion budget in 1983 ranged from $19.5 million for Spain to $81.6 million for Italy (Table 6.4). If we express these budgets as a percentage of countries' exports (f.o.b. values) – admittedly a simplistic relationship – the highest proportionate expenditure occurred in Italy and Spain (0.1 %) and the lowest in France and Belgium (0.04 %). Some budgets have remained at similar levels in absolute figures (i.e., United Kingdom's BOTB net cash expenditures were $73.25 million in 1987, against $77.55 million in 1983), while others increased dramatically during the same period (i.e., Spain's ICEX expanded seven fold to $146 million).

Table 6.4: Promotion budget and exports (1983)

Country	Exports (mill. $)	Promotion (mill. $)	Percentage
France	91,100	36	0.04
Belgium	51,700	23	0.04
U. K.	91,400	78	0.08
Italy	72,700	82	0.11
Spain	19,780	20	0.10

Source: A Comparative Analysis of Public Export Promotion Support in Spain and E.E.C. Countries – Ministry of Industry and Energy (1985).

SPAIN'S EXPORT PROMOTION SYSTEM: I.C.E.X.

The Spanish export promotion organization was set up at the end of 1982 under the name of Instituto Nacional de Fomento a la Exportación (INFE) as an agency of the Ministry of Economy and Finance. Its mandate was to promote exports with public funds. Previously some of INFE's tasks (such as documentation, trade fairs and missions, etc.) were carried out in different departments of the Ministry, albeit with limited promotion tools, excess of bureaucracy and little coordination.

The export organization was reorganized in 1987 and re-named to Instituto Español de Comercio Exterior (ICEX). Under a new Export Promotion Plan, assistance to exporters including services provided by some 79 commercial offices around the world would be better coordinated. Another reason for restructuring export support was the impending internal European market integration after 1992.

The main programs and instruments of ICEX to fulfil the Export Promotion Plan are:

1. Information to domestic and foreign firms, on:
    - trade statistics and regulations (tariff, customs)
    - potential Spanish exporters (around 60,000 are on the OFFERES data base)
    - Trade opportunities to about 1,500 subscribers (BISE)

> • Foreign market data, collected by the Commercial Offices abroad.
2. Advice, courses and publications:
> • Contracts and arbitrage, standards and technical specifications, packing and transport.
> • Training courses in foreign trade with Universities and private institutions. Availability of scholarships.
> • Magazines, news and market research studies. Yearly census of Spanish exporters.
3. Trade Fairs:
> • Financial support for exhibitions under national pavillion, groups or individual firms.
> • Assistance in the organization of domestic sectoral exhibitions
4. Export firms assistance:
> • New exporters association (ANEX)
> • Market prospects and promotion campaigns abroad
> • Set up of commercial firms and export trading companies abroad
> • Technological research linked to international contracts
5. Sectoral plans, financial support to:
> • Inbound and outward trade missions
> • Sectoral promotion plans (advertising campaigns and exhibitions)
> • Investments abroad

The public resources used by ICEX in pursuit of these objectives have increased fast and steadily from 2.8 billion ptas ($19.5 million) in 1983 to 18 billion ($146 million) in 1987. In contrast with other export promotion organizations (such as U.K.'s BOTB), ICEX has applied its budget mainly to services providing direct support to exporters. For example, in 1984 and 1985, in excess of 90 percent of the budget was spent on trade fairs and sectoral plans in specific countries and regions. Table 6.5 illustrates how the Spanish export promotion budget for the years 1984 and 1985 was applied to different services and programs.

In 1987, the total ICEX budget represented around 0.4 percent of Spanish f.o.b. export value, up from 0.1 percent in 1983. The Export Promotion Plan predicates further rapid growth of this budget in order to reach 1.0 percent of the export value by 1992 (i.e., 0.6 percent in 1988, 0.7 percent in 1989, 0.8 percent in 1990, 0.9 percent in 1991). It is noteworthy that the plan appears to be on target with a budget to exports ratio of between 0.5 and 0.6 percent or 22 billion ptas (approx. U.S. $200 million) for 1988.

Table 6.5: Spanish export promotion budget (1984-1985) ($ mill.)

Service or Program:	1984	1985
Information	1.72	1.67
Courses	0.83	1.25
Advising	0.38	1.18
Trade Fairs	12.19	12.35
Assistance	6.62	12.41
Sector Plan	8.54	12.38
Total	30.29	41.23

Source: Spanish Institute of Foreign Trade (ICEI, before INFE) 1985.

With the aid of export data since 1961, and the experience of ICEX's export promotion budget, both exports and the promotion budget were estimated to 1992. While details of the forecast methodology are discussed in the appendix, it is noteworthy that exports would expand to some $45 billion, or twice the export value achieved in 1984 (Table 6.6).

Considering the size of Spain's economy, the export promotion budget of ICEX compares favourably with that of other export promotion organizations in other E.E.C. countries.

The fact that ICEX is a relatively new institution has an inherent advantage in that its focus is clear and its programs and services aim to support export development by responding to the needs of target use groups. For example, a positive image based on quality and competitiveness of Spanish products needs to be supported, special emphasis is placed on small and medium-sized exporters, and last but not least, investment to further develop the export infrastructure receives emphasis.

Table 6.6: Spanish exports and promotion budget (1983-1992)

Year	Exports ($ mill.)	ICEX budget ($ million)	Export promotion as % of exports
1983	19,593	19.5	0.10
1984	22,722	30.3	0.13
1985	23,478	41.2	0.17
1986	26,600	67.8	0.25
1987	33,978	146.1	0.43
1988*	33,815	200.0	0.59
1989*	36,503	255.0	0.70
1990*	39,295	315.0	0.80
1991*	42,192	380.0	0.90
1992*	45,192	452.0	1.00

* = forecast of exports and budget.
Source: See Appendix to the chapter.

The results of promotion efforts are not immediate and a lag occurs between export promotion expenditure and effect on exports. Such lags stem from the gestation period implicit in particular export promotion measures, for example the expense of a trade fair may only result in sales in the following year. When exports and export promotion budgets are viewed together in the same year or with a one year lag, the trend line shows an increasing slope. In other words, export promotion expenditures and exports are positively related. We must be careful not to suggest direct causality, particularly in the short term, since many other factors influence the export decision and involvement of the individual firm. Measuring the impact of export promotion and the effectiveness of such efforts, both of firm and national level, is highly complex and beyond the scope of this chapter. A comprehensive discussion of this issue can be found in Seringhaus and Rosson (1989).

SUMMARY AND CONCLUSIONS

Until recently, tariffs were seen as the main barriers to exports. In the 1970s nontariff barriers (NTB) became a feature of international trade. While GATT worked to reduce tariff levels, NTBs actually increased the overall level of protection. NTBs are less visible than tariffs and their effects in trade flows are more difficult to estimate (GATT took the first measures about NTB only in 1979). Countless NTBs are applied by countries, however, the OECD countries consider technical and safety specifications (standards and homologation) to be the main ones, while Eastern European and developing countries seem to be more worried about quotas and subsidies. For the latter countries, tariffs are still the main barrier of trade.

Paradoxically, as some countries try to protect their markets from foreign competition, they encourage exports through public promotion policies, which are generally of three types:

1. Fiscal (tax exemptions, VAT reimbursement, etc.)
2. Financial (credit and export credit insurance)
3. Promotion (Information, Assistance, Trade missions and fairs, etc.)

The latter is one of the main tools used by governments to increase their export performance, often through publicly funded export promotion organizations.

A comparison of export promotion systems used in seven E.E.C. countries (France, Belgium and Luxembourg, United Kingdom, Germany, Italy and Spain) shows that, except for Germany, where the chambers of commerce and trade associations have the main role in supporting exporters, the organization of export promotion through public agencies is very similar. The instruments and policies used by these agencies are also mainly traditional and their differences appear to lie mainly in the effectiveness of their policies and the public resources available to support exporters.

The financial resources available to these agencies for the promotion of exports differs widely between countries. The budgets of some new agencies like Spanish ICEX are growing very rapidly, both in absolute and relative terms, while other more traditional organizations, such as the British BOTB, have maintained stable budget levels in recent years, attempting to improve the quality and efficiency of services. Most of the resources are used to help exporters abroad (through trade fairs and missions, travel and marketing facilities, etc.) instead of more basic services as market information and research at home.

A review of the main export promotion systems in the E.E.C. suggest that the organizations use similar instruments but employ them in different ways, according to the tradition of government and private sector interaction in each country.

Spain's ICEX was set up late in 1982 and has since expanded both in terms of personnel and budget to cope with the increasing demand for promotion services in a highly competitive and changing trade environment. The new Export Promotion Plan foresees an export promotion budget of 1 percent of exports in 1992, or approximately $450 million, some twenty-two times the budget of 1983. The intent of this plan is to create a solid export basis and to improve the quality image of Spanish exports both within the E.E.C. and in other foreign markets. The impact of export promotion on export volume is not immediate due to the many other factors affecting sales abroad. Even in the long term such impact must not be overestimated, since the basic factors of competitiveness in exports still depend on innovation, quality and price.

APPENDIX

Based on export data since 1961 and the target percentage of export promotion budget provided under the Export Promotion Plan, export volume was projected using three different models. While all models achieved high R-squared, the best fit was achieved using the quadratic model. The following tables provide the estimation models and their equations, a summary of the fit, and actual and estimated export volumes generated with the three models.

Table 6A.1: Estimated fitted models using least squares

1. Estimated exponential model   i for t=1, 2, ... , 27
    $Y=517.10 (1.17957)^t$
    Compounded growth rate=18.0 per cent
    Exponential trend is highly significant (t-statistic=30.012)

2. Estimated linear model   i for t=1, 2, ... , 27
    $Y=-6267.3 + 1180.16t$
    Linear trend is highly significant (t-statistic=14.010)

3. Estimated quadratic model   i for t=1, 2, ... , 27
    $Y=770.46 - 275.921t + 52.003t^2$
    Linear trend is marginally significant (t-statistic=-1.507)
    Quadratic trend is highly significant (t-statistic=8.196)

Table 6A.2: Summary of the fit for the three models

	Exponential model	Linear model	Quadratic model
Mean absolute percent error	18.6	123.4	18.6
Standard error	4,313.309	3,409.362	1,785.310
R^2	.9730	.8870	.9703

Source: Prepared by author.

Table 6A.3: Table of actual and estimated export volume

Time	Actual Y	Exponential trend	% Error	Linear trend	% Error	Quadratic trend	% Error
1961	710	610	14.1	-5087	816.5	547	23.0
1962	736.67	719	2.4	-3907	630.4	427	42.0
1963	735	849	-15.5	-2727	471.0	411	44.1
1964	935	1001	-7.1	-1547	265.4	499	46.6
1965	970	1181	-21.7	-366	137.8	691	28.8
1966	1253.33	1393	-11.1	814	35.1	987	21.2
1967	1379.48	1643	-19.1	1994	-44.5	1387	-0.6
1968	1588.67	1938	-22.0	3174	-99.8	1891	-19.0
1969	1900	2286	-20.3	4354	-129.2	2499	-31.5
1970	2387.14	2697	-13.0	5534	-131.8	3212	-34.5
1971	3058.74	3181	-4.0	6714	-119.5	4028	-31.7
1972	3801.55	3752	1.3	7895	-107.7	4948	-30.2
1973	5195.67	4426	14.8	9075	-74.7	5972	-14.9
1974	7072.28	5220	26.2	10255	-45.6	7100	-0.4
1975	7690.3	6158	19.9	11435	-48.7	8332	-8.3
1976	8721.97	7263	16.7	12615	-45.0	9668	-10.9
1977	10204.05	8568	16.0	13795	-35.2	11109	-8.9
1978	13044.16	10106	22.5	14976	-14.8	12653	3.0
1979	18191.57	11921	34.5	16156	11.2	14301	21.4
1980	20663.88	14061	32.0	17336	16.1	16053	22.3
1981	20209.06	16586	17.9	18516	8.4	17909	11.4
1982	20063.72	19654	2.5	19696	1.8	19870	1.0

Table 6A.3: Table of actual and estimated export volume (cont'd)

Time	Actual Y	Exponential trend	% Error	Linear trend	% Error	Quadratic trend	% Error
1983	19593	23078	-17.8	20876	-6.5	21934	-11.9
1984	22722	27221	-19.8	22057	2.9	24102	-6.1
1985	23478	32110	-36.8	23237	1.0	26374	-12.3
1986	26600.6	37875	-42.4	24417	8.2	28750	-8.1
1987	33978	44676	-31.5	25597	24.7	31231	8.1
1988	-	52699	-	26777	-	33815	-
1989	-	62162	-	27957	-	36503	-
1990	-	73324	-	29137	-	39295	-
1991	-	86490	-	30318	-	42192	-
1992	-	102021	-	31498	-	45192	-
1993	-	120340	-	32678	-	48296	-

Source: Computed by author.

REFERENCES

Anjaria, Shailendra J., Kirmani, Naheed and Petersen, Arne B. (1985). *Trade Policy Issues and Developments*, International Monetary Fund, Washington, D.C.

Bekerman, Marta (1986). *Promotion de Exportaciones. Una Experiencia Latinoamericana: El caso de Brasil.*, Comercio Exterior, vol. 36 No. 5, Mexico.

Cahiers francais no. 229 (1987). *Le Commerce International*, Paris.

Crespy, Guy (1988). *Strategies et Competitivites Dans L'industrie Mondiale*, Observatoire des Strategies Industrielles, Ed. Economica, Paris.

De Vries, Barend A. (1979). *Export Promotion Policies*, World Bank Staff Working Papers No. 313, Washington D.C.

Garcia Bianco, J.L. (1985). La Politica de Promoción Comercial Española., Información Comercial Española no. 624-625, Madrid.

Granell, Francesc (1979). *La Exportación y los Mercados Internacionales*, Hispano Europea, Barcelona.

Instituto Español de Comercio Exterior (1988). *Servicios a la Exportación*, Madrid.

Instituto Nacional de Fomento de la Exportación (1985). *Objetivos y Programas*, Madrid.

Machado, Carios (1988). "Export Assistance: Yes or No? And if Yes, What Kind?" Symposium on the Importance of Trade Promotion and Assistance, Washington D.C.

Manzanares, Rafael (1983). "Instrumentos de fomento de la exportación", Información Comercial Española, Julio-Agosto, Madrid.

Ministerio de Industria y Energia (1987). *España en Europa, un Futuro Industrial*, Madrid.

OECD (1987). *The Export Credit Financing Systems in OECD Member Countries*, Paris.

Requeijo, Jaime (1987). *Introducción a la Balanza de Pagos de España*, Madrid.

Rhee, Young Whee (1985). *Instruments for Export Policy and Administration. Lessons from the East Asian Experience*, World Bank Staff Working Papers No. 725, Washington D.C.

Secretaria General Técnica del Ministerio de Industria y Energia (1985). *Análisis Comparativo de las Ayudas Públicas a la Exportación en la CEE y en España*, Madrid.

Seringhaus, F.H. Rolf and Philip J. Rosson (1990). *Government Export Promotion: A Global Perspective*, London: Routledge.

Sodersten, Bo (1982), *International Economics*, Hong Kong: The MacMillan Press Ltd.

U.S. Department of Commerce (1988). "Export Now. It Makes Good Business Sense", *Business America,* Washington D.C.

Wheeler, Colin (1988). "Stimulating the Scottish and United Kingdom Economies through Export Promotion Programmes", Symposium on the Importance of Trade Promotion and Assistance, Washington D.C.

CHAPTER SEVEN

Italian Exporting SMFs and Their Use of Support Services

Roberto Sbrana and Monica Siena Tangheroni[*]

SUMMARY

The focus of this study is on the support services offered by private and public institutions in Italy to small and medium-sized export firms. Previous research in this area has focused on the internationalization of Italian SMFs and the availability of export support services.

Since exporting is becoming more and more important for Italian firms generally it is timely to analyze export support and how effective it is for small firms entering foreign markets. This chapter is based on the evaluation by small firms of non-financial support services offered by private and public institutions, using data from a survey of 116 exporting Italian SMFs associated with export consortia. After a description of the characteristics of the SMFs interviewed, the use and the helpfulness of support services are analyzed and conclusions offered.

INTRODUCTION

Italian industry consists largely of small and medium-sized firms (SMFs) which represent almost all the manufacturing units, especially in the production of traditional goods (textiles, fashion, leather & shoes, furniture, tiles, etc.). In these industries the great majority of firms are artisan-based, with

---

[*]   University of Pisa, Pisa.

less than 10 employees (Varaldo 1987), principally settled in the so called "third Italy" (Piore-Sabel, 1980). Despite this characteristic, Italy enjoys a leading position in the international arena founded largely on the export of products manufactured by these "fragmented industries".

One might assume that, because small size is often considered an obstacle to export activity, the international success SMFs have enjoyed is due to a wide range of public and private services which help small manufacturers to overcome their own limitations. This chapter then deals with some relevant aspects of the export activity of Italian SMFs and seeks to determine the extent to which support services offered by public and private institutions help them to successfully perform in international markets.

Export activity of Italian SMFs has been the subject of ongoing research by many scholars since these companies have a relevant role in export trade (Bonaccorsi, 1987). Some of this research deals also with the institutions supporting SMFs in their export activity, pointing out the nature of these institutions and the type of services they can offer.

The recent Italian literature covers the subject in different ways. Some research deals with general characteristics of the internationalization of SMFs with only minor reference to the institutions offering export support services (Gerby Sethi 1979, 1982). Other studies are empirical in nature, focused on export support services or export performance of SMFs limited to one geographic area of Italy (Fornasari 1986, Crescini 1986, Quaglia 1986, Reid 1987). Finally, some research efforts concern the analysis of public and private institutions offering support services to exporting SMFs (Finpiemonte-Ceris 1981, Bittante 1985).

Our study represents therefore a new approach, since it examines the support services used by SMFs rather than those offered by the institutions. In other words, our emphasis is not on macroeconomic dimensions, rather we consider the public policy and support services in the microeconomic context of firm behavior. Moreover, our research endeavours to bring out the entrepreneur's opinion about available support services and their level of usefulness.

This chapter consists of the following sections:
1. methodology;
2. characteristics of respondent firms;
3. export orientation in SMFs;
4. sources of export growth;
5. foreign market information sources;

6.   the use of support services by SMFs;
7.   conclusions.

METHODOLOGY

For the purpose of sample selection two key characteristics were specified: first, the firms had to be current exporters, second, they had to be small or medium-sized, with 200 or less employees.

No industry sectors were specified as a broad representation of small business was sought. Federexport[1] assisted in providing names and addresses of small and medium-sized firms to be included in the sampling frame. Through Federexport contact was established with some consortia of small firms. Consortia executives assisted in identifying and selecting firms most willing to participate in the survey. The decision to use consortia executives as a participant motivator was taken to achieve the best possible response rate, given that the usual willingness of Italian firms to participate in surveys is very low. This may have introduced a "distortion" in the sample, by influencing some of the aspects of the study, to a small extent, as we will see later.

The questionnaire used in this study was adapted from one used in a Canadian study on export practices (Seringhaus 1987). The underlying rationale was two-fold. First, to adapt a proven research instrument, second, to develop some comparable data for subsequent analysis.

The Canadian questionnaire was translated and adapted to the Italian situation. Highlights of the main areas of adaptation are:

1.   Simplification or exclusion of some questions. In fact previous research with mail questionnaires among to Italian SMFs suggests that the average level of the entrepreneur's cultural and educational background does not permit the asking of questions beyond a certain complexity or specificity without the benefit of a personal interview. For these reasons we decided also to avoid questions about financial problems. In addition, our experience suggests that small firms would have been reticent in giving such information in a mail questionnaire.

---

[1]   Federexport is the National Association of Export Consortia. This federal institution had 151 associated Italian export consortia in 1987.

2. The adaptation of the section concerning the institutions offering
    support services to exporting firms required substitution of Italian
    organizations and services.

3. The majority of questions did not ask for data or quantitative
    information that the respondent generally would not have on hand.
    All questions were "closed questions" and asked for a qualitative
    evaluation of export related dimensions. It was decided to use the
    summated Likert scale format which has also been referred to as
    "analysis of satisfaction" methodology (Resmini 1987), which
    requires that the respondent evaluate his or her agreement or
    disagreement with the various statements in the questionnaire,
    using a graduated scale.

A structured mail questionnaire consisting of 21 questions was sent
with an introductory letter, as well as a pre-stamped enveloped to facilitate the
return, to 250 SMFs distributed throughout Italy, however, with proportional
concentration in the more industrialized northern and central areas. The number
of valid and complete questionnaires received was 116, which represents a 46.4
percent response rate. This percentage is very high if we consider the usual
return rates in similar studies conducted by mail in Italy and in other countries
(Gerbi Sethi 1979, 1982).

CHARACTERISTICS OF RESPONDENT FIRMS

Analysis of the 116 questionnaires shows that about two-thirds of the
firms produced consumer goods, while the remaining third produced industrial
goods. The average size of respondent firms shows that 61.2 percent have less
than 50 employees, 23.3 percent have from 51 to 99 employees and only 15.5
percent have 100 employees or more. The high proportion of small firms in the
sample reflects the fragmented structure of the Italian manufacturing industry.
Notwithstanding their small size, these firms are generally very dynamic and
efficient. They are able to sell their own products successfully on international
markets (a typical example is the great success on international markets achieved
by "made in Italy" products of the fashion industry). In many cases these firms
have been involved in export markets for many years (Gerbi Sethi 1979).
Indeed, the sample corroborates this and more than 53 percent have been

exporting for 10 years or more both to countries within Europe and overseas, while only about 5 percent are recent exporters (less than 2 years). Export represents, therefore, a traditional activity for the majority of small Italian firms.

The last noteworthy sample characteristic is the extent of firms' export involvement. For the sample as a whole, some 41 percent of total sales are exported. Approximately 15 percent of firms export more than 75 percent of their production. This underlines both the success with which Italian firms have developed export markets and the threat posed by extensive dependence on foreign markets. Moreover, it is significant to observe that the respondent firms expect to further increase their export involvement over the next few years. The average percentage of export sales two years ago was 36 percent, while the same figure foreseen two years hence is 44 percent.

Table 7.1: Present markets of export activity

Geographic areas	Percentage of exports (n = 116)
E.E.C. Countries	57.2
Western Europe other than E.E.C.	10.2
Eastern Europe	1.7
U.S.A.	10.3
Canada	3.5
Central and South America	3.2
Africa and Middle East	7.4
Asia	5.1
People's Republic of China	0.3
Australia and New Zealand	1.1
Total	100.0%

Source: Prepared by authors.

The majority of export activity is concentrated in E.E.C. countries (57.2%), and to a lesser extent other Western European Countries (10.2%) and the U.S.A. (10.3%). The other geographic areas, while sometimes important to individual firms, play a secondary role.

RESULTS

Export Orientation in SMFs

As suggested earlier, the respondent firms have a very positive orientation toward exporting. In other words, the export activity is not accidental, but is a structural element in their sales policies (Silva 1979). The sample firms largely view export activity as a new opportunity, because of market expansion and standardization. Support for this statement is found in the following research results:

- notwithstanding the importance of the home market, which accounts for about 59 percent of total sales, 57 percent of the firms concentrate the majority of their efforts on export activity;
- 87 percent of firms declared that export trade is becoming more and more an important activity;
- 65 percent of firms indicate that the export decision and research of new markets are regularly planned;
- 93 percent of the firms are planning to increase the number of their foreign markets in the next few years;
- there is widespread expectation that export profits will increase significantly in the next two years. Some 58 percent agree with this statement. 9 percent think that export profits will decrease, with the remaining firms (33%) not expecting to change.

This positive export orientation is particularly interesting as competitive conditions that characterize the Italian market are expected to become more intense compared to those abroad. About 39 percent of the firms assert that competition is harder in Italy than abroad, with about 18 percent expressing a contrary opinion. This may be explained to some extent in that Italian markets are often seen as saturated while export markets are expanding, thus offering a good opportunity for further growth of the firm.

Sources of Export Growth

We asked the firms which sources of export growth were important in the past and which ones they foresee to be relevant in the future.

Other than 'past' and 'future' the time dimension was not defined and it should be recognized that respondents' perception of time has some influence on their responses. In general, as shown in Table 7.2, a broad shift in the relative importance of factors is noted. Whether or not this reflects a learning curve is not clear, however, one can argue that experience conditions the response to the 'future'.

The emphasis of what is important has shifted. While technology is still the most important growth factor, export marketing know-how is the second-most important (was fourth in the past), and seeking new markets for proven products ranks third (was second in the past).

The three largest changes in perceived importance of growth factors were 'own technology' (to 76.5%), 'export marketing know-how' (to 69.9%) and 'adoption of other technology' (to 48.2%). While all noted changes were statistically significant, the foregoing three growth factors clearly emphasize the importance of technology and know-how in today's international business environment.

Table 7.2: The importance of different sources of export growth

Sources of export growth	% of responses "very important" (n = 116)		Statistical significance*
	Past	Future	
Own technology	43.9	76.5	.001
Adopt others technology	24.7	48.2	.001
Firm's export marketing know-how	37.0	69.9	.001
Information from external sources	26.0	41.9	.001
Support services of public and private institutions	15.0	32.7	.001
Increase of foreign markets for present products	42.1	61.2	.001
Selling new products to old markets	36.6	58.9	.001
Selling new products to new markets	40.0	56.7	.001

* T-test, two-tailed, used to test statistical significance.
Source: Prepared by authors.

It is interesting to note that all export growth sources asked about except one are seen by respondents as "positive" factors (that is, the number of answers to "fairly important" and "very important" exceeds the number of answers to "not important" and "of minor importance"). The only case in which the negative answer exceeds the positive one concerns the use of support services offered in the past by public and private institutions. This suggests that the success of Italian SMFs in the international market is not due to public support policies (ie. activities of institutions that exist to help SMFs in their export performance), but exclusively to the firms' own activities and efforts (Scott 1983). Thus, while support services were not well regarded in the past, it is also evident that firms expect them to become more important in the future (Gerbi Sethi 1982).

Foreign Market Information Sources Used by SMFs

As we have pointed out earlier, information and marketing know-how are considered a very important factor in export growth, especially in the future. Several questions in the questionnaire sought to discover which information sources firms use and how important these are.

It is possible to assert that the firms use traditional tools to obtain information on foreign markets. This is probably related to their small size which does not allow them to use more sophisticated tools to analyze foreign markets. Information sources were considered in the context of "preparation for exporting" and "entering new export markets". No statistically significant difference is noted between results concerning "preparation" and those concerning "entering", we therefore limit our discussion to the latter.

Participation in international trade fairs (85.3%) was the most important information source, closely followed by personal visit to markets (81.8%) (see Table 7.3). Intermediaries and contacts, such as foreign firms and agents also featured as a major information source (77.5%). Such sources know the market environment of their own countries very well and can support SMFs with relevant and useful information to enter or develop markets (Secchi 1983). Therefore, these are very particular tools. They are different from more traditional market research approaches since they are based on the personal skill of the entrepreneur to perceive opportunities offered by foreign markets rather than on quantitative methods for an objective analysis of the same markets (Seringhaus 1987).

Similarly to its limited importance as a growth source, public or private institutions also are of relatively little importance as an information source. The most frequent criticism of the information given by the institutions concerns lack of precision and currency. Their market research is often industry based and broad, ignoring the existence of important segments within industries. Respondents thus regard the information from this source as unreliable and often useless, leaving the firm to its own initiative to obtain appropriate foreign market information.

Table 7.3: The importance of different information sources in the export process

Information sources	% stating source as "fairly" or "very" important in entering new export markets (n=116)	Statistical significance*
Participation in fairs and exhibition	85.3	58.88
Personal visits to markets	81.8	63.65
Foreign firms or agents	77.5	36.38
Our own market research at home	59.4	10.14
Our own market research abroad	58.7	11.46
Public or private institutions	46.8	1.75

* Chi-square test for statistical significance conducted by comparing positive answers ('fairly important' and 'very important') to negative answers ('not important' and 'of minor importance').
Source: Prepared by authors.

Use of Support Services by SMFs

This section deals with support services available to the exporting SMFs, and considers their use and helpfulness. Emphasis is on the so-called "soft" support services, that is, non- material aids to firms, such as promotional programs, market research, export consulting, export vocational training, assistance for participation in international trade fairs, etc. These are typically included in the set of support services provided by institutions. More "material" kinds of support services, such as financial and insurance services, were excluded because they involve many complex problems that are beyond the aims of this chapter (Lanzara Sbrana 1984).

Table 7.4: Firms' use and opinions regarding the helpfulness of the different institutions offering export services (n = 116)

Private and public Institutions	% of respondents using service	% of respondents rating service as useful
Industrial association	18.3	27.9
Banks	19.8	19.0
Consortia	29.1	35.2
Service centres	2.7	6.9
Trading companies	7.4	15.7
I.C.E	24.0	23.6
Chamber of Commerce	14.0	21.1
Local Government:		
• Region	0.9	4.7
• Province	0.9	2.3

Source: Prepared by authors.

The institutions providing export support services differ both in their nature and in their territorial jurisdiction. Some of them are public, others are private (industrial associations, consortia, etc.). Some institutions are national (such as I.C.E. or the National Institute for Foreign Trade), others are regional, provincial or local (such as chambers of commerce, provincial offices of industrial associations, consortia, etc.) (Finpiemonte-Ceris 1981).[2]

---

[2] *I.C.E.* (National Institute for Foreign Trade) is a public central body dependent on the Ministry for Foreign Trade. Its particular tasks concern export promotion and Italian products promotion abroad.

Chambers of commerce are public institutions at the local level, which depend on the Ministry of Industry, Trade and Handicraft. They carry out various activities involving the economic sector besides the industrial one. Therefore, export promotion is not their unique activity; on the contrary it is just one of many other activities carried out by these local bodies.

Regions and Provinces are public political institutions at the local level. They principally deal with administrative work in the area of their influence. As to support services to exporting firms, they generally offer training courses and data banks.

Industrial associations are private organizations operating locally. In general their area of influence overlaps that of chambers of commerce. They are a grouping of local entrepreneurs and carry out a variety of functions.

The extent of use of support services among firms is very low (Table 7.4). In all cases the number of firms that use export support services of a certain institution in a systematic manner is much lower than the number of firms that do not, or only rarely, use them. Keeping this fact in mind, two institutions are worth mentioning: consortia (29%) and I.C.E. (24%). As pointed out earlier, the interviewed firms are all associated with consortia. This fact may have influenced their answers leading to a halo effect concerning the usefulness of their association. On the other hand, it is surprising that only about one-third of respondents find consortia useful.

The high number of unanswered questions is disturbing, especially questions related to the usefulness of the support services offered (about 27% of firms cannot estimate the usefulness of support services, because they have probably never used them) (Bittante 1985).

Overall, 49.5 percent of respondents indicated that export support services offered by the various institutions are not useful; 32.5 percent think they are of very little use; only 18 percent consider them very useful (Table 7.5).

The institutions whose support services are considered the most useful are consortia (35%), industrial associations (28%) and I.C.E. (23%) (Table 7.6). Finally, considering the types of "soft" support services used by the sample firms, the service most appreciated is the one that organizes participation in international fairs and exhibitions, closely followed by information and market research, visits to markets, and promotion and advertising. Trade fair services are provided mainly by the consortia themselves and I.C.E. For the other three services, in addition to the latter two institutions, industry associations and chambers of commerce also feature as providers. All the other kinds of soft support services listed in the questionnaire showed a very low usage level among respondents.

Local banks are private credit institutions, operating locally. They sometimes offer export support services to the firms which are their own clients. This principally occurs in the areas with a high number of export SMFs.

Services centres are established by public or private institutions and sometimes include firms and consortia, in order to set up more specialized operators able to offer real services to the local firms.

Table 7.5: Performance rating of public and private
institutions offering export services (n = 116)

	% using services			% finding services helpful		
	None	Somewhat	Very	None	Somewhat	Very
In general	53.7%	33.0%	13.3%	49.5%	32.5%	18.0%
Public institutions	60.3	29.1	10.6	55.7	30.3	14.0
Private institutions	48.3	36.2	15.5	44.6	34.2	21.2

Source: Prepared by authors.

Overall then, these results offer a very meagre picture of the role played
by private and public institutions in the provision of export support services in
Italy.

CONCLUSIONS

This chapter provided some insight into the export behavior of SMFs
in Italy and the role played by export support organizations. On one hand the
structure of the questionnaire provided useful and relevant data concerning some
aspects of export behaviour, while on the other hand the findings point to the
need to gather information about the causes that underly the present situation.
Despite this limitation, we are able to draw the following conclusions.

First, there is a lack of knowledge among SMFs concerning the support
services offered by the various institutions. This fact may be supported by the
high number of non responses among users and the sizeable group of non-user
firms. This situation probably reflects the size of enterprises and the scarcity of
specialized and qualified employees knowledgeable in existing support services
and their use.

Second, there is a prejudice towards support services offered by public
institutions and private institutions because their services are too generic and not
customized, such as the services offered by industrial association offices, private

Table 7.6: Usage of different services across institutions (% of firms requiring the single service)

Services Requested	Users No.	Users %	Consortia	Industry Assoc.	Distributors & Agencies	Banks	Chambers of Commerce	I.C.E.	Public Institut.	Others	Total
Promotion and advertising	51	16.9	38.2**	11.7	3.9	-	15.9	8.0	2.1	20.2*	100
Participation in Trade Fairs and exhibitions	77	25.5	38.6	11.4	3.0	-	10.0	18.6	7.1	11.3	100
Personal visit to markets	52	17.2	44.2	17.3	2.0	2.0	11.6	15.3	3.8	3.8	100
Information and market research	59	19.5	33.8	12.9	3.3	4.8	8.1	24.2	3.3	9.6	100
Consulting services	24	8.0	47.6	14.3	9.4	4.8	-	14.3	-	9.6	100
Training seminars	17	5.6	17.7	34.4	-	-	21.9	17.7	-	8.3	100
Documentation and procedures services	22	7.3	24.2	28.6	-	24.2	14.2	4.4	-	4.4	100
TOTAL	302	100.0	-	-	-	-	-	-	-	-	-

* = including magazines: 9.5%
** = read as follows: 38.2% of companies reporting usgae of promotion and advertising services, did so through consortia.
Source: Prepared by authors.

service centres and also by some consortia. In all these cases the services offered both by private and public institutions are not tailored to the needs of the firm. This surely is a contributing factor to the low usage among SMFs. Furthermore, institutions are considered very slow in providing support and their research and data too old and obsolete (Scott 1983). In any case, the unwillingness to use services offered is most evident for public institutions. This generally reflects the Italian attitude of considering them inefficient and useless. Their services are also considered less helpful than others. About 40 percent of the firms indicated they used public support services to a certain extent, but some 86 percent were of the opinion that the services are either somewhat helpful or not helpful. This means that a lot of firms view the services negatively without ever having tried them. In the case of support services offered by private institutions the difference between the two percentages is smaller (52% against 79%), but equally concerning.

Third, there is overlap of services offered by various public and private institutions. A "division of labour" and coordination among the institutions providing export support services seems lacking. Each institution offers its own range of services without taking into consideration similar services carried out by other institutions, even in the same area of influence. This situation undoubtedly produces a waste of effort and resources, with a consequent reduction in efficiency.

Undoubtedly, Italian public and private institutions have a potentially higher service capacity and should be able to deliver a more sophisticated range of export support services to the SMFs. Indeed, the services most used are very simple tools and can hardly meet the needs of firms to increase their involvement in an international environment that is becoming more and more dynamic and demanding. Thus, at an industrial policy level, a review of the purpose and role of export support services for SMFs is necessary. In this vein it would thus be useful: (1) to conduct a preliminary analysis of the needs of the firms that can be met by support services; (2) to strongly involve firms interested in the various support programs. Moreover, we think that the offer of services should be more personalized and customized in order to be of immediate availability to SMFs; (3) to widely inform the entrepreneurs about the existence of support services through more extensive promotion.

ACKNOWLEDGEMENTS

This study was carried out with the aid of a grant from C.N.R. (National Council of Research), project number 86.01174.10. The authors thank Professor R. Varaldo for his helpful and useful suggestions. Acknowledgement is owed also to Dr. Iacopo E. Inghirami for his special help in the computer processing of the data.

REFERENCES

Bittante, E. (1985). "I servizi reali a sostegno dell internazionalizzazione: una analisi comparata dell intervento pubblico", *Commercio*, No. 21, pp. 149-175.

Bonaccorsi, A. (1987). "L'attivita esportativa delle piccole e medie imprese in Italia: una rassegna delle indagini empiriche", *Economia e Politica Industriale*, No. 54, pp. 229-267.

Crescini, M. (1986). "Le politiche di sostegno delle esportazioni nelle Marche: un'indagine quantitativa", *Economia Marche*, No. 2.

Ceris, Finpiemonte (1981). *Strutture di intermediazione e assistenza sui mercati esteri per le piccole e medie imprese*, Milano: F. Angeli.

Fornasari, C. (1986). "Primi risultati di una indagine campionaria sulle imprese esportatrici modenesi", in M.L. Fornaciari Davoli-G. Pini, *Piccole e medie imprese ed esportazioni*, Milano: Fiuffre.

Gerbi Sethi, M. (1979). *Imprese italiane di fronte alle esportazioni*, Milano: F. Angeli.

Gerbi Sethi, M. (1982). *Piccole e medie imprese di fronte alle esportazioni* Milano: F. Angeli.

Lanzara, R. (1987). "Strategic Differentiation and Adaptation among Small and Medium-Sized Italian Exporting Manufacturers", in P.J. Rosson and S.D. Reid, Eds, *Managing Export Entry and Expansion*, New York: Praeger, pp. 41-53.

Lanzara, R. and R. Sbrana (1984). "Export Trade Government Policies and Italian Small Firms", *Economia Aziendale*, Vol. 3, No. 2, pp. 117-130.

Piore, M.J. and C.F. Sabel (1980). "Italian Small Business Development: Lessons for U.S. Industrial Policy", in J. Zysman and L. Tyson, eds,

American Industry in International Competition, Ithaca: Cornell University Press, pp. 391-421.

Quaglia, F. (1986). "Politiche regionali di sostegno all export: un confronto tra diversi modelli organizzative, *Economia Marche*, No. 2.

Reid, S.D. (1987). "Export Strategies, Structure, and Performance: An Empirical Study of Small and Italian Manufacturing Firms", in *Managing Export* in P.J. Rosson and S.D. Reid, Eds, *Managing Export Entry and Expansion*, New York: Praeger, pp. 335-357.

Resmini, L. (1987). "Efficacia dei servizi pubblici a sostegno dell internazionalizzazione", *Commercio*, No. 27, pp. 157-179.

Seringhaus, F.H.R. (1987). "The Role of Trade Missions in Export Expansion: a Comparison of Users and Non Users", in P.J. Rosson and S.D. Reid, eds, *Managing Export Entry and Expansion*, New York: Praeger, pp. 187-198.

Seringhaus, F.H. Rolf (1986). "The Impact of Government Export Marketing Assistance", *International Marketing Review*, Summer, pp. 55-66.

Scott, W.G. (1983). "Imprese minori: esportare per crescere", *L'impresa*, No. 1, pp. 21-28.

Secchi, C. (1983). "Radiografia della PMI che opera con l'estero", *L'impresa*, No. 1, pp. 29-36.

Silva, F. (1979). "L'impresa esportatrice", *Giornale degli economisti*, No. 1, pp. 35-65.

Varaldo, R. (1987). "The Internationalization of Small and Medium-Sized Italian Manufacturing Firms", in P.J. Rosson and S.D. Reid, Eds, *Managing Export Entry and Expansion*, New York: Praeger Publishers, pp. 203-222.

Varaldo, R. (1987). "Le industrie con prevalenza di piccole imprese nella realta produttiva italiana", in *Scritti di Economia Aziendale per Egidio Giannessi*, pp. 1169-1186.

PART III

Evaluating the Role of Public Organizations in Export Promotion

INTRODUCTION

Part III of the book deals with the performance of public organizations as revealed by evaluation studies. In Chapter eight, Rosson and Seringhaus report on Canadian government-supported participation of exporters in international trade fairs. General evaluation measures show positive results from participation. When attention turns to specific types of companies, however, the results are inconsistent. Thus, closer matching of companies and trade fairs appears necessary.

Diamantopoulos, Schlegelmilch and Inglis investigate the export promotion services available to and used by Scottish companies in Chapter nine. Users revealed that, on the whole, export support fell short of their expectations. The data suggest that companies using export servicesare not discernably different from non-users in demographic and export terms Public organizations are advised to develop and deliver "better quality" support of a more specialized nature, that is based on companies' needs rather than on tradition.

In Chapter ten, Lanzara, Varaldo and Zagnoli expand the discussion of export support organizations to consider consortia in an Italian context. Export consortia have a useful role to play for the smaller company, which gain from the pooling of expertise and resources, as well as from government financial support. Similar to individual companies, consortia need to be nurtured most in the early stages of exporting, and public sector financial support might best be provided for product and market research.

De Mortagnes and Van Gent draw from a number of evaluation studies undertaken in the Netherlands. They conclude in Chapter eleven that the less-than-optimal functioning of export promotion stems from two factors:

inadequate understanding on the part of public organizations, and a lack of awareness and knowledge of available support by industry. The authors also draw attention to needed changes in export promotion occasioned by Europe 1992. Further, they argue that greater cooperation between government, industry and universities would help improve export promotion systems.

CHAPTER EIGHT

International Trade Fairs: Firms and Government Exhibits

Philip J. Rosson and F.H. Rolf Seringhaus[*]

SUMMARY

International trade fairs are important marketing events for countless firms around the world. Yet despite being important, surprisingly little empirical research has been undertaken in this area. This chapter helps to fill the void. It focuses on international trade fair exhibits that have been organized by government, and examines the behaviour and results of 367 firms exhibiting at 48 international trade fairs in the 1984-86 period. The analysis proceeds at two levels. First, the entire sample is considered so as to provide some benchmark data. Second, recognizing the heterogeneity of firms in the sample, this is followed by analysis of three distinct types: first-time, expanding, and continuing exporters. Trade fairs are found to produce good overall results but considerable variation exists among the participating firms. Continuing exporters generate the most consistent sales, while first-time exporters do less well in sales terms but appear to learn much from participation. Expanding exporters do least well as a group – producing very inconsistent sales and not seeming to benefit so much from the trade fair experience. These results are discussed and possibilities for improving government programming are suggested.

---

[*] Dalhousie University, Halifax, and Wilfrid Laurier University, Waterloo respectively.

INTRODUCTION

Trade fairs bring buyers and sellers together at thousands of locations each year. Despite their obvious importance, however, relatively little attention has been paid to trade fairs in the marketing literature. International trade fairs have attracted even less attention among writers. This chapter tries to fill part of this void. It examines firms' experiences when they form part of a government-initiated exhibit at a trade fair in a foreign market.

The chapter has five sections. In the first, the literature on trade fairs, the export decision process, and government export support is briefly reviewed. The second section describes the study methods. The third section provides a summary description of the firms sampled. The study findings follow in section four, where "before" and "after" the trade fair data are presented. Finally, in section five, these results are discussed.

LITERATURE REVIEW

Trade fairs

Trade fairs (or shows, exhibitions, expositions) are a big and growing business, as a few statistics demonstrate. In the U.S. for example, some 9,000 fairs were held in 1984 (a doubling from 1976), attracting: 90,000 participants, 37 million attendees, and generating $8 billion of expenditure. Moreover, more than one-half of these fairs sold all available space and had to refuse requests for an additional two million square feet of space (Faria & Dickinson 1985b). Trade fairs rank as the third biggest promotional expense (after television and newspaper advertising) for U.S. firms (Bello & Barksdale 1986). In the People's Republic of China, the number of trade fairs has grown from a handful to 200 in 1984 (Isham 1985). The number of trade fairs is increasing world-wide, with growth rates highest in sectors such as electronics, and regions like South East Asia.

Trade fairs vary considerably as to size and drawing power. At one extreme are world events such as the Paris Air Show and Frankfurt Book Fair, while at the other are the agricultural and home shows that take place in most communities. The former are clearly international trade fairs but what of the latter? Even the smallest and most local trade fairs are likely to feature foreign products, but usually it is the product's local retailer or distributor that exhibits rather than its producer. For the majority of exhibitors then, these are mostly domestic affairs. As a working definition here, we might consider trade fairs to be "international" when a significant percentage of exhibitors are foreign manufacturing or service firms which take space and staff their own booths.

Trade fair benefits/difficulties. The key feature of a trade fair is that it brings numerous, interested buyers and sellers in contact at one location. Profiles of trade fair attendees indicate that most have buying influence in their organizations. As a result, attendees spend an average of 10 hours in conversation with exhibitors, and it is not unusual for 70 percent of attendees to have made a sizeable purchase from one or more of the fair exhibitors within 12 months. Furthermore, fairs can help in communicating with, and selling to, hard-to-reach customers. Typically, 80 percent of all booth visitors would not otherwise be contacted by firm salespersons (Couretas 1984).

Bonoma (1983) argues that the trade fair arena permits firms to satisfy selling and nonselling objectives. The former include:

- identification of prospects
- gaining access to key decision makers
- disseminating facts about products, services and personnel
- selling products
- dealing with current customer problems.

Nonselling objectives include:

- maintaining image with competitors, customers, the industry, the press
- gathering competitive intelligence
- maintaining and enhancing firm morale
- product testing.

Clearly then, trade fairs can satisfy various firm needs, not just selling to existing or known customers. Other writers suggest that market exposure and "waving the firm flag" are frequent and reasonable motives for taking part in trade fairs (Bello & Barksdale 1986).

Against these positive features of trade fairs it must be noted that participation costs have escalated in recent years. Space costs have risen by 70 percent in the last 10 years, while other costs have doubled, leading to average exhibit costs of $35,000 and personnel costs of $17,500 in 1985 in the U.S. However, trade fairs still compare well with the cost of an industrial sales call; comparative costs being $68 for a fair contact versus $205 for a sales call (Faria & Dickinson 1985b). Aside from cost escalation, other negative aspects of trade fairs are frequently mentioned. These include: (1) unknown effectiveness; (2) difficulty of measuring efficiency; and (3) the use of fairs as rewards for managers and customers rather than as a sound marketing tool (Bonoma 1983). Consequently, some firms view participation "as a necessary evil rather than as an opportunity to be exploited" (Bello & Barksdale 1986).

Running an effective exhibit is sometimes difficult because the sheer size of many fairs makes for "a crowded, cluttered and confusing environment. Both buyers and sellers must cope with a lot of competing and conflicting marketing noise..." (Konopacki 1985). This often means that it is difficult to communicate effectively with buyers and to consummate transactions. One study of 200 exhibitors at a major U.S. international trade fair indicates that firms which are more committed to exporting and staff their booths with personnel knowledgeable about selling to foreign buyers, experience fewer communication difficulties with buyers or transaction (logistics, financing, credit) problems (Bello & Barksdale 1986).

Firms' use of trade fairs. A number of studies have tried to discover the types of firm that use trade fairs. Two are looked at briefly here. The first examined trade fair decision making essentially as a two-step process where the first decision concerns whether to participate, and the second how much to spend given participation (Lilien 1982). The data (on 131 U.S. industrial products) suggest that a product is more likely to use trade fairs as a promotional medium if:

- it is technically complex
- it is carried in inventory
- the associated sales level is high
- there are many people involved in the purchase decision process which is under close review
- purchase frequency is high.

Given a decision to use a trade fair, the level of spending is likely to be greater for:

- a product early in its life cycle, whose
- sales are high, with
- aggressive plans and
- lower customer concentration.

The importance and usage of trade fairs was examined in a second study of 653 firms exhibiting at 41 fairs in the U.S. (Faria and Dickinson 1985a). Major findings were that firms according the greatest importance to trade fairs were:

- industrial product manufacturers, and those
- with sales of more than $100 million
- employing middlemen
- with a moderate number of product lines and
- with a market share of more than 20 percent.

Participation in trade fairs was greater for:

- consumer products manufacturers, and those
- with sales of $100 million or more
- selling to retailers
- with five or more product lines, and
- with market shares over 20 percent.

The above authors find these results logical, explaining them in terms of the marketing task facing the firms, the benefits which trade fairs offer, and the ability of firms to successfully present product lines in a fair environment.

Choosing the trade fair. With many trade fairs available each year and a limited budget, it is clearly important for firms to select the best fairs at which to exhibit. Not only has the number of trade fairs grown steadily but, as a result of emerging product areas – often tied to technology advances – there has been a trend towards more specialized fairs. These more specialized fairs are often an outgrowth from larger, broader-based fairs. A number of specialized research firms and trade fair associations provide information on fairs, typically rating these as to audience quality, audience activity and exhibit performance (Cox, Ciok & Sequeira 1986). A recent survey of firms yielded the following listing of criteria used in trade fair selection: audience quality, audience quantity, display location and logistical aspects (Faria & Dickinson 1985b). Some similarity to the above listing is seen, but there are differences too.

Exhibiting well. Considerable practical material is available on how to get the best results from exhibiting at a trade fair. The international Trade Centre of UNCTAD/GATT, for example, has produced useful information guides on this subject. These publications offer very specific advice concerning booth design, product display, booth selling, as well as more general tips for success (see Bendow 1981, for example). A recent study of U.S. firms revealed trade fair success to be more likely when the following factors are evident (Kerin & Cron 1987). The firm:

- has a large number of products
- has a large number of customers
- has written objectives for the fair
- uses vertical (as opposed to horizontal) fairs.

In summary, one view of the steps necessary to achieve trade fair success is (Weinrauch 1984):

1. Provide management support
2. Set specific, primary and realistic objectives
3. Do a market analysis and adequate research
4. Select a specific trade show that coincides with your market targets
5. Plan an adequate budget
6. Develop pre-show promotion
7. Create a professional staff for the booth
8. Learn how to sell and effectively negotiate during the exhibition
9. Carefully and immediately follow-up on trade show leads
10. Evaluate and measure the performance and results of a trade show.

We are unable to test these ideas in this chapter but do provide some benchmark data on firms' experiences at international trade fairs – the role that fairs play in their foreign marketing, and the results that are achieved.

The Export Decision Process and Government Programme Targeting

Firms' participation in international trade fairs should be viewed in the context of the export decisions they must typically make. The most fundamental step, of course, if the decision about whether to expand operations through exporting or in the home market (see Figure 8.1). For the firm that chooses exporting, the second decision to be resolved is what market(s) should be targeted for entry. Next comes the decision how the product/service is sold and distributed. These decisions have to be resolved before any business can flow from foreign customers. The fourth decision is faced periodically as export experience develops and performance assessments suggest the need for change.

Governments around the world have developed export promotion programs to help firms make these decisions and so improve their chances of foreign market success. Explicitly or implicitly, these programs serve a variety of firm types. As others have done (Czinkota 1982, Barrett & Wilkinson 1985), we argue that the firm's export development stage is a useful way of thinking about how these programs are, or can be, targeted. The development stage will probably define a firm's experience and needs and, hence, its requirements for assistance, better than anything else. Elsewhere, we have identified five types of firm that government export programmes are aimed at, and describe these briefly below (Seringhaus & Rosson 1990):

1. *non-exporters* – firms with exportable products/services that have never thought of, or have shown no desire to export
2. *failed exporters* – firms with previous export experience that led them to withdraw from foreign market(s)
3. *first-time exporters* – firms that are aware of foreign market opportunities and sense that these might help them meet their growth objectives
4. *expanding exporters* – firms that wish to move their products/services into one or more new markets
5. *continuing exporters* – firms that are interested in fine-tuning their export operations as a result of current and projected performance levels.

See the export decision process and five exporter types in Figure 8.2. We consider the final three of these exporter types in this chapter.

Figure 8.1:   The export decision process

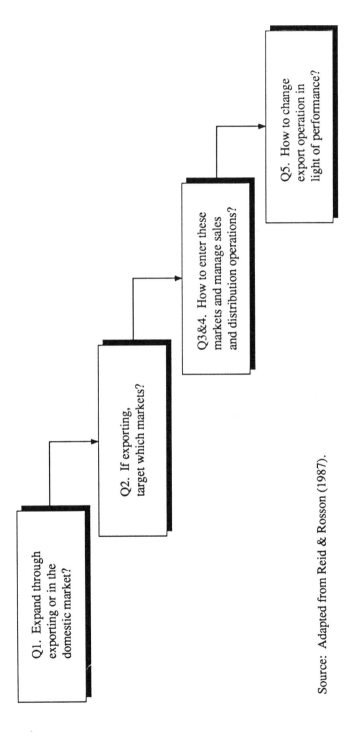

Q1. Expand through exporting or in the domestic market?

Q2. If exporting, target which markets?

Q3&4. How to enter these markets and manage sales and distribution operations?

Q5. How to change export operation in light of performance?

Source: Adapted from Reid & Rosson (1987).

How do trade fairs help these firms' in their export decision-making? Our views are summarized in Figure 8.3. "First-time exporters" have an interest in exporting but must decide whether to move ahead in this direction. Exhibiting at a trade fair is usually not an appropriate way to resolve this issue, because this signals that orders will be taken and products/services supplied to interested foreign customers. Attending a trade fair to investigate the market is another matter, as is participation on a trade mission to the market of interest. Trade fair participation can be helpful for "expanding exporters" in assessing: market potential, barriers to entry, alternative entry methods, and prospective trading partners. Why do we distinguish between the helpfulness of fairs to first-time and expanding exporters when both are essentially focusing on a new foreign market? The answer lies in the question that each type of firm is attempting to resolve: the question for first-time exporters is "Should I export?", whereas that for expanding exporters is "Does this market seem right for me?". Expanding exporters will also often use trade missions to make the same determination. Trade fair attendance can be very beneficial for "continuing exporters". This is a useful venue for renewing contacts, deepening relationships, and broaching ways to improve existing strategy. Where changes are regarded as necessary, again the fair provides an arena in which to check out this idea, and take action. In a general sense then, we regard trade fair participation as most useful for firms that are at later points in their export development – expanding and continuing exporters rather than first-time exporters. We now turn to the study and the testing of some of these ideas.

METHODS

The data reported here was collected as part of an evaluation of the Promotional Projects Program (PPP). This program is an important part of the Canadian federal government's strategy for export development. The PPP covers government-initiated trade fair exhibits, outgoing and incoming missions, and in 1985-86 had a budget of about $15 million. The objective of the evaluation essentially was to: assess the effectiveness of the PPP, profile user firms, and gauge firms' views of its usefulness. The evaluation study was conducted in three major stages: (1) an exploratory research phase resulting in a planning report; (2) a mail survey of recent trade fair and mission participants; and (3) analysis of

Figure 8.2: Exporter types and the export decision process

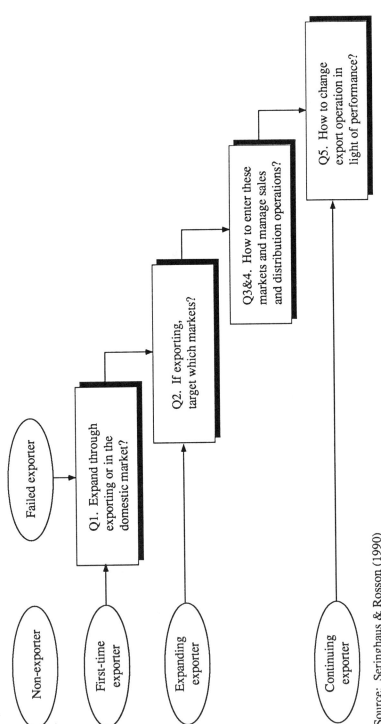

Source: Seringhaus & Rosson (1990)

Figure 8.3: Exporter types and trade fairs

Exporter type	Key questions to resolve	Decisions to be made	Role played by trade fair
First-time exporter	Should exporting be initiated?	• Growth potential from exports vs. domestic • Problems to be overcome to tap export potential • Likely cost/benefit of export involvement	• Trade fair not appropriate for these firms
Expanding exporter	Which market(s) should be entered? What market entry method is best?	• Determine market potential and barriers to entry • Choose between feasible market entry options • Selection of foreign market partner	• Chance to present product/ service to the market and test response prior to entry decision • Check out competitors • Make useful future contacts with buyers and partners
Continuing exporter	How can performance be maintained/ improved?	• Need to adjust/change existing operations • Decide what new initiatives look best	• Vehicle to renew contacts and solidify position • Chance to test new ideas prior to final decisions • Opportunity to scout for new partners

Source: Prepared by authors.

the survey data, culminating in a final report. The survey methodology used in the evaluation is now detailed.

The target population for the study consisted of firms which participated, with Department of External Affairs support, in trade fairs and missions in the period fiscal year 1984/5 to the first half of 1986/7. Sampling of this population was in two stages, first of the trade fairs and missions (or events), and then of participants within events. This meant that a detailed analysis of factors contributing to the success of events and firms was made possible.

The sampling of events was stratified by type of event (trade fairs, outgoing missions and incoming missions); geographic area (5 categories); and industrial sector (3 categories). Some 48 trade fairs, 18 outgoing and 11 incoming trade missions were sampled. A random selection process within each sampled event led to a sample of 570 firms being drawn. On average, about nine firms per trade fair and five per mission were sampled. A response rate of 90 percent was achieved, allowing for an overall accuracy of estimates to within ± 5 percent for most of the variables examined.

A preliminary questionnaire was developed after a review of the literature, consultation with Department of External Affairs (DEA) trade officers, and discussions with export firms and trade fair organizers. This was pre-tested with a sample of 25 firms, with telephone follow-up of non-respondents and return of all questionnaires by special delivery mail. This process led to a number of changes in the final questionnaire.

The survey procedure ensured that the correct respondent for the survey was identified prior to the first mailing of the questionnaire. Verification of the correct respondent, full mailing address and telephone number, as well as the language of preference (English or French) for the questionnaire, was achieved through a telephone screening survey. Firms were not surveyed unless an appropriate respondent could be found, that is, someone who could accurately report on the event in question. The survey process included three mailings, including a postcard reminder, as well as a telephone reminder where necessary.

Respondents were guaranteed full confidentiality in both the covering letter and introduction to the questionnaire. They were informed that: first, only the researchers would ever see the specific answers from any respondent (DEA staff would be provided only with statistical summaries); and second, all questionnaires would be destroyed after the data had been entered into the computer. A supplementary survey of 30 firms was conducted after the survey proper, to test the reliability of survey results, especially for certain questions requiring judgemental (as opposed to categorical) responses. The test-retest reliabilities of these data were typical for contemporary surveys.

SAMPLE CHARACTERISTICS

In the balance of this chapter, we refer only to the sample of firms that participated in international trade fairs – these numbered 367. This sample of firms was national in scope, with adequate regional and sectoral representation. We first profile trade fair users in general terms, before considering their exporting characteristics (see Table 8.1). An overwhelming number of firms were manufacturers (85%), with trading companies and distributors (19%), and service providers (13%) making up the balance of the sample. In terms of firm size, the majority were small to medium-sized (total sales of $2-50 million – 54%), followed by very small firms (<$2 million – 32%), and large firms (>$50 million – 14%). The average age of the firms was 24 years, with 13 years of exporting experience.

The dependence of the sampled firms on exporting varied considerably, with almost six in ten firms earning more than 20 percent of total sales from foreign markets. The geographic scope of the firms' operations was wide, with the United States (89%), Asia/Pacific (61%), and Western Europe (60%) the dominant destination points for shipments, and the average number of countries sold to 12.

Regarding exporting firm types, more than one-half of the firms were continuing exporters, defined as those that had been selling to the market the trade fair reached for three or more years. Somewhat more than two in ten firms were either first-time exporters (making their first attempt to export), or expanding exporters (having some export experience and attempting to enter a new market). These distinctions were made earlier and we return to them again below. First, however, we present and discuss the findings for the entire sample.

FINDINGS

Before the Trade Fair

In this section, we describe the behaviour of the sampled firms prior to the trade fair in the market(s) in question. This provides some sense of where the firms are starting from and what they hoped to achieve through participation.

Perhaps surprising is the fact that almost one-half of the firms had either no (35%) or less than one year (10%) of experience in marketing to the

Table 8.1: Characteristics of sampled firms

Characteristic	

Type of firm (n=359)
- Manufacturer 85.2%
- Trading company/distributor....................................19.2%
- Service provider 13.1%

Total annual sales (n=358)
- <$2 million 31.5%
- $2 - 49.9 million 54.4%
- >$50 million..14.0%

Average date of:
- Establishment (n=356) 1963
- Starting to export (n=334)....................................1974

Export intensity (exports as percent of total sales) (n=351)
- <20%...41.0%
- 20 - 69% 41.0%
- >70%...18.0%

Export focus
- Number of countries exported to (n=341) 11.5
- Areas exported to: (n=353)
  - United States..88.7%
  - W. Europe 59.5%
  - E. Europe 14.4%
  - Asia/Pacific..60.6%
  - Latin America..42.8%
  - Africa/Middle East...36.8%

Exporter type (n=247)
- First-time exporter...20.1%
- Expanding exporter...23.2%
- Continuing exporter...56.7%

Source: Prepared by authors.

market(s) reached by the trade fair (Table 8.2). Surprising, because fairs are usually regarded as a promotional method for established sellers. The balance of the sample is made up of firms with 1-3 years experience (20%), or more than 3 years experience (36%). These more experienced firms make up the bulk of those reporting their level of marketing effort in the 12 months prior to the trade fair as either moderate (40%) or major (22%). This leaves a good-sized group

Table 8.2: Firms' behaviour prior to the trade fair

Behaviour

Activity in market prior to trade fair
- Length of time exporting to market (n=351)
    - not at all..34.8%
    - <12 months 9.6%
    - 1-3 years..19.7%
    - >3 years 35.6%
- Level of marketing effort, prior 12 months (n=346)
    - none 13.3%
    - minor...25.1%
    - moderate..39.6%
    - major...22.0%
- Average annual sales,
  12 months prior to trade fair – $000 (n=243) $40

Objectives for trade fair (n=355)
- Testing market for demand,
  acceptance and competitiveness 71.5%
- Identifying or appointing agents/
  representatives/distributors 51.0%
- Obtaining quote or bid opportunities................................31.0%
- Making immediate sales to final users...............................24.5%
- Making immediate sales to dealers....................................27.0%
- Securing licensing/joint venture arrangement.....................13.5%
- Making business contacts 78.9%
- Maintaining presence in market.......................................51.8%
- Meeting regular customers and agents/
  representatives/distributors 45.1%
- Introducing a new product to the market...........................44.5%

Source: Prepared by authors.

(38%) with no or only minor marketing effort in the run-up to the fair. This, of course, reflects the sizeable group of export newcomers in the sample, as does the average of $40,000 in sales in the year prior to the fair.

Next, we consider the objectives stated for the trade fair by firms. Trade fairs are seen to fulfil a variety of different functions. The dominant objectives of firms involve making business contacts (79%) and market and competitive testing (72%). Also important are market maintenance (52%), foreign partner selection (51%), meeting buyers and partners, and new product introduction (45% each). It is particularly interesting to note the lower endorsement of immediate sales objectives – seeking bid opportunities, dealer and final user sales are objectives for less than one-third of all firms. This finding is consistent with the view expressed by writers such as Bonoma (1983). Finally, relatively few firms in this sample attended the trade fair with a view to securing a licensing or joint venture arrangement.

These data show that among the firms participating in the trade fairs sampled, considerable diversity of background and interests is evident. We now turn our attention to the results achieved by these firms.

After the Trade Fair

Trade fair results can be measured in a number of different ways and we employ four here. Although sales may not be the dominant objective for firms exhibiting at trade fairs, there is the expectation that these will flow in the future. We therefore use sales as one measure. Various types of sale were considered, specifically actual on-site sales, actual sales within 12 months, and other firm and committed future sales. These types of sale are summed to produce a single measure here. The second indicator of trade fair results employed is the extent to which the trade fair helped firms to achieve their stated objectives. A third measure reports the number of foreign market partners appointed. As seen earlier, finding such persons or organizations is important for many firms in that it paves the way for future sales. Finally, we also report on a range of post-fair activities. This is another result that will impact on future rather than present sales. We now discuss the results in the order they appear in Table 8.3. Results for the entire sample are presented first, followed by those for three different types of firm – first-time exporters, expanding exporters, and continuing exporters.

The Whole Sample

In reporting the extent to which firms met their trade fair objectives, scores of (1) poor, (2) good, and (3) excellent were averaged for the sample firms. The results were best for firms using the fair to meet customers and partners (2.33), followed by those with market maintenance (2.31), business contact (2.18), and new product introduction (2.15) objectives. Two dominant objectives mentioned above appear less well served by trade fairs, namely market and competitive testing (2.02), and foreign partner selection (1.77). Sales and licensing/joint venture arrangement objectives are not achieved so often.

Table 8.3: Firms' results from the trade fair

Results

Assessment of trade fair in helping to meet objectives
(1=poor, 2=good, 3=excellent)
- Testing market for demand, acceptance and competitiveness (n=290).................................2.02
- Identifying or appointing agents/ representatives/distributors (n=220)..........................1.77
- Obtaining quote or bid opportunities (n=167)............1.65
- Making immediate sales to final users (n=158)..........1.25
- Making immediate sales to dealers (n=158)...............1.56
- Securing licensing/joint venture arrangement (n=106) 1.78
- Making business contacts (n=316)...........................2.18
- Maintaining presence in market (n=233) 2.31
- Meeting regular customers and agents/ representatives/distributors (n=216)........................2.33
- Introducing a new product to the market (n=198) 2.15

Number of agents/representatives/distributors appointed (n=336)...........0.37
Sales impact: (n=367)
- Average total sales related[a] to trade fair ($000)...........$376
- Companies with sales greater than $1 million...........3.3%
- Companies with no sales.....................................48.8%
- Companies with sales greater than own costs...........41.4%

Note: [a] Sales following participation in the trade fair.
Source: Prepared by authors.

A second measure of trade fair success is the extent to which foreign partners are found. Agent/representative/distributor sign-ups were relatively low for the sample firms, averaging a little more than one partner for every three firms going to a trade fair.

The sales data provide some intriguing results. On the surface, the average sales related to firms' trade fair participation looks good. At $376,000 this is more than nine times the average for pre-trade fair sales – a significant increase. However, a single measure is inadequate here. Table 8.3 shows that considerable variability exists in firms' results. A small number of firms (3%) do very well, grossing over $1 million in sales. However, a very large number (49%) do poorly, achieving no sales at all, while a further 10 percent of firms fail to cover their trade fair participation costs (on average $10,000). Thus, almost six in ten firms fail to break even.

The last set of results focus on firms' activities following the trade fair. This is based on the idea that for many firms, exhibiting at a trade fair will expose them to new ideas about how to operate in the market in question. In other words, whether sales are achieved or not, there is a considerable learning experience which will affect future sales. Again, we present results for the entire sample of firms. One encouraging aspect of trade fair participation is that almost one-third of firms report increased efforts in the market following the trade fair. A series of specific marketing initiatives were presented to respondents. The most frequent changes reported as directly resulting from the trade fair were related to markets (more trips to market – 27% of firms), products (product changes – 21%; new products – 19%), and promotion (more promotion – 15%; more trade fairs – 12%). Other changes frequently were of an organizational or effort kind. In this latter category, it is clear that trade fair participation sometimes triggers a more realistic view of the present market opportunity and/or a will to examine others. Thus it appears that exhibiting at a trade fair has results which cannot be captured solely through sales measures.

In the absence of much writing on international trade fairs, these data provide a benchmark against which others might be compared. We have seen that firms engage in trade fairs for different reasons, at contrasting stages in their international development, and that their performance can be judged in various ways. The purpose in presenting the data in aggregate form is that first, it gives some overall sense of firms' behaviour and results and, second, this tends to be the way that many governments evaluate export promotion programmes of this type. However, we have noted that government programmes serve a diversity of firms. Recognizing this fact, we now consider the trade fair results achieved by three such types of firm – first-time exporters, expanding exporters, and continuing exporters. The method used to categorize sample firms to these is shown in Table 8.4.

Table 8.4: Three types of exporter

Exporter type	Length of time exporting to market prior to the trade fair[a]	Extent to which trade fair provided a first learning opportunity about exporting[b]
First-time exporter (n=38)	Not at all	To a great extent
Expanding exporter (n=80)	Not at all	Not at all
Continuing exporter (n=129)	More than 3 years	Not at all

Notes: [a] Six-point scale, ranging from (1) Not at all, to (6) More than 5 years.
         [b] Three-point scale, ranging from (1) Not at all, to (3) To a great extent.
Source: Prepared by authors.

Three Types of Exporting Firms

Some 247 firms were categorized as first-time (38), expanding (80), or continuing exporters (129), and the results that follow are based on this smaller sample of firms' responses to various questionnaire items. Table 8.5 shows the results these types of exporting firms achieved, using the same four measures as above. We discuss each in turn.

Considering first the extent to which the trade fair enabled the firm to achieve its stated objectives, we find that with only one exception (i.e., finding foreign partners), continuing exporters rate trade fairs most highly, with first-time exporters second, and expanding exporters last. The second measure of success is the number of foreign partners signed-up and here there is almost no difference across the three exporter types. The number of partners signed by continuing exporters, only slightly lower than others, may be surprising. One might expect market newcomers (first-time and expanding exporters) to be in greater need of partners than an established seller. These data may reflect, however, the need for firms to regularly add to or fine-tune their overseas selling and distribution networks. Thus, while the two other exporter types must establish market partners, continuing exporters seek to refine their foreign operations.

Table 8.5: Results from the trade fair by exporter type

Results	Exporter type		
	First-time	Expan-ding	Contin-uing

Assessment of trade fair in helping to
meet objectives (1=poor, 2=good, 3=excellent)
- Testing market for demand, acceptance
  and competitiveness (n=132)................2.12........1.89........2.63
- Identifying or appointing
  agents/representatives/
  distributors (n=101) ....1.77........1.12........1.74
- Obtaining quote or bid
  opportunities (n=75) ....1.50........1.36........1.79
- Making immediate sales
  to final users (n=69).............................1.21........1.07........1.32
- Making immediate sales
  to dealers (n=70)..................................1.31........1.25........1.71
- Securing licensing/joint venture
  arrangement (n=41).............................1.75........1.50........1.90
- Making business contacts (n=145)........2.10........2.06........2.25
- Maintaining presence in
  market (n=112) ....2.27........1.82........2.43
- Meeting regular customers and
  agents/representatives/
  distributors (n=105) ....2.08........1.94........2.47
- Introducing a new product to
  the market (n=87)..............................2.06........1.82........2.28

Number of agents/representatives/
distributors appointed (n=158)........................0.4..........0.4..........0.3
Sales impact: (n=164)
- Average total sales related[a] to
  trade fair ($000)...............................$82.......$822..........$730
  - excluding very large sales.............$82.........$33..........$115
- Companies with sales > $1 million........ 0%..........2.6%......4.3%
- Companies with no sales...................51.5%.....68.4%.....39.8%
- Companies with sales > own costs......30.3%.....18.4%.....54.8%

Note: [a] Sales following participation in the trade fair.
Source: Prepared by authors.

Table 8.5: Results from the trade fair by exporter type (cont'd)

Results	Exporter type		
	First-time	Expanding	Continuing

Follow-up activities:
- Companies that have increased effort in market (n=157)

	First-time	Expanding	Continuing
Companies that have increased effort in market (n=157)	60.0%	41.7%	15.4%

- Companies that have done additional marketing or made changes in market as a *direct* result of trade fair participation: (n=156)

	First-time	Expanding	Continuing
- modified products to better suit market	29.0%	14.3%	20.0%
- introduced new products to market	19.4%	8.6%	20.0%
- gone to more trade fairs	29.0%	0%	7.8%
- gone on trade mission	19.4%	0%	2.2%
- made more trips to market	22.6%	14.3%	22.2%
- established offices in market	0%	0%	1.1%
- purchased marketing studies	0%	0%	2.2%
- increased promotion/advertising	12.9%	11.4%	10.0%
- made organizational changes to better focus efforts	16.1%	8.6%	12.2%
- reduced level of effort	9.7%	5.7%	2.2%
- withdrawn from market	3.2%	2.9%	1.1%
- started to explore other markets	25.8%	5.7%	10.0%

Note: [a] Sales following participation in the trade fair.
Source: Prepared by authors.

When the sales impact of trade fair exhibiting is turned to, the results contrast much more. As might be expected, first-time exporters produce far less sales. With an average of $82,000, their sales are one-tenth those of expanding exporters and one-ninth those of continuing exporters. However, the superior performance of these two latter groups is somewhat misleading, for a small number of very large sales distort the average. When one expanding exporter's ($30 million) and three continuing exporters' sales ($7.5, $11.1 and $37.2 million) are excluded, average sales for these drop to $34,000 and $115,000 respectively. Going beyond simply considering average sales yields interesting results! Poor sales performance is almost as unevenly distributed as large-scale sales. Firms with no sales are quite high across all three groups but, at 68 percent, highest for expanding exporters. This group also has the lowest percentage (18%) of firms "breaking-even" (or generating enough sales to cover their trade fair costs). The picture that emerges from these particular results is one of greater and more consistent performance by continuing exporters than by first-time exporters. These results are exactly as anticipated. The expanding exporter results are more surprising, however, with lower overall performance by a high number of firms.

Finally, we turn to firms' post-fair initiatives. A strong pattern emerges, with first-time exporters showing the most activity. Six in ten of these firms report increased efforts, and this group generally does the most additional marketing or makes the most change as a result of participating at the fair. The initiatives most frequently undertaken include: product modification (29%) and new product launches (19%); more trade fair exhibits (29%), trade mission participation (19%), and visits to the market (23%); and investigation of other foreign markets (26%). Continuing exporters also instigate product change and more market visits but, as established firms in the market in question, only about one firm in six increased its marketing effort in the wake of the fair. As might be expected, some four in ten expanding exporters indicate increased post-fair efforts. The changes induced by trade fair participation are lower for this group however, with product modification and market trips among the more frequent responses.

SUMMARY

The behaviour and results of firms participating in government-initiated trade fair exhibits may be summarized as follows. In general terms, a variety of firms participate, and existing sales in the market covered, on average, are low. The participating firms have diverse objectives for trade fairs and some of these are satisfied well through their involvement. The "harder" results show that foreign partners are signed-up and sizeable sales increases are registered. However, there is substantial variation with a large number of firms that do not recover their costs. Considerable learning and refocusing of efforts appears to take place after the trade fair, at least for some firms.

When individual types of exporter are considered, strong behaviour patterns and results emerge. Continuing exporters fare best in concrete terms – achieving their objectives more readily and producing higher and more consistent sales results. First-time exporters also achieve their objectives reasonably well, but rather than generating high sales, these firms learn and adapt their operations as a result of the fair experience. Finally, expanding exporters do the least well – producing very uneven results and, seemingly, not learning so much from their participation.

DISCUSSION AND CONCLUSIONS

The above results indicate that the sample firms did well at government-initiated trade fair exhibits, at least in an overall sense. However, as might be expected, the results vary substantially from one firm to the next. The results provide a preliminary idea about firms' trade fair participation which, it is hoped, will be supplemented by other studies. As is the case with most exploratory studies, more questions are raised than answered. We highlight a few of these questions by way of conclusion, and add some comments.

Perhaps the most interesting finding in this study is the almost 60 percent of firms that fail to recover their participation costs. In the absence of other studies, this percentage seems high. Whether it is a cause for concern is another matter; some might argue that for export newcomers, the experience is more important than sales *per se*. Whatever the case, it is clear that there is room for improvement. A number of decision steps are implicated here, beginning with, for example, the selection of the fairs themselves. We have no data on practices here and so are unable to comment further. Nor do we know precisely how firms are selected to participate in the chosen trade fairs. Our data does suggest, however, that some firms do not prepare well before, or follow-up after the trade fair. Some 4 percent of firms stated that they had no specific objectives for the fair, and 10 percent did not pursue contacts or take other initiatives on returning home from the fair. This suggests that some of the selected firms were not "export ready" or lacked the motivation to exploit the opportunity the fair presented. How exhaustively these points can be checked out prior to the fair is a moot point, but it is clearly important.

These points concern individual firm selection. A related question is "What types of exporter should be targeted for trade fair exhibits?" We saw earlier that continuing exporters were the most consistent sales performers at trade fairs, followed by first-time and expanding exporters. In sales terms then, targeting the former would create the greatest sales impact per program dollar. What of the other two exporter types examined? We argued above that in addition to continuing exporters, trade fairs could be useful to expanding exporters. This sample of expanding exporters showed very wide variations in trade fair sales. As well, relatively few changes were set in motion by this group, implying little learning from the fair experience or low motivation to proceed further. Consequently, we must reserve judgement on the appropriateness of trade fairs for this exporter type. Our final group – first-time exporters – appear to achieve reasonable sales from the fair and to learn considerably from participation. This is intriguing because our view is that for most firms of this type, trade missions are a better vehicle for testing out export markets than a trade fair.

It is apparent from this discussion that there is scope for improved targeting of firms for trade fair participation. Depending on the objectives government officials have for the fair – short-term sales, learning for the longer-term, or some mix of these two – different exporter types and individual firms may be selected to participate. We look forward to more field studies of international trade fairs, as well as other forms of government export promotion.

REFERENCES

Barrett, Nigel J. and Ian F. Wilkinson (1985). "Export Stimulation: A Segmentation Study of the Export Problems of Australian Manufacturing Firms," *European Journal of Marketing*, Vol. 19, No. 2, pp. 53-72.

Bello, Daniel C. and Hiram C. Barksdale (1986). "Exporting at Industrial Trade Shows," *Industrial Marketing Management*, Vol. 15, pp. 197-206.

Bendow, Bruce (1981). "Before You Enter a Trade Fair," *International Trade Forum*, (October-December), 10-13, pp. 28-30.

Bonoma, Thomas V. (1983). "Get More Out of Your Trade Shows," *Harvard Business Review*, (January/February), 75-83.

Cox, Jonathan M., Robert S. Ciok and Ian K. Sequeira (1986). "Trade Show Trends," *Business Marketing*, (June), p. 142 *et passim*.

Couretas, John (1984). "'Unknown Prospect' Unmasked at Trade Shows," *Business Marketing*, (July), p. 33.

Czinkota, Michael R. (1982). *Export Development Strategies: U.S. Promotion Policy*, New York: Praeger.

Faria, A.J. and J.R. Dickinson (1985a). "What Kinds of Companies Use Trade Shows Most – And Why?," *Business Marketing*, (June), p. 150 *et passim*.

Faria, A.J. and J.R. Dickinson (1985b). "Behind the Push to Exhibit at Trade Shows," *Business Marketing*, (August), p. 99, 100, 102.

Isham, Robert C. (1985). "The China Trade Show," *Sales and Marketing Management*, October 7, p. 50, 52-3.

Kerin, Roger A. and William L. Cron (1987). "Trade show Functions and Performance: An Exploratory Study," *Journal of Marketing*, Vol. 51 (July), pp. 87-94.

Konopacki, Allen (1985). "Capturing Power Buyers on the Trade Show Floor," *Meetings and Conventions*, Special Piedmont Supplement, Vol. 10, pp. 42-52.

Lilien, Gary (1982). "A Descriptive Model of the Trade-Show Budgeting Decision Process," *Industrial Marketing Management*, Vol. 12 (February), pp. 25-9.

Reid, Stanley D. and Philip J. Rosson (1987). "Managing Export Entry and Expansion: An Overview," in Philip J. Rosson and Stanley D. Reid, Eds., *Managing Export Entry and Expansion*, New York: Praeger, p. 6.

Seringhaus, F.H. Rolf and Philip J. Rosson (1990). *Government Export Promotion: A Global Perspective*, London: Routledge.

Weinrauch, J. Donald (1984). "Role and Utilization of Trade Shows for International Trade," *Proceedings*, Southern Marketing Association, New Orleans, November 14-17, pp. 284-287.

CHAPTER NINE

Evaluation of Export Promotion Measures: A Survey of Scottish Food and Drink Exporters

A. Diamantopoulos,* Bodo B. Schlegelmilch* and K. Inglis**

SUMMARY

Based on a survey of Scottish food and drink companies, this chapter provides empirical evidence on the use and managerial evaluation of a wide range of export assistance bodies and the services they offer. The results show (1) which export promotion bodies are most frequently approached for assistance, (2) which bodies are perceived to be most/ least helpful, (3) which particular forms of export assistance are most frequently used by food & drink exporters and (4) which forms of export assistance offered by export promotion bodies are rated as being of high/ low quality. In addition, it is investigated whether differences exist between exporting firms which receive some form of assistance from export promotion organisations and those which do not. The implications of the findings for providers of export promotion are discussed and policy recommendations are made.

INTRODUCTION

This chapter focuses on the usage and evaluation of a wide range of public and private export promotion measures. The issues are analyzed in the

---

*   University of Wales, Swansea.
** CACI Inc., Edinburgh .

context of the Scottish food and drink industry in an attempt to eliminate, as far as possible, the influence of geographic- and industry- specific differences on the usage and evaluation of export promotion. The industry chosen is a major export earner for Scotland, accounting for about one-quarter of all Scottish manufactured exports (Standing Commission on the Scottish Economy 1988).

Initially, various definitions of export promotion are discussed and comparisons of export promotion expenditures in different countries are made. This is followed by a description of the main organizations that provide export assistance in Britain. The data and variables used for the empirical investigation are then discussed in the methodology. Subsequently, the analysis focuses on the use and perceived overall effectiveness of various organizations as a source of export assistance as well as on the use and evaluation of specific export marketing services. Both types of information are combined to identify whether certain organizations were preferred for certain services and to obtain insight into the interaction between the overall ratings of export promotion bodies and the evaluation of their specific services. In addition, an attempt is made to identify potential differences between users and non-users of export assistance. A discussion of the results and recommendations for providers of export promotion ends the chapter.

BACKGROUND

The promotion of export activities through government and other public or private bodies has received wide attention from both policy makers and academic researchers (for comprehensive literature reviews, see Seringhaus 1985, 1987). This interest reflects, on the one hand, a recognition of the potential usefulness of export promotion for individual companies and, on the other hand, the view that export promotion policies have a major impact on firms' competitive position abroad (House of Commons 1980) and, thus, to the economic well-being of a country.

From a theoretical point of view, the economic role of export promotion may be seen as contributing to the international division of labour by involving as many companies as possible in international trade. However, export promotion is not unanimously regarded as positive but is also sometimes viewed as a stumbling block to free trade. In this context, Krebs (1977) includes export promotion, together with import restrictions, into a basket of "beggarmy-neighbour-policy" measures; similarly Borchert (1977) points out that certain export promotion policies, such as cheaper interest rates for exporters, can have a trade effect similar to import duties; finally, Beyfuss (1984) stresses that export promotion can be in conflict with free trade objectives.

In this context, it is interesting to compare the official export promotion expenditure in different countries. Such a comparison not only reflects differences in the perceived economic usefulness of such policies, but also reveals divergent political convictions regarding the desirability of free trade as well as the role of the government in promoting exports. Table 9.1 contains this information for some of the major export nations.

Table 9.1: Official export promotion expenditure in different countries

Country	Export promotion as % of exports	Index versus Britain	Export promotion per capita ($U.S.)	Index versus Britain
Britain	1.8	100	$31.0	100
Italy	0.6	33	$8.0	26
France	1.4	78	$25.0	81
West Germany	0.02	1	$0.5	2
Singapore	0.09	5	$7.4	24
South Korea	1.7	94	$9.7	31
Japan	0.7	39	$7.9	31
USA	3.5	194	$32.0	103
Canada	1.8	100	$53.0	171

Source: Compiled by the authors based on information from the National
        Swedish Industrial Board (1984).

From an individual company's point of view, doubts about the potentially trade distorting effects of export promotion are largely irrelevant as long as such concerns do not result in serious limitations of the export promotion services on offer. Rather, companies are primarily concerned with the reputation of bodies providing export assistance and with the quality of the different services available through such bodies. However, the usefulness of export promotion in terms of its impact on firms has been questioned in the past (Tookey 1964, Cunningham & Spigel 1971, Reid 1984, Gronhaug & Lorentzen 1983). A possible explanation for this may be the lack of a generally recognised definition of export promotion (Beyfuss 1984). Suggestions range from rather narrow definitions which include only those measures that actually improve the international competitiveness of exporters (Lefevre 1970), through contributions that attempt to distinguish between market-conform (e.g., information, contacts) and market-inconform export promotion measures (e.g., export subsidies) (Glastetter 1979), to still wider definitions that include all public policy measures actually or potentially enhancing export activities either from a firm, industry, or national perspective (Seringhaus 1985).

Indeed, reviewing 21 empirical studies which attempted the measurement of export marketing assistance to firms, Seringhaus (1986) concluded that the uncertainty about the impact of export marketing assistance is directly related to the differences in the methodology and measurements used in the respective studies. Developing an evaluation paradigm, he is particularly critical of the use of global, overall measures of export assistance rather than specific and individual measures, arguing that the former have resulted in ambivalent and ambiguous findings.

Analyzing the extent to which the wide range of public and private export promotion on offer is used and evaluated by firms, this chapter attempts to overcome this measurement problem. Both a global evaluation of the organizations that provide export assistance and a specific evaluation of the various services they offer is conducted. This is expected to shed some light on the relationship between both types of measures.

EXPORT ASSISTANCE IN BRITAIN: THE INSTITUTIONAL FRAMEWORK

Britain has a number of organizations that provide export promotion in one form or another. The most important are the British Overseas Trade Board (BOTB), the Export Credits Guarantee Department (ECGD), and, for the particular industry under investigation, the British Food Export Council (BFEC). In addition, there are a number of institutions that provide export promotion as just one of many other services they offer. These include chambers of commerce, banks, trade associations and various Scottish based quasi-governmental institutions (e.g., the Scottish Development Agency (SDA) and the Scottish Council for Development and Industry (SCDI)).

The British Overseas Trade Board (BOTB) is based in London and has ten regional offices throughout the country. It employs about 2,000 people half of which are based abroad and formally fall under the Foreign Commonwealth Office (FCO). During 1986/87 the total BOTB net expenditures were £45 million to which a further £53 million has to be added for the costs of the FCO commercial overseas staff that engaged in export promotion (BOTB, 1987). It is mostly the smaller companies that use the BOTB services as shown by the fact that over 80 percent of the BOTB's funds have been drawn by companies with fewer than 200 employees (National Swedish Industrial Board 1984). Among the large number of services offered are the Export Intelligence Service, which is a computerized data base of export opportunities constantly updated by overseas staff and matched to the specific requirements of subscribing companies; the Overseas Trade Fairs Service that can provide travel grants as well as exhibition stands and display aids at reduced rates; the Export Marketing Research Scheme which offers free advice on how to set up overseas market research and supports specific projects financially; and the Outward Missions Scheme that supports exporters interested in joining a trade mission going abroad.

The Export Credits Guarantee Department (ECGD) is a government department which has about 1,800 employees of whom 700 are stationed in London, 700 in Cardiff and the remaining 400 in ten regional offices. Its aim is to promote exports by providing insurance against a range of overseas trade risks plus guarantees to UK banks that enable exporters to have access to finance at preferential fixed rates of interest. The ECGD covers roughly one-third of all British exports. However, if oil and barter transactions are excluded, the ECGD is involved in 70 to 80 percent of all export orders with credit arrangements over more than 2 years (National Swedish Industrial Board 1984). Among its services are the Comprehensive Short Term Guarantee which covers sales on credit terms not exceeding six months; the Supplemental Extended-Terms Guarantee which is available to holders of Comprehensive Short Term Guarantees and covers credit terms between six months and five years; and the Foreign Currency Contracts Endorsement, which protects policy holders who invoice in foreign currency against extra losses through participation in the forward exchange market of foreign borrowing. The ECGD usually strives to insure the entire export turnover of a company. However, none of the policies offer a complete insurance against risk, but rather limited cover up to 90 percent of loss from buyer risks and 95 percent loss from political risk.

The British Food Export Council (BFEC) was established in 1971 through the initiative of 60 founding member-companies who decided to set up a marketing organization to co-ordinate some of their export efforts. In 1983, "Food from Britain" (FFB) was established by the British Government. Following a re-organization in 1986, the stated objective was to promote the concept of quality and range of British food and drink and to "open up channels for information and intelligence, as well as acting as a clearing-house for data, contacts, ideas and advice" (BFEC 1988). The BFEC is particularly active in their four target markets, France, Germany, Benelux and the U.S.A., with local FFB offices promoting British foodstuffs in these countries (Marketing Week 1986).

Chambers of commerce are located in a number of cities and towns and provide information on a large variety of export issues, including regulations, and standards, tariffs, transport, packaging, documentation and exhibitions. They also organize trade missions and, in some cases, are authorized to issue certificates of origins for exporters.

Banks frequently provide detailed information and advice to current or potential exporters. A typical example is the Midland Bank, whose International Division through its 16 branches offers information on export documentation, methods of payment, export credit insurance, export finance and foreign currency transactions as well as advice on export marketing issues. Similar services are provided by virtually all major U.K. banks.

The Scotch Whisky Association (SWA) with offices in Edinburgh and London represent the interests of whisky distillers, whisky being the number one Scottish export (accounting for no less than 21 percent of total manufactured exports in 1986 (Standing Commission on the Scottish Economy 1988)). Major SWA activities include the assembly of regular statistics on the industry, the provision of market information and the supply of data on market entry barriers.

The Scottish Development Agency (SDA) is a quasi-government organization (in 1987 about two-thirds of the £140 million income represented government funds) with the objective to "help build a strong economy and a better quality of life in Scotland" (SDA 1988). In this function, it spends about 16 percent of its income on advisory services and has established an export marketing group to cater for the specific needs of exporters.

The Scottish Council for Development and Industry (SCDI) has some 1,100 subscribing members. One of its objectives is to assist companies develop international markets by, for example, organizing overseas trade missions, seminars and conferences on export related issues and publishing market guides.   In 1987, the SCDI in conjunction with the Scottish Development Agency created "IRIS", an international research and information to suit companies' individual needs through on-line computer access to over 500 commercial databases worldwide (SCDI 1988).

Before turning to the analysis of the survey data, the next section briefly covers the methodology and variables.

METHODOLOGY

Data

The data for this study was gathered by a postal questionnaire sent to a stratified random sample of a computer listing of 224 Scottish exporters of food and drink products.   The sampling frame, which was provided by the Scottish Council for Development and Industry, grouped exporters into thirteen sectors reflecting the major product categories within the industry.   Stratification by these sectors resulted in the selection of 116 exporters out of which 51 replied in response to the mailed questionnaire (see Table 9A.1 in the Appendix for details).   Forty-eight of these replies were usable, yielding a satisfactory effective response rate of 41%.

Variables

The variables used in this study fall into three main categories, notably firm demographics, export characteristics and export assistance variables.

Firm Demographics comprise sales turnover, number of employees and the age of the companies concerned.   Sales turnover and the number of employees were measured at ordinal and ratio level respectively.   They were included to investigate whether firm size affected the use of export assistance. Company age, measured at ratio level, was employed as a proxy for industry experience, to explore whether younger firms are more likely to use export promotion services than more established firms.

Export characteristics include indicators of export intensity, export experience, export initiation, size and organization of export manpower, number and location of export markets, range of products exported and product adaptation. Export intensity was measured as proportion of total sales while export experience was expressed in years and as a dichotomous variable registering whether the company perceives itself as a "regular" or "irregular" exporter. Export initiation indicates whether exporting started as a consequence of external factors (e.g., inquiries from abroad, declining home market) or as a deliberate market development strategy. Size and organization of export staff refers to the number of export employees and the existence of a separate export department. The number of export markets was included to explore whether the usage of export promotion might differ between companies that concentrated their resources on a relatively small number of markets (market concentration strategy) and those that served a large number of export markets (market spreading strategy). The location of these export markets relates to seven geographical regions and involves a simple count of the number of different regions to which exports were made. The respondents were also asked to indicate whether they exported the full range of products or limited their export operations to specific product items only; although an admittedly crude measure, it provides a subjective indication of the "exportability" of a company's product range. Finally, product adaptation, was operationalized as a dichotomous variable, indicating whether products destined for export markets were modified in any way (e.g., by changing constituent product ingredients, altering the packaging, and/or using a different brand name); further methodological details on the export characteristics variables are contained in Diamantopoulos and Inglis (1988).

Most of the variables used reflect export marketing know-how, which has been found to be inversely related to the need for export promotion assistance (Seringhaus 1987). Czinkota (1982) found a link between the export development process and the perception of export services, in that more experienced exporters were observed to be ambivalent about export assistance. Bilkey (1978) suggested that export promotion programmes should be tailored to different stages of export market involvement. However, it has also been reported that exporters continued using assistance services despite a build-up of experience (Mayer & Flynn 1973, Cullwick & Mellallieu 1981). In this context, it is interesting to note that high usage has found to be positively correlated with the perceived helpfulness of export promotion (Seringhaus 1983, Cullwick & Mellallieu 1981). It should also be mentioned that, in general, exporting firms (especially smaller ones) make only limited use of the available services (Rabino

1980, Reid 1984, Parson and Foster 1978, Simpson et al. 1981), that the helpfulness of government services is sometimes judged negatively by firms (Gronhaug & Lorentzen 1983), and that export promotion organizations have had difficulties in adapting their services to problems facing the smaller firm (Cannon 1977).

Export assistance variables are subdivided into two groups, namely those which reflect the firms' usage and evaluation of export promotion bodies and those which record the usage and evaluation of specific export assistance services. A list of the twelve bodies and nine services investigated in the study is included in the Appendix as Table 9A.2. The usage/popularity of each export promotion body and export assistance service was measured by a simple count of the number of companies that had received assistance from the body concerned or used a particular service. The perceived quality of the bodies/services was assessed by 5-point semantic differential-type scales, ranging from 5="very good" to 1="useless". In addition, the firms in the sample were asked to indicate the "best" and "worst" export promotion bodies and the "best" export assistance service according to their experience.

ANALYSIS

Firm Demographics

Initially, some descriptive statistics were calculated to obtain an overall picture of the kind of companies included in the sample. The median company age was found to be 63.5 years, the median number of employees was 138.5 and the median sales turnover was £3 million. One-third of the companies were founded over one hundred years ago, the number of employees ranged from a minimum of three to a maximum of 7,500 and the large majority of companies reported sales turnovers in excess of £2 million.

Providers of Export Assistance

The first analysis undertaken focused on the use and perceived effectiveness of various export promotion bodies as a a source of export assistance; 40 (83%) of the firms in the sample used some form of export assistance while only 8 (17%) did not draw on outside bodies for advice. Table 9.2 displays the results for those organizations most often consulted for export assistance.

Table 9.2: Use and rating of bodies providing export assistance

Body[a] (ranking order: popularity)	Exporters using the body		Overall rating	Times considered	
				Best	Worst
	n	%[b]	mean	%	%
British Overseas Trade Board	32	80	3.5	22	9
Chamber of Commerce	25	63	3.8	16	4
Export Credits Guarantee Department	22	55	3.3	14	23
British Food Export Council	12	30	3.6	17	17
British Banks' Intelligence Unit	8	20	3.6	13	13
Export Agency in the U.K.	8	20	3.1	13	0
Scottish Development Agency	5	13	2.8	20	20
Scottish Whisky Association	5	13	4.0	60	0

Note: a Only the most popular bodies are listed. Results pertaining to the remaining institutions are available from the authors on request.
      b Proportion of all users of export assistance.
Source: Prepared by authors.

The results indicate that the British Overseas Trade Board (BOTB) is used most widely for export assistance by the Scottish food & drink companies in the sample. Indeed, no less than 80 percent of the companies that used export assistance dealt with the BOTB. The overall rating of 3.5 (between average and good) also shows that, on average, companies have positive views of the BOTB. This is also reflected by the fact that 22 percent of the companies rated the BOTB as the best provider of export assistance. In contrast, however, 9 percent of the firms that used the BOTB perceived it as the body that proved least helpful.

The second most widely used source of export assistance is the chamber of commerce, providing export assistance to 25 (63%) of the firms that took export advice. Again, the average level of satisfaction is high, with 16 percent of companies even perceiving it as the best source for export assistance.

With 22 (55%) mentions, the Export Credits Guarantee Department (ECGD) ranks third among the bodies providing export assistance. Although the overall rating of 3.3 is average, nearly a quarter of the companies (23%) that have used the ECGD regarded it as the worst source for export assistance.

The British Food Export Council was used by a third of the companies that sought export assistance and ranks fourth in popularity among the export promotion bodies. Ranks five and six are occupied by the British Banks' Intelligence Unit and U.K. Export Agencies, each having been used by eight (20%) of the companies concerned. The Scottish Development Agency (SDA) follows at rank seven, having been used by five (13%) of the companies. With a rating of 2.8, it is the only body which received a quality rating of below average. In contrast, the Scottish Whisky Association, also used by five companies, received an overall rating of "good" (4.0); moreover, 60 percent of its users classified it as the best source for export assistance.

Export Services

The second analysis focused on the specific export marketing services which had been requested by the companies using the export promotion bodies investigated above. Table 9.3 summarizes the results pertaining to the seven most widely used export marketing services.

There appear to be no material differences in the popularity of the above services; all are used by 19 to 23 companies (about half of the companies receiving export assistance). The provision of initial contacts with customers and advice on overseas laws and regulations are the two services with both the highest mean ratings and the largest number of mentions as "best service". Advice on product specifications was sought by 19 (48%) of the companies; with a mean of 2.7 (between "not good" and "average"), the quality of this service received the lowest overall rating. Finally, it is worth noting that there were no "best" mentions for marketing research abroad, despite this being one of the most widely sought services from export promotion bodies.

Table 9.3: Use and rating of export assistance services

Service (ranking order: popularity)	Exporters using the body		Overall rating	Times considered best service
	n	%[a]	mean	%
Financial assistance	23	58	2.8	77
Marketing research abroad	23	58	3.0	0
Initial contacts with customers	22	55	3.5	23
Advice on laws/regulations	22	55	3.5	18
Distribution facilities	22	55	2.8	9
Market assessment	21	53	3.3	10
Product specifications	19	48	2.7	0

Note: a   Proportion of all users of export assistance.
Source: Prepared by authors.

Combined Export Promotion Body/Export Service Evaluation

In the third analysis, the data gathered on export promotion bodies and export assistance services were combined to show (1) which bodies were used for which particular services, (2) how each specific service provided by a particular body was rated by the companies using that body/service combination, and (3) whether and how the ratings for specific services differed for firms that rated the overall performance of the export promotion body as "good" or "poor". To conduct this analysis, the 5-point semantic differential scales employed to measure the overall rating for each body and service were dichotomized so that "average", "not good" and "useless" were combined into a single "poor" category, while the "good" and "very good" scale points were recoded into a "good" category. Consequently, it became possible to extract the following information for each body/service combination:

Figure 9.1: Combined evaluation of export promotion body
and assistance service

Export assistance service

	Good	Poor
Good Export promotion body	Proportion of firms perceiving the body *and* the specific service as "good".	Proportion of firms perceiving the body as "good" but the specific service as "poor".
Poor	Proportion of firms perceiving the body as "poor" but the specific service as "good".	Proportion of firms perceiving the body *and* the specific service as "poor".

Source: Prepared by authors.

Table 9.4 provides this information for the 8 bodies by 7 services matrix. To facilitate easy comparison, the figures are expressed as proportion of the total number of firms in each body/service combination, although the number of companies per cell (reported in brackets) is sometimes rather small.

With 25 mentions each, the most widely used BOTB services were the provision of initial contacts with customers and advice on distribution facilities. The former service also obtained the best overall rating, being perceived as "good" in 64 percent of its 25 mentions. However, it should concern the BOTB that of the seven services investigated, five were regarded as "poor" by the majority of its users. The performance of the BOTB was perceived to be particularly weak with regard to their overseas marketing research service and the provision of product specifications (with 74 percent and 75 percent of all mentions respectively rating these services as "poor"). In this context, it has to be emphasized that these results reflect the views of Scottish food and drink exporters and cannot be generalized across different industries without further investigation.

Table 9.4:   Perception of individual export promotion bodies and services - percent

Export assistance service

Export promotion		1 g	1 p	2 g	2 p	3 g	3 p	4 g	4 p	5 g	5 p	6 g	6 p	7 g	7 p
British Overseas Trade Board	g	22	22	22	13	44	4	30	5	24	16	32	5	10	20
	p	8	48	4	61	20	32	30	35	8	52	13	50	15	55
		(n=23)		(n=23)		(n=25)		(n=23)		(n=25)		(n=22)		(n=20)	
Chamber of Commerce	g	13	27	20	20	25	19	46	8	20	20	43	0	8	34
	p	13	47	0	60	19	37	23	23	7	53	7	50	8	50
		(n=15)		(n=15)		(n=16)		(n=13)		(n=15)		(n=14)		(n=12)	
Export Credits Guarantee Department	g	14	22	34	8	34	8	13	17	17	25	18	18	10	30
	p	0	64	0	58	8	50	8	42	0	58	18	46	0	60
		(n=14)		(n=12)		(n=12)		(n=12)		(n=12)		(n=11)		(n=10)	
British Food Export Council	g	30	30	25	38	20	30	40	30	20	30	50	12	14	43
	p	10	30	0	37	40	10	20	10	10	40	0	38	29	14
		(n=10)		(n=8)		(n=10)		(n=10)		(n=10)		(n=8)		(n=7)	
British Banks' Intelligence Unit	g	17	33	0	33	0	40	14	29	0	33	17	16	0	33
	p	0	50	0	67	0	60	29	28	0	67	17	50	0	67
		(n=6)		(n=6)		(n=5)		(n=7)		(n=6)		(n=6)		(n=6)	

Table 9.4: Perception of individual export promotion bodies and services - percent (cont'd)

Export assistance service

Export promotion		1		2		3		4		5		6		7	
		g	p	g	p	g	p	g	p	g	p	g	p	g	p
Export Agency in the U.K.	g	14	14	25	13	25	13	13	25	25	13	38	0	25	12
	p	0	72	0	62	37	25	50	12	0	62	25	37	25	38
		(n=7)		(n=8)		(n=8)		(n=8)		(n=8)		(n=8)		(n=8)	
Scottish Development Agency	g	0	20	0	25	0	20	0	25	0	20	25	0	0	25
	p	40	40	25	50	40	40	25	50	20	60	25	50	25	50
		(n=5)		(n=4)		(n=5)		(n=4)		(n=5)		(n=4)		(n=4)	
Scottish Whisky Association	g	0	50	25	25	0	50	50	0	25	25	25	25	0	50
	p	0	50	0	50	0	50	25	25	0	50	0	50	0	50
		(n=4)		(n=4)		(n=4)		(n=4)		(n=4)		(n=4)		(n=4)	

1 = Financial assistance
2 = Marketing research abroad
3 = Initial contacts with customers
4 = Advice on overseas laws/regulations

5 = Distribution facilities
6 = Market assessment
7 = Product specifications

Source: Prepared by authors.

Chambers of commerce represent the second most frequently utilized source of export assistance. With 16 reported usages, the most frequently obtained service was, as for the BOTB, the establishment of initial contacts with customers. The service resulting in the largest proportion of satisfied users was the provision of advice on overseas laws and regulations, with 69 percent of its users rating it as "good". Market assessments provided by the chambers of commerce are perceived to be "good" by 50 percent of its users. However, similarly to the results of the BOTB, the other services offered by chambers of commerce are all perceived to be "poor" by the majority of their users. This holds particularly for advice on product specifications and conducting marketing research abroad, which received "poor" ratings from 80 percent or more of their users. Again, these results replicate the findings on the BOTB in that the two services rated worst for chambers of commerce are identical with the ones rated worst for the BOTB.

Moving on to the Export Credits Guarantee Department (ECGD), not surprisingly the service most widely used was financial assistance. However, it is remarkable that 85 percent out of its users rated this ECGD service as "poor". Contrary to prior expectations, the advice of the ECGD has also been sought in a number of other areas, though the perception of these services is less than complimentary for the ECGD. Their advice on these services was rated as "poor" by between 58 percent (initial contacts with customers) and 90 percent (product specifications) of the users. In interpreting these results, one has to bear in mind that advice outside the area of export finance is not within the remit of the ECGD and presumably only given as a by-product of talking to exporters about financial matters.

With ten mentions each, the export assistance services most widely sought from the British Food Export Council (BFEC) were financial assistance, initial contacts with customers, advice on overseas laws and regulations as well as on distribution facilities. Initial contacts with customers and advice on overseas laws and regulations were also the two services with the highest proportion of satisfied users (60%). This provides further evidence of the important role these two services play in export assistance.

British Banks' Intelligence Units were most often used for advice on overseas laws and regulations, and their assistance in this matter was perceived to be "good" by 43 percent of its users. However, overall their export assistance services appear to be not well regarded by Scottish food and drink companies, as evidenced by the fact that four of the seven services investigated did not show a single satisfied user!

Export Agencies were also approached for advice on a wide variety of issues. Out of the seven services investigated, three show a higher proportion of satisfied than dissatisfied users, i.e., initial contacts with customers, advice on overseas laws and regulations, and market assessment. Although more than 50 percent satisfaction in three out of seven services might not be regarded as a good performance rating, it has to be emphasized that the number of services with a majority of satisfied users is higher than in any of the bodies discussed above.

The Scottish Development Agency (SDA) was most often approached for advice on financial assistance, initial contacts with customers and distribution facilities. Noticeable is the relatively high proportion of mentions that rated the SDA as a "poor" source for export advice but companies subsequently perceiving the specific services obtained as "good". Still, the majority of users appear to be dissatisfied with their services.

The Scottish Whisky Association (SWA), finally, was not widely used for export assistance. This is surprising given the importance of whisky exports for Scotland in general and the prevalence of companies from the drinks industry in our sample in particular. When used, the services of the Scottish Whisky Association were also perceived to be "good" in the minority of mentions only.

A complementary perspective on the perceived quality of each service delivered by a particular body was obtained by restructuring the information presented in Table 9.4. This was achieved by subtracting the "poor" from the "good" mentions and dividing by the total number of mentions (i.e., users of the service). Hence, favourable overall evaluations of a given service are represented by positive values whereas unfavourable evaluations are represented by negative values; within this scheme, the extreme values of 1 and -1 indicate that every user of the service concerned was satisfied or dissatisfied respectively, while a value of 0 indicates a 50/50 split between satisfied and dissatisfied users. The results of this analysis are shown in Table 9.5.

Table 9.5 shows that a considerable number of users are dissatisfied with the provision of four of the seven investigated services, regardless of the bodies that provided these services! Specifically, not a single positive score could be recorded for financial assistance, overseas marketing research, advice on distribution facilities and product specifications. As to the provision of initial contacts with customers, advice on overseas laws and regulations and market ass-

Table 9.5: Service quality delivered by export promotion bodies

Export promotion body	Financial assistance	Marketing research abroad	Initial contacts with customers	Export assistance services Advice on overseas laws/ regulations	Distribution facilities	Market assessment	Product specifications
British Overseas Trade Board	-0.39	-0.48	0.28	0.22	-0.36	-0.09	-0.50
Chamber of Commerce	-0.47	-0.60	-0.13	0.38	-0.47	0.00	-0.67
Export Credits Guarantee Department	-0.71	-0.33	-0.17	-0.17	-0.67	-0.27	-0.80
British Food Export Council	-0.20	-0.50	0.20	0.20	-0.40	0.00	-0.14
British Banks' Intelligence Unit	-0.67	-1.00	-1.00	-0.14	-1.00	-0.33	-0.10
Export Agency in the U.K.	-0.71	-0.50	0.25	0.25	-0.50	0.25	0.00
Scottish Development Agency	-0.20	-0.50	-0.20	-0.50	-0.60	0.00	-0.50
Scottish Whisky Association	-1.00	-0.50	-1.00	0.50	-0.50	-0.50	-1.00

Source: Prepared by authors.

essments, at least some export promotion bodies scored positive ratings, i.e., satisfied the majority of their users. The results in Table 9.5 also demonstrate that some bodies are unable to claim satisfaction for the majority of their users even for a single service they provided. In this context, particularly poor profiles are displayed by the Export Credits Guarantee Department, Banks and the Scottish Development Agency.

Differences Between Users and Non-Users of Export Assistance

Following the examination of the use and evaluation of export assistance among the sample firms, an attempt was made to identify potential differences between users and non-users of export assistance in terms of demographic and export characteristics. To this end, chi-square tests were employed to compare the two groups of firms on nominal-scaled variables and Mann-Whitney-U tests for all other variables (Table 9A.3 in the Appendix). The results indicate that there is practically no difference in terms of firm demographics or export characteristics between users and non-users of export assistance, a single exception being the greater number of export markets served by the user group (p<.10). However, even this result may be dismissed as a chance event rather than an instance of systematic variation. Using a 10 percent level of significance, one would expect 1-2 significant results purely by chance when undertaking comparisons on thirteen variables. At this stage a word of caution is necessary: while the results provide no evidence to the contrary, it would be unwise to state conclusively that users and non-users of export promotion in this industry cannot be differentiated in terms of the export characteristics investigated. Although this may indeed be the case, the lack of statistical significance may be a result of artifacts in the data, specifically. the grossly unequal sample sizes of forty users and eight non-users and the small number of firms comprising the data base of this study. It may be prudent, therefore, to reserve judgement as to the existence and magnitude of differences between the two groups of exporters.

CONCLUSIONS AND IMPLICATIONS

While readily acknowledging the limitations of the present study, i.e., single industry data, limited sample size and dominance of companies from the drinks (whisky) industry, one cannot but conclude that the picture painted by the results is hardly complementary for the providers of export assistance. While the vast majority of the exporters in the sample sought export assistance in one form or another (thus indicating the desirability of export assistance), the quality of the assistance obtained did not, on the whole, match the expectations of its users. Some export promotion bodies, for example the Export Credits Guarantee Department and the Scottish Development Agency, are perceived by their users as being totally inadequate. And the same holds for a number of specific services on offer, such as overseas market research and advice on distribution facilities abroad. The latter finding is particularly disturbing since, in many instances, it is the services that are sought most often which attract the strongest criticism.

Turning attention to the comparison between users and non-users of export assistance, no differences could be identified between the two groups of companies either in terms of firm demographics or export characteristics. Assuming that the inability to detect any differences is not due to artifacts in the data, it would appear that the mere use of export assistance is not a major differentiating factor of export behaviour. Perhaps more important is the specific type of export assistance received (i.e., the specific "bundle" of export promotion services tapped by the firm), which is likely to differ according to the firm's export development stage (Czinkota 1982).

Taken collectively, the findings of this study indicate the following actions for organizations that provide export promotion:

1. Providers of export promotion should be more concerned with the quality of their existing export assistance services. To this end some efforts should be made to evaluate the success of their programmes as perceived by their clients. It would be particularly useful to unearth the criteria used by exporting firms when judging providers of export assistance and the specific services available. In this context, it is encouraging to note that some bodies are already undertaking such evaluation exercises; for example, the authors are aware of a study commissioned by the British Overseas Trade Board to obtain feedback from the users of its Export Marketing Research Scheme.

2. Providers of export promotion should carefully review the scope for greater specialization in terms of service provision. Such specialization would help ensure that different export assistance bodies could concentrate on different export assistance services and,

thus, build expertise in specific areas. This could only benefit the quality of the services provided to firms seeking export assistance.

3. Providers of export promotion should investigate the extent to which present and potential exporters seek other kinds of export assistance which are not currently available from export promotion bodies. It should be considered how marketing research can best be conducted to identify new services needs; the scope for collaboration and/or coordination with different organizations in the design of new services should be investigated; and the match between qualifications of staff and the requirements of new services should be evaluated.

APPENDIX

Although a chi-square test could not be performed to objectively determine the extent of bias introduced in the sample as a result of non-response (due to the small number of cases in each cell of the contingency table), it appears that the obtained response does not vary widely from the composition of the original sample frame. The fact that four product sectors are not represented in the final sample is not particularly worrying, given the low export orientation of these sectors.

Table 9A.1: Sample breakdown and non-response analysis

Product sector	Total no. of firms (1)	No. of exporters (2)	% of firms exporting (3)=(2)/(1)	No. of firms in sample (4)=(2)X(3)	No. of responses
Grain milling	19	1	5.3	1	0
Bread/flour confectionery	43	3	7.0	1	0
Biscuits	20	12	60.0	7	3
Bacon curing, meat & fish	153	75	49.0	37	18
Milk & milk products	31	9	29.0	3	1
Sugar	3	2	66.7	1	1
Cocoa, chocolate & sugar confectionary	20	12	60.0	7	5
Fruit & vegetables	26	12	46.2	6	2
Vegetable & animal oils and fats	12	1	8.3	1	0
Other food industries	25	12	48.0	6	1
Brewing & malting	25	9	36.0	3	1
Soft drinks	40	8	20.0	2	0
Other drink industries	113	68	60.2	41	16
Total	530	224	42.3	116	48

Source: Prepared by authors.

Table 9A.2: Bodies and services investigated in the study

Bodies investigated in the study
1. British Overseas Trade Board (BOTB)
2. Chambers of commerce
3. Export Credits Guarantee Department (ECGD)
4. British Food Export Council (BFEC)
5. British Banks' Intelligence Units
6. Export agencies in the U.K.
7. Scottish Development Agency
8. Scottish Whisky Association
9. Scottish Council for Development and Industry (SCDI)
10. Purchasing Agents in the U.K.
11. Seafish Industry Authority
12. Scottish Agricultural Export Council (SAEC)

Services investigated in the study
1. Financial assistance
2. Overseas marketing research
3. Establishment of initial contacts with customers
4. Advice on overseas laws and regulations
5. Advice on available distribution facilities
6. Market assessment
7. Product specifications
8. Establishment of an overseas sales force
9. Exhibitions and overseas trade fairs

Source: Prepared by authors.

Table 9A.3: Comparison of users and non-users of export assistance

Export characteristics	Users	Median Non-users	Significance of M-W-U*
Company age (years)	67	18	ns**
Number of employees	188	70	ns
Sales turnover (£ million)	3	2.5	ns
Export intensity (% of total sales)	20.5	20.5	ns
Number of export markets served	9.5	5	p<.10
Number of regions served	3	2	ns
Export experience (years)	10	10	ns
Number of export staff	4.5	2	ns

	Percentage		Significance of Chi-square
Export experience (regular exporters)	85	75	ns
Range of products exported (full range)	48	38	ns
Product adaptation (yes)	80	63	ns
Export initiation (started deliberately)	60	38	ns
Export department (yes)	60	63	ns

*   The choice of the Mann-Whitney-U (M-W-U) test was based partly on measurement considerations (i.e., some variables were measured on ordinal scales) and partly on the fact that the non-user group consisted of only eight companies, implying that the distributional assumptions of parametric procedures (such as a t-test for the difference between means) would have been violated (Siegel, 1956).

**   ns = not significant.

Source: Prepared by authors.

ACKNOWLEDGEMENTS

The authors would like to express their thanks to the editors and the anonymous reviewer for the helpful comments on an earlier draft of this chapter.

REFERENCES

Beyfuss, J. (1984). "Formen staatlicher Exportfoerderung", in E. Dichtl and O. Issing, Eds., *Exporte als Herausforderung fuer die deutsche Wirtschaft*, Koeln: Deutscher Instituts verlag GmbH.

Bilkey, W.J. (1978). "An Attempted Integration of the Literature on the Export Behavior of Firms", *Journal of International Business Studies*, Vol 9, Summer, pp. 34-46.

Borchert, M. (1977). *Aussenwirtschaftslehre – Theorie und Politik*, Opladen: Westdeutscher Verlag.

British Food Export Council (1987). *Let's Get the Most out of Britain,* London.

British Overseas Trade Board (1987). *British Overseas Trade Board Report 1986*, London.

Chapman, N. (1986). "Why the FFB is Flying the British Flag in Europe", *Marketing Week*, (October), pp. 50-53.

Cannon, T. (1977). "Developing the Export Potential of Small Firms: The Role of Government and Banking Services", Sixth Annual Conference of the European Foundation for Management Development, Paris.

Cullwick, T.D.C. and J.P. Mellallieu (1981). "Business Attitudes to Government Export Services and Export Marketing Behavior", *New Journal of Business*, Vol. 3, pp. 33-54.

Cunningham, M.T. and R.I. Spigel (1971). "A Study in Successful Exporting", *British Journal of Marketing*, Vol. 5, (Spring), pp. 2-12.

Czinkota, M.R. (1982). *Export Development Strategies*, New York: Praeger Publishers.

Diamantopoulos, A. and K.N. Inglis (1988). "Identifying Differences Between High- and Low-Involvement Exporters", *International Marketing Review*, Vol. 5, No. 2, pp. 52-60.

Glastetter, W. (1979). *Aussenwirtschaftspolitik*, Koeln.

Gronhaug, K. and T. Lorentzen (1983). "Exploring the Impact of Government Export Subsidies", *European Journal of Marketing*, Vol. 17, No. 2, pp. 5-12.

House of Commons (1980). "Proceeding of the Special Committee on a National Trading Corporation", First Session of the Thirty-Second Parliament, Issue No. 29.

Krebs, G. (1977). *Angewandte Aussenwirtschaftstheorie und -Politik*, Koeln: Fachhochschule.

Lefevre, D. (1970). *Staatliche Ausfuhrfoerderung und das Verbot wettbewerbsverzerrender Beihilfen im EWG Vertrag*, Baden-Baden.

Mayer, C.S. and J.E. Flynn (1973). "Canadian Small Business Abroad: Opportunities, Aids and Experiences", *Business Quarterly*, (Winter), pp. 33-47.

McFarlane, G. (1978). "Scots Queen's Award Winners Don't Excel", *Marketing*, (April), pp. 27-32.

National Swedish Industrial Board (1984). *Export Promotion by Governments in Nine Countries*, Stockholm.

Parsonm, M. and P. Foster (1978). "Notes on the Motivation and Methods of the Small Exporter", *Industrial Marketing Digest*, Vol. 3, No. 2, pp. 130-135.

Rabino, S. (1980). "An Examination of Barriers to Exporting Encountered by Small Manufacturing Companies", *Management International Review*, Vol. 20, No. 1, pp. 67-73.

Reid, S.D. (1984). "Information Acquisition and Export Entry Decisions in Small Firms", *Journal of Business Research*, Vol. 12, (June), pp. 141-157.

Scottish Council Development and Industry (1988). *Programme 1988*, Edinburgh.

Scottish Development Agency (1988). *Annual Report 1987*, Glasgow.

Seringhaus, F.H.R. (1983). "Government Export Marketing Assistance in the Early Phase of the Internationalization Process of the Firm", paper presented at the Ninth Annual Conference of the European International Business Association, Oslo.

Seringhaus, F.H.R. (1985). "Private/Public Sector Interaction: How Effective is Export Assistance by Government". Proceedings of the Annual Conference of the European Marketing Academy (Bielefeld, West Germany), pp. 119-128.

Seringhaus, F.H.R. (1986). "The Impact of Government Export Marketing Assistance", *International Marketing Review*, Vol. 3, No. 2, pp. 55-66.

Seringhaus, F.H.R. (1987). "Export Promotion: The Role and Impact of Government Services", *Irish Marketing Review*, Vol. 2, pp. 106-116.

Siegel, S. (1956). *Nonparametric Statistics for the Behavioural Sciences*, Intern. Ed, Tokyo: McGraw-Hill Kogakusha, Ltd.

Simpson, C.L., D.A. Roy and D.L. Loudon (1981). "Use and Perception of External Support Facilities in the Initial Export Activity Among

Smaller Manufacturing Firms in the Southeastern United States",
presented at the Annual Meeting of the Academy of International
Business, Montreal, October, pp. 15-17.

Standing Commission on the Scottish Economy (1988). *Interim Report*,
Glasgow: Fraser of Allander Institute.

Suntook, F. (1978). "How British Industry Exports", *Marketing*, (June), pp. 29-
34.

Tookey, D.A. (1964). "Factors Associated with Success in Exporting", *The
Journal of Management Studies*, vol. 1, (March), pp. 48-66.

Vernon, I. and J. Ryans (1975). "The Awareness and Selection of an Export
Incentive: The DISC Case", *Baylor Business Studies*, (February- April),
pp. 19-26.

CHAPTER TEN

Public Support to Export Consortia: The Italian Case

Riccardo Lanzara, Riccardo Varaldo, Patrizia Zagnoli[*]

SUMMARY

This chapter focuses on the Italian experience with export consortia, examining the evolution of the phenomenon from 1981 to 1987. In the first section the distinctive characteristics of export consortia are identified and compared with those of various public and private Italian institutions for export support. A discussion follows on the role played by public intervention in the development of this particular form of collaboration among firms. Different types of export consortia are described in order to build up a model able to interpret their process of development. Finally, summary comments are provided and practical suggestions are offered for the revision of Italian public policies towards export consortia.

INTRODUCTION

Forms of collaboration between small and medium-sized firms (SMFs) may vary considerably in type and in purpose. Often, this sort of cooperation leads to the creation of formal institutions of an associative kind. Export consortia may be included in this category of institutions; they are of particular economic importance in view of the role that they may play in the

---

[*]   Scuola Superiore di Studi Universitari e di Perfezionamento, S. Anna, Pisa.

internationalization processes of SMFs. "Export grouping schemes are one of the many approach that offer the hope of better exploiting the untapped export potential of smaller companies" (Welch & Joynt 1987, p. 55).

Distinctive characteristics of export consortia are compared with those of various other institutions, both public and private, which support exportation. Then follows a discussion of the role that public intervention has played in the development of this particular form of association between firms. The different forms of export consortia are subsequently described, and a model is proposed to interpret the process of development of these forms. In the final section, Italian public intervention is criticized, and some ideas are expressed about the possible revision of public policies towards export consortia.

THE POSITION OF EXPORT CONSORTIA AMONG INSTITUTIONS SUPPORTING EXPORTATION

On the local and national level, several institutions exist in Italy which offer aid to exporting firms, especially those of small size. This demonstrates the growth in the general attention paid to the phenomenon of exportation.

Following a primary, broad classification, exporting institutions may be divided into public and private ones. The services offered may, in turn, be divided into two main kinds (1) financing and insurance; (2) real services (promotion, market research, etc.).

The combination of the type of organization and the services offered makes it possible to distinguish most of the types of bodies which offer assistance to exporters, including consortia (see Figure 10.1).

Public operators

SACE and Mediocredito Centrale. Until the end of the 70's, the structure of assistance for exporting firms in Italy was far too inadequate, in spite of the great interest shown for exportation by Italian firms, even of small size (Varaldo 1987). As a result, Italian exporting firms were at a clear disadvantage compared with their international competitors. The latter could benefit from easier insurance and financial conditions, and other facilities were in general far more favourable (Lanzara & Sbrana 1984, pp. 119-120). In order to overcome this weakness in its intervention schemes in favour of exportation, the government decided to introduce a number of legislative arrangements. The first of these was the so-called Ossola Act, which was passed on May 24th, 1977. This act introduced forms of insurance against risks of a commercial and political nature associated with export activities, such as insolvency, exchange rate fluctuation, etc.[1]

Figure 10.1: Types of export-supporting operations

	Finance, insurance	Real services
Public operators	- S.A.C.E. - Mediocredito	- I.C.E. - Chambers of Commerce
Private operators	- Local banks - Private insurance companies	EXPORT CONSORTIA

Source: Prepared by authors.

The Act established the creation of a single Government body – S.A.C.E. (Special Section for Export Credit and Insurance) – which brings together those insurance and evaluation aspects which were previously divided among a large number of different public institutions. It further decreed that financing facilities for exporters were to be managed by a central banking institute, the Mediocredito Centrale (Medium Term Credit Central Institute).

I.C.E. and Chambers of Commerce. A second group of public organizations supplies "real services" to firms. Foremost among these is the I.C.E. – Instituto per il Commercio con l' Estero (Institute for Foreign Trade) –

---

[1] The Ossola Act has been recently updated by a new Act (Act no. 83, February 21st 1989) which has introduced more financial facilities.

which is a central body dependent on the Ministry for Foreign Trade. On the local level, there are the chambers of commerce, which depend on the Ministry of Industry, Trade and Handicraft. Both of these institutions carry out various activities, such as market research, promotion, organizational support for participation in international fairs and exhibitions, management education, financial consultancy, etc. The main purpose of these interventions is to support firms in their exporting activities, and, more generally, to promote Italian products abroad.

Private organizations

Local banks and industrial associations. Private organizations generally offer the same services as public ones. Those worthy of mention as regards export financing are the banking institutes, particularly those operating on a local level, and the industrial associations. However, as will be described further on, both play a limited role. Far more important is the activity of insurance carried out by some private companies, who have entered the market of export risk coverage. Even when public insurance is possible, the time needed to guarantee, or to receive payment of an indemnity, is often so long that all real benefits for the firm disappear. Private insurance companies are more flexible, and are spread all over the country, with the result that they can grant insurance and pay indemnity very quickly.[2] It is interesting to note that it is the SMFs in particular that apply to these private insurance companies: this shows the trouble that they have in referring to the supporting public structures (Espansione 1983).

Consortia. A "consortium" can be defined as an "ad hoc or ongoing, informal or formal, sometimes 'shell', association of two or more business/governmental/financial entities to profitably pursue, generally on a competitive basis, one or more common commercial activities which are either complementary to, an extension of, or in addition to the regular activities of its members" (Dhawan & Kryzanowski 1978, p. 9).

The inadequacy of export-supporting structures in Italy made it difficult up to the end of the 70's for these forms of association to develop among firms.

---

[2]   In some cases, the time required for coverage is less than 48 hours, and indemnities are paid no longer than 60 days after the accident (Espansione 1983, 130).

Certain laws existed which severely hindered the emergence of consortia, inasmuch as firms taking part were subject to unlimited liability as regards the tasks undertaken by consortia.

It was only at the beginning of the 80's that Act no. 240, passed on May 21st, 1981, introduced a series of measures favouring the creation of consortia among SMFs, especially those involved in the export trade. This act provides both for fiscal concessions of a general nature, regarding payment of VAT, tax concessions on profits reinvested, etc. and for grants and cheaper credit for the acquisition of fixed investments and/or corporate investments in market research, patents, etc.

The Act contains unquestionable improvements compared with similar arrangements made before 1981. In spite of this, however, the number of export consortia created among SMFs is still extremely limited, especially when compared with the overall number of exporting firms in Italy. In 1982, the consortia listed in the National Association of Export Consortia (Federexport 1988)[3] totalled 115, while the number of SMFs taking part was 5,091, equal to 5 percent of the total number of exporting firms (more than 91,000) (Lanzara & Sbrana 1984, p. 118). In 1987, while the number of consortia that were members of Federexport had risen to 151, the total number of firms taking part had gone up to 6,801. This figure, however, is still very low when compared with the total number of exporting firms, which, in 1984, was calculated to be just over 80,000 (I.C.E. 1986). This shows that only a very small minority of SMFs make use of the consortium in order to export. One of the reasons for this phenomenon lies in the nature of Italian SMFs: most of the owner-managers were originally artisans, and their activities were born and developed from their manual and technical capacities. Many of them base their market success on particular, personal "recipes", which differentiate their product from those of competitors. For example, in the leather industry the recipes of tanning are "unwritten", and consist in learning by doing – a specific invisible asset of the entrepreneur. Consequently, SMFs are used to operating individually, and

---

[3]   Federexport was set up in 1974 for the purpose of: (1) representing the export consorzia vis-a-vis the government authorities, the central and peripheral institutions and administrations and the mass media; (2) promoting the setting of new consortia and the further growth of the existing ones; (3) coordinating the activities of the consortia and contributing to the improvement of their operating techniques in order to promote greater participation of SMFs in international trade. Federexport does not perform any commercial agency or intermediation functions, so that its intervention or assistance is entirely free of commission or charges of any kind.

are afraid that the disclosure of their "secrets" might have a negative effect on the competitiveness of their products.

BENEFITS AND PROBLEMS OF EXPORT CONSORTIA

Export consortia are used in quite a few countries with varying degrees of success. In Europe, the Italian experience is quite unique and many European countries are now evaluating and trying to imitate it. More over it must be pointed out, as we mentioned above, that the number of export consortia created among SMFs in Italy is still very limited.

The lack of a wide experience and the lack of empirical research[4] make it difficult to evaluate the pros and cons of this kind of institution. It is, however, possible to highlight in a general way the major potential benefits and problems that can be derived/encountered by a member firm from participating in an export consortium (Table 10.1).

As regards benefits, it must be noted that Italian consortia are generally support organizations for SMFs which have limited export experience and are in the early stages of export market entry or expansion.[5] Firms with considerable export experience generally avoid participating in consortia. In fact, in this case firms are compelled to share their previous experience and know-how with other member firms.

On the other side, most of the possible problems encountered within/by a consortium stem from differences among members and between members and the consortium itself. These contrasts require that the general manager of a consortium should be an outsider with veto power. If this condition is not satisfied, the general manager will not be able to resolve disagreements adequately among consortium members (Dhawan & Kryzanowski, 1978 p. 34). In this case, the consortium will not work or will operate with enormous difficulties.

---

[4] An interesting empirical survey was conducted on the potential benefits and problems of forming and operating Canadian-based consortia (especially in the areas of agro-industry and high technology) (Dhawan & Kryzanowski, 1978). Unfortunately, in Italy no such empirical research has been undertaken.

[5] The type of consortium designed to supply a complete technology project (turnkey or project management consortium) is still very rare in Italy.

Table 10.1: Six major potential benefits and problems
encountered within/by export consortia

Benefits	Problems
1. Strong organization for market penetration	1. Lack of consortium entrepreneurship
2. Easier entry by reducing initial market barriers	2. Lack of delegation of firm management authority
3. Easier entry by reducing the necessary initial investment	3. Disagreements in defining consortium strategy
4. Economies of scale in export support services	4. Decision-making
5. Activation of new export channels	5. Sales allocation among members
6. Strong organization for participation in fairs and exhibitions	6. Distribution of profits

Source: Prepared by authors.

THE FINANCING OF CONSORTIA: THE ROLE OF PUBLIC INTERVENTION

The financial resources at the disposal of export consortia derive from both external and internal sources. Internal resources covered 68 percent of the expenses sustained by the Federexport consortia in 1986 (Federexport 1988), while the remainder was subsidised either by the government or by other bodies outside the firms. This means that consortia may be considered to be organizations that are largely financed either by contributions from the firms associated, in the form of an annual membership fee, or by the proceeds of their own activities. Thus we cannot speak of structures that are totally state-assisted or completely dependent on some external institutions. In actual fact, consortia may be considered on the one hand as intermediary organisms between firms and public and private financing, and on the other as instruments for the management and coordination of financial resources.

The contributions of external financial sources is, however, of considerable importance. This stems from the fact that consortia are often born from initiatives of local bodies and organizations. Industrial associations, chambers of commerce, and various other bodies interested in the development of SMFs have assisted many consortia during the start-up phase, and continue to provide financial and technical support for their activities.

Another external source, which is undoubtedly the most important one, is represented by annual contributions from the government, made in conformity with the above mentioned Act number 240, of 1981. Figure 10.2, which refers to the Federexport consortia, shows that these contributions, together with those of local and regional public bodies, increased their percentage of total external financing, respectively from 42.0 percent and 10.4 percent in 1981 to 60.2 percent and 15.0 percent in 1987.

It may be noted (see Figure 10.3) that public contributions account for practically all external financing: the percentage of this source of financing passed from 74.3 percent in 1981 to 89.1 percent in 1987; in particular, public contributions made in conformity with Act. no. 240 accounted for 60 percent of this financing in 1987, with the government thus becoming the main external financing body.

The criteria on which state financing is based take into consideration on the one hand the structural and organizational solidity of consortia (stability of the premises and of the staff), and on the other, the level of promotional activity, that is to say, the real ability to offer services to firms. This ability is evaluated exclusively on the basis of the expenses shown in the profit and loss account of the previous year. Another parameter which is normally taken into consideration for the assignment of state contribution is the number of firms that belong to the consortium: the more there are, the higher the contribution is. As will be noted, these criteria adopted to determine financing do not make any reference to the actual performance of the consortium in terms of proceeds of sales and/or profit. An evaluation is made only of the stability of the initiative and the dimensions of the consortium in terms of level of expenses sustained and the number of firms belonging to it. It would therefore seem legitimate to conclude that government contributions tend to ignore the potential profitability of the initiatives, and favour consortia that have already reached the take-off phase.

Figure 10.2: Contributions from external financing sources made to consortia belonging to Federexport
(million lira, %)

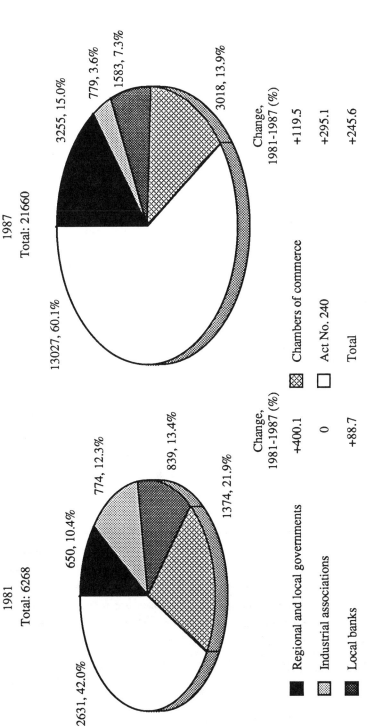

1981
Total: 6268

1987
Total: 21660

13027, 60.1%

3255, 15.0%

779, 3.6%

1583, 7.3%

3018, 13.9%

2631, 42.0%

650, 10.4%

774, 12.3%

839, 13.4%

1374, 21.9%

	Change, 1981-1987 (%)
Regional and local governments	+400.1
Industrial associations	0
Local banks	+88.7

	Change, 1981-1987 (%)
Chambers of commerce	+119.5
Act No. 240	+295.1
Total	+245.6

Source: Federexport 1988.

The experience of public incentives in favour of consortia has, however, proved to be extremely valid, making an effective contribution to the development and the consolidation of activities. Since coming into force, Act no. 240 has been used to assign contributions for a total value of 49.4 thousand million lira (Federexport 1988, p. 43). In 1987, the sum made available under Act no. 240 was 22 thousand million lira, of which 44 percent (or 9.6 million lira) was assigned to Federexport consortia, compared with a total request of 10.4 thousand million lira. The average contribution (see Table 10.2) to each single Federexport consortium was more than 86 million lira, compared with a maximum contribution permitted by the law of 100 million. On average, the contribution assigned covers about 26 percent of the total expenses sustained by Federexport consortia.

Even though this level has gone down since 1981, it is still highly significant, and gives an idea of the importance that the government gives to forms of association among firms involved in exportation.

THE MAIN ACTIVITIES OF EXPORT CONSORTIA

Another interesting aspect is the analysis of the expenses sustained by consortia. Figure 10.4 shows the two main expenses for firms belonging to Federexport: staff (wages, social contributions, leaving indemnity, etc.) and promotional activities (exhibitions and fairs, advertising, market research, etc.).

The most important expense is that of promotional activities, which has gone up in the last few years from 60.2 percent in 1982 to almost 68 percent in 1987. This underlines the fact that in spite of the increased volume of activity, the organizational structure of consortia tends to maintain limited dimensions: in 1986, the average number of employees per consortium was slightly less than three (2.97), while the average number of external consultants was about half that figure (1.54). Thus, the consortium proves to be an extremely flexible structure, whose expenses are predominantly variable in nature, and therefore linked with the volume of activity and the services that are offered to member firms.

Figure 10.3: Financial sources for consortia belonging to Federexport: Distribution between public and private institutions (million lira, %)

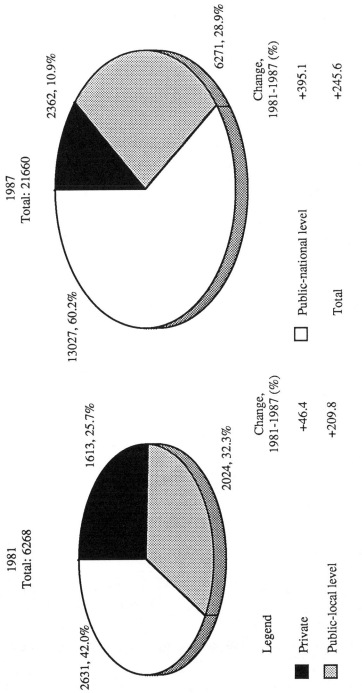

1981
Total: 6268

1987
Total: 21660

2631, 42.0%

1613, 25.7%

2024, 32.3%

2362, 10.9%

13027, 60.2%

6271, 28.9%

Change,
1981-1987 (%)

+46.4

+209.8

Change,
1981-1987 (%)

+395.1

+245.6

Legend

■ Private

▨ Public-local level

□ Public-national level

Total

Source: Federexport 1988.

Table 10.2: Federexport consortia expenses and public support
(1981 - 1987)

	1981	1987
Government financial support		
(Act 240) (million lira)	4250	13027
Consortia total expenses (million lira)	13678	49462
Government support/expenses	31.1%	26.3%
Government support / No. of consortia*		
(million lira)	51.8	86.3

Note: * Number of export consortia that applied for financial support.
Source: Federexport 1988

Figure 10.5 shows the division of the promotional expenses. As can be seen, the greatest expense is represented by participation in exhibitions and fairs (60.9%), which is obviously connected with the second largest expense, travel (20.0%).

Expenses for advertising and market research are much lower, making up less than 20 percent of the total. This is due to the fact that participation in trade fairs, with the presentation of one's products, offers a very important opportunity for SMFs, not simply to receive orders, but to carry out a product test,[6] and, at the same time, market research on current trends in international markets, by means of personal contact with agents and customers.[7] Thus, the consortium becomes an important structure in order to give firms of smaller dimensions the chance to take part in international trade fairs.

CHARACTERISTICS AND SCOPE OF EXPORT CONSORTIA

An analysis of export consortia reveals the importance of two kinds of parameters: (1) the structural characteristics; and (2) the scope of the consortia.

---

[6]   Leather and footwear firms provide a classic example of the use of exhibitions and trade fairs to test new products (see Lanzara 1988).

[7]   A good example is offered by the wood-working machine sector: firms use international exhibitions to carry out market research, often based on personal contact between owner-managers and customers or agents (see Meliani 1988).

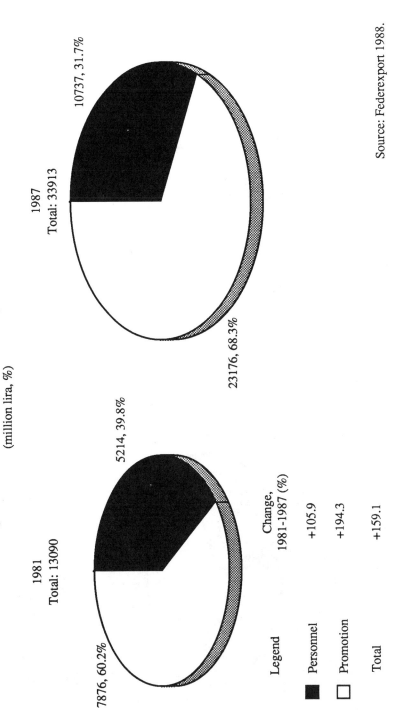

Figure 10.4: Main Federexport consortia expenses
(million lira, %)

1981
Total: 13090

5214, 39.8%

7876, 60.2%

1987
Total: 33913

10737, 31.7%

23176, 68.3%

Change, 1981-1987 (%)	
Personnel	+105.9
Promotion	+194.3
Total	+159.1

Legend

■ Personnel

□ Promotion

Source: Federexport 1988.

Figure 10.5: Distribution of promotional expenses of Federexport consortia (million lira, %)

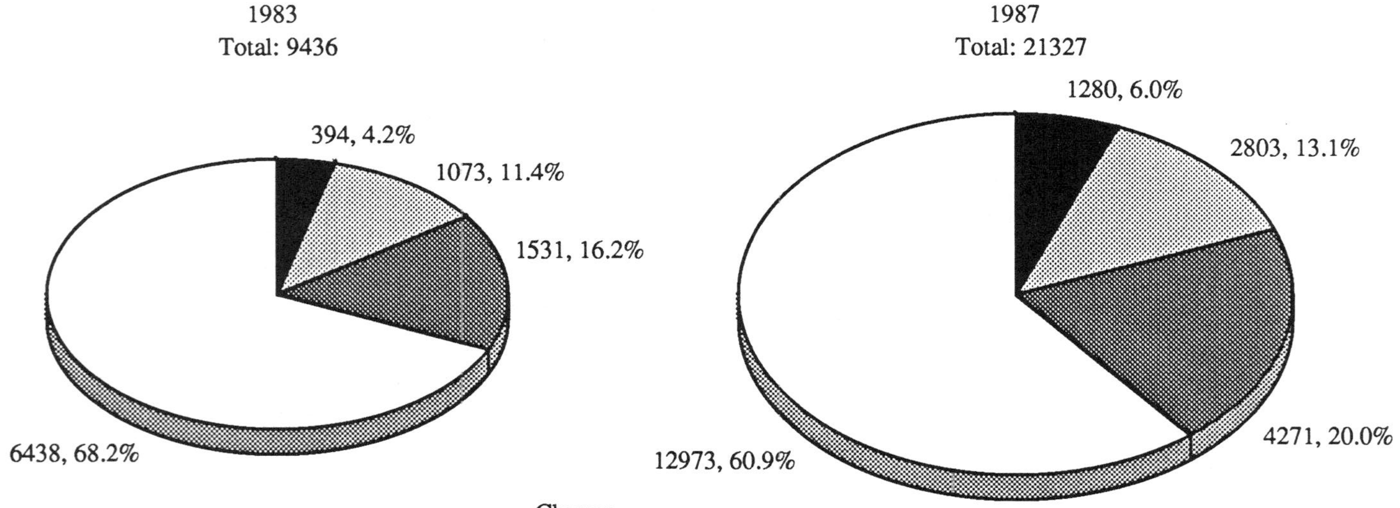

1983
Total: 9436

1987
Total: 21327

6438, 68.2%

394, 4.2%

1073, 11.4%

1531, 16.2%

2803, 13.1%

1280, 6.0%

4271, 20.0%

12973, 60.9%

Change,
1983-1987 (%)

+224.9

+161.2

+179.0

+101.5

+126.0

Legend

Market research

Advertising

Travel

Exhibition and trade fairs

Total

Source: Federexport 1988.

The structural characteristics of consortia include:
1. the number of associated firms;
2. private and public nature of the constituent partners;
3. product diversification of export consortia;
4. complementary between associated firms;
5. legal form of export consortia.

As regards the number of associated firms, we can identify small consortia (from 0 to 10 associated SMFs), medium-sized (11 to 50 SMFs), and large ones (more than 50 SMFs).[8] Larger export consortia generally have greater heterogeneity of products among the firms.

Consortia may be made up only of private SMFs, or they may have a mixed private/public nature. Especially in the start-up stage of export consortia, the support of the local chamber of commerce, the Regional government, or the County administration can be essential in order to promote collaboration among SMFs, and to activate promotional services.

In terms of product diversification, consortia can be classified as multisectorial or monosectorial. Multisectorial consortia are very heterogeneous in terms of the industrial sectors represented. On the contrary, monosectorial consortia are made up of firms that are homogeneous in terms of their products.

Another key aspect of export consortia is the degree of complementarity among firms. Complementarity among associated firms is high when they manufacture different, but complimentary products, which contribute to an integrated, complex final product, or which can be supplied as an integrated package of different models, materials, uses, etc. On the contrary, a low degree of complementarity means that the associated SMFs supply products that belong to different sectors, or a wide range of similar products which have little connection with one another in terms of potential customers and users.

Lastly, let us consider the legal form of consortia. The juridical and substantial nature of consortia would seem to be particularly well exploited when the consortium provides consultancy and pre-export services, and the responsibilities of export activities are still singly managed by each associated

---

[8] In 1982, the size distribution, in terms of number of associated firms, of the 115 export consortia belonging to Federexport registered 35 in the group 0-10, 45 in the group 11-50, and 35 with more than 50 associated SMFs. Only 5 export consortia had more than 200 associated SMFs.

firm. The consortia provide internal services for the associated SMFs, without having to direct external relationships.

The nature of consortia tends to change, depending on the task or the activities that they have to carry out. Consortia that manage not only the promotion but also the sales activities tend to change their nature from consortia to independent incorporated trading companies.

The scope of consortia characterised by external activity goes from simple promotion or sales to more complex forms that involve both promotion and sales activities. The "purely" promotional consortia can be of two different kinds:

1. the overall services consortia, where the SMFs are associated in order to obtain public financial support, and to share some basic services, such as telex, telefax, translations, and so forth.
2. 'real' promotion and selling consortia, which not only provide some basic service, achieving economies of scale that a single firm could not obtain, but are also active in advising the SMFs. Generally, they provide information about legal and economic conditions of potential export markets, access to trade fairs, promotional trips, joint advertising campaigns, etc.

The incidence of promotional expenditure in direct activities, such as trade fairs and promotional trips, as previously mentioned, shows that the mentality of the artisan still survives in the promotional field, as well. SMFs and consortia seem to prefer to contact the market directly by means of a sort of "visual test", instead of using modern, systematic marketing tools.

The combination of export promotion and export selling in a new, specialized firm with its own brand name implies a real entrepreneurial attitude and activity, which, for many different reasons, may be difficult to activate. These consortia buy the product from the manufacturing companies and, in order to sell, have to elaborate their own export strategies and organise themselves as real, new, autonomous companies.

TYPOLOGY OF EXPORT CONSORTIA

Combining the degree of complementarity among associated firms and the degree of diversification of export consortia, we have constructed a simple matrix of four squares, or typology of export consortia (see Figure 10.6).

A high degree of product diversification and a low degree of complementarity among associated firms characterize generic multisectorial consortia (Square 1).

The generic multisectorial consortium is the typical kind found in the early stages of development of this form of association; it includes companies involved in very heterogeneous activities. In these cases, the consortium can provide basic promotional services, such as telex, translation, etc., which are useful, though not closely connected with the exporting and the market strategy of every single associated firm (see Figure 10.7 for an example of this type of consortium).

Figure 10.6: Typology of export consortia

Complementarity among associated SMFs

	Low	High
High	Generic multisectorial (1)	Complementary multisectorial (3)
Low	Generic monosectorial (2)	Specialised monosectorial (4)

Product diversification of export consortia

Source: Prepared by authors.

Generic monosectorial consortia start as a result of collaboration among companies of the same sector that produce similar products, and are often located in the same area (Square 2). As the product diversification inside the consortium and the degree of complementarity among associated SMFs are both low, the consortium can activate information and services from the more simple (translation, telex, etc.) to more complex ones (finance and insurance advisory service, technical information, search for new markets, promotion of the product image, trade fairs, etc.), all in the area of general promotional activities. Obviously, the SMFs associated in generic monosectorial consortia are normally competitors. This means that sometimes, there is no real willingness to collaborate among the partner firms. In addition, some of them may try to take over the activities of the consortium in order to direct them towards their own particular goals. Or, more commonly, the collaboration can be overwhelmed by the leadership of a few firms, clearly harming the aims of collaboration. This is particularly the case in generic monosectorial consortia where firms are frequently asymmetric in terms of their market power, and their products are placed on the same markets.

Complementary multisectorial consortia of SMFs that belong to different but complementary sectors are focused on obtaining an integrated promotional activity, in terms of supplying final services to the user (e.g., integrated supplies for the house, such as furniture, lamps, glass and metal accessories), or coordinated images and designs (e.g., fashion-coordinated products, such as garments, shoes, jewellery, etc.) (Square 3). They are able to offer and to promote the supply of packages of products and/or services, which are vertically or laterally integrated. These consortia register a low level of internal conflict among associated firms, because they play on the degree of collaboration, rather than competition, among the SMFs involved.

Low product diversification and high complementarity characterize specialized monosectorial consortia (Square 4), which are able to achieve a high degree of specialization in their activities, providing both promotional and sales services. In these cases, consortia are really a complete specialized centre for services, entitled to exercise the role of an autonomous company whose work is the fulfilment of export activities. In order to achieve their aim effectively, these consortia, which become profit centres, need to be based on associations of SMFs that are not in conflict with one another, and, on the contrary, can gain an advantage from cooperating, in view of the high degree of complementarity of their products or services. This can happen when the SMFs are: (1) specialized in particular products or parts of products which are complimentary; or (2) able to supply a complete product or a complete realization.

Figure 10.7: Examples of Italian consortia

Generic multisectorial consortium

Name: Bergamo Export
Location: North of Italy (Lombardia)
Year of constitution: 1969
Size - Associated firms (1987): 252
     Firms total number of
       employees (1987): 12,000
Sectors covered:
 - Foodstuffs
 - Sport goods
 - Paper products
 - Chemical and pharma-
    ceutical products
 - Supplies for con-
    struction industry
 - Electronics, optical and
    precision instruments
 - Plant and technology
 - Gift articles
 - Gold and silversmiths
 - Miscellaneous products
    (toys, optical goods, etc.)
 - Textile and clothing
 - Engineering and machinery
 - Furniture and interior
    design goods
 - Boats and boating equipment

Specialised monosectorial consortium

Name: Consite
Location: North of Italy (Lombardia)
Year of constitution: 1978
Size - Associated firms (1987): 7
     Firms total number of
       employees (1987): 820
Sectors covered:
 - Plant and technology

Generic monosectorial consortium

Name: Conciatori Toscani
Location: Centre of Italy (Toscana)
Year of constitution: 1982
Size - Associated firms (1987): 10
     Firms total number of
       employees (1987): 300
Sectors covered:
 - Tanning of skins and leather

Complementary multisectorial
consortium

Name: Consorzio Moda Firenze
Location: Centre of Italy (Toscana)
Year of constitution: 1983
Size - Associated firms (1987): 5
     Firms total number of
       employees (1987): 200
Sectors covered:
 - Footwear and accessories
 - Textiles and clothing

Source: Federexport.

Specialized monosectorial consortia are designed to play an effective role in export promotion, and in selling for the "customer" associated companies. This means that they are based on a delegation of power and decision-taking in order to manage the business of the associated companies.

DEVELOPMENT STAGES OF EXPORT CONSORTIA

The stages of development of export consortia can be analyzed by considering the Federexport statistics. According to Federexport data, export consortia of SMFs increased from 16 in 1974 to 151 in 1987 (+843%), and the number of associated companies increased from 1,000 in 1974 to 6,801 in 1987 (+580%).

In the early years of activation of this form of export collaboration, consortia were mainly characterized by multisectorial features. Two-thirds of them were the result of the association of small firms which were active in different sectors of production. The average number of associated firms was around 70-80 per consortium (see Figures 10.8 and 10.9).

The goal in that period was to increase the number of SMFs involved in exporting. In this perspective, many local chambers of commerce assisted in starting up export consortia which were generally multisectorial, and characterized by a mixed private/public nature.

At this early stage in the development of the export consortia life cycle, entrepreneurs still identified with their own companies, and they rarely set up collaboration with other firms in the fields of management, marketing or commercialization. Consequently, "external" public support was essential to promote collaboration among firms, and to activate basic promotional services. On the one hand, generic promotional services represent the easiest form of collaboration among different "entrepreneurial individuals", since they do not directly affect the export strategy or the performance of the products of every single firm. On the other hand, it is not convenient for single SMFs to carry out the basic promotional activities provided by export consortia, since they cannot achieve a sufficient economy of scale. On the contrary, an export consortium can allow companies to have specialized and specific services available.

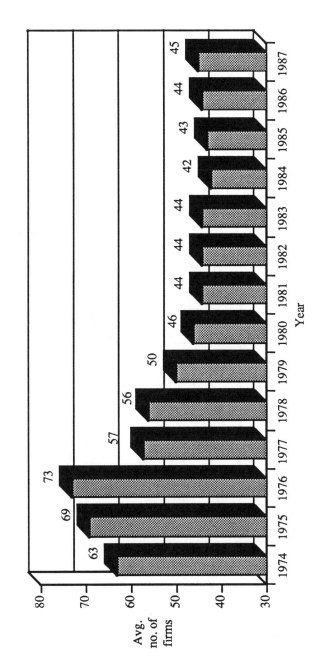

Figure 10.8: Average number of consortia associated firms, 1974 - 1987

Source: Federexport 1988

Figure 10.9: Typology of export consortia, 1974 - 1987

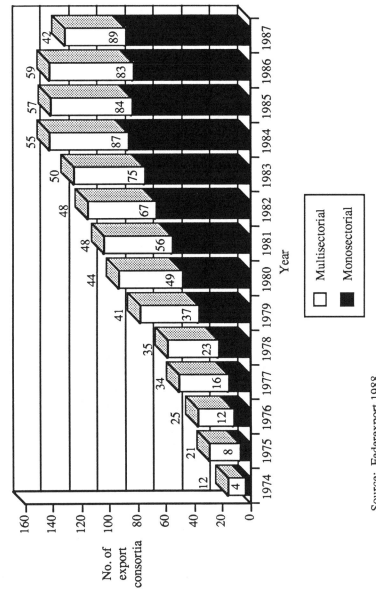

Source: Federexport 1988

At the end of the 70's, export consortia showed a turn-around in the sectorial variety, as well in the average number of firms associated. The more recent period in the development of export consortia has been mainly characterized by monosectorial, and also specialized consortia, with a reduced number of SMFs per consortium.

By 1980, 53 percent of consortia were monosectorial, and the average number of firms associated was about 40. This marks the beginning of the most recent stage of development in the evolution of export consortia. At this point, the goal is the consolidation of the export activities of SMFs. They have to face increasingly global market conditions, where competitive rules are becoming more and more complex. They need to change their export activities from ad hoc to systematic. In order to cope with complex specialized export functions, export consortia are tending to become more and more highly organized and specialized on particular promotion, sales and distribution activities. The highly competitive environment pushes associated companies to reduce the level of "entrepreneurial individuality", and to collaborate more intensively in a common effort to manage the complex variables of the marketing mix.

The number of specialized consortia is increasing. The same trend towards a greater level of specialization may be observed in multisectorial export consortia, which tend to be characterized by a decreasing variety of sectors represented, in which every company can be classified in different sectors, but the products are complementary to each other. Their products compete in different markets, but their respective added value can increase if they are offered as a package that constitutes a complex, articulated supply.

Furthermore, in these difficult market conditions, it is often necessary to be able to mange complex integrated export activities, such as, for example, barter, countertrade, buyback, etc. At this point, consortia reveal their intrinsic limits, and many of them tend to become autonomous trading companies, in order to cope with these complex exchange conditions.

RETHINKING PUBLIC SUPPORT FOR EXPORT CONSORTIA

The analysis of financial support for export consortia has shown that the public sector, on the national and the local level, increased its support from 74.3 percent of the total external financial support in 1981, to 89.1 percent in 1987. At the same time, the structural and typological characteristics of export consortia revealed a clear trend towards a reduction in sectorial variety of the associated firms, and an increasing complementarity of SMFs and specialization and qualification of the promotional and sales services supplied.

This analysis leads to at least three considerations for change:

1. The need to reduce generic public support to export consortia, based on expense levels. At the last stage of the export consortia life cycle, it is becoming more and more clear that financial support is not useful *per se,* but can produce positive results only if it is directed to effective, highly qualified services, and is selective in sponsoring those export consortia that are dealing with the most advanced issues.

2. These aims can be achieved by considering the various levels of requirements that characterize the different stages of the export consortia life cycle. It might be more productive, in fact, to correlate public financial support with the age of export consortia. Public support should be intensive and more concentrated in the initial stages of export consortia, in order to help in organizing the delicate, and complex start-up phase, in terms of physical location, trained personnel, promotional services, etc. After the start-up stage, public financial support should be provided for "real" selective services, such as market research, joint advertising, new product research, countertrade, technology transfer to foreign markets and so on.

3. The desirable development of public support should be increasingly based on structural and operational aspects of the performance of export consortia, rather than on expenses already sustained. This *ex-post* procedure of financial support is not related to the strategy of export consortia. On the basis of our analysis, we would suggest focusing public financial support on the evolutionary structure of consortia, thus linking it with new aims and prospects, such as an analysis of new products, new market opportunities, and organization of their own distribution network.

REFERENCES

Dhawan, K.C. and L. Kryzanowski (1978). *Export Consortia, A Canadian Study*, Montreal: DEKEMCO Ltd.

Espansione (1983). No. 162, November.

Federexport (1988). *Consorzi export in Italia*, Roma: Confindustria.

I.C.E. (1986). "La struttura delle esportazioni italiane", Roma.

Lanzara, R. (1988). "I rapporti strategici con le imprese conciarie", in R. Varaldo, Ed., *Il sistema delle imprese calzaturiere*, (Torino, Giappichelli editore), pp. 41-53.

Lanzara, R. and R. Sbrana (1984). "Export Trade: Government Policies and Italian Small Firms", in *Economia Aziendale*, Volume III, Number 2, August, pp. 117-30.

Meliani, R. (1988). "Il marketing internazionale delle imprese produttrici di macchine per il legno", unpublished Tesi di laurea, Dipartimento di Economia Aziendale, Universita' Degli Studi di Pisa.

Varaldo, R. (1987). "The Internationalization of Small and Medium-sized Italian Manufacturing Firms" in P.J. Rosson and S.D. Reid, Eds, *Managing Export Entry and Expansion*, New York: Praeger Publishers, pp. 203-22.

Welch, L.S. and P. Joynt (1987). "Grouping for Export: An Effective Solution", in P.J. Rosson and S.D. Reid, Eds., *Managing Export Entry and Expansion*, New York: Praeger Publishers, pp. 54-70.

Zagnoli, P. (1984). "D.P.R. 902/1976 e L. 240/1981 e loro applicazioni in Toscana", paper presented at the Conference on *L'innovazione tecnologica nell' impresa toscana*, Chianciano Terme, October.

CHAPTER ELEVEN

International Marketing and Government Export Promotion in the Netherlands

Charles Pahud de Mortanges and Aart P. Van Gent[*]

SUMMARY

This chapter deals with the strengths and weaknesses of the Netherlands' public export promotion and assistance efforts. According to several surveys the respondents' expectations often exceeded what the government had to offer.

It is argued that the below-average evaluation of services by the public export promotion and assistance agencies is, in part, due to their lack of theoretical and managerial knowledge of international business in general, and international marketing in particular. To fill this void, we propose a closer interaction between public export promotion and assistance agencies, private industry, and academia. Rather than simply providing a window for passing information, the agencies must begin to think and act more like managers and consultants who can offer assistance over the entire exporting process.

The current preparations for a newly integrated European market after 1992 has put the activities of individual government export promotion agencies in a different perspective. However, the agencies will not necessarily become redundant with respect to their E.E.C. activities. Instead, their efforts must then concentrate more on aiding companies to find (or redefine) their market positions within a new Europe.

---

[*]   University of Limburg, Maastricht and Nijenrode, The Netherlands School of Business, Breukelen, respectively.

INTRODUCTION

The Netherlands sends well over half of all the goods and services it produces across its borders and could thus be considered one of the most successful exporting nations in the world. How much of this success can be attributed to the promotional efforts of the public sector?

The conceptual framework of this chapter is an integral part of the relationships shown in Figure 11.1. Thus, the basic question is: What knowledge/expertise is required for (successful) export management and how can public export promotion and assistance agencies best provide it? First, this chapter gives an overview of the organization and operations of the main Dutch government agency involved in assisting in the selling of goods and services abroad. Second, we will discuss the results of several surveys which attempted to measure the effectiveness of such assistance. Although the surveys were undertaken by third parties, the interpretation and discussion of the results are ours. General conclusions drawn from these studies will address the awareness, usage and effectiveness of the services provided by public agencies. It is our hypothesis that discrepancies between the normative and the positive are, primarily, due to a lack of theoretical knowledge of the government officials planning, organization and implementation of export promotion on the one hand, and a similar lack of knowledge manifested by private industry on the other. It is very difficult to help a person who doesn't know how to ask the right questions. There seems to be a convergence of an increasing need of specific export knowledge, and the development toward specialization of such knowledge within the fields of international marketing and international business. Subsequently, we will argue that there is a need for greater transferability of knowledge in the areas of international business and international marketing in general, and exporting in particular, between academia, the public sector, and the private sector.

THE DUTCH EXPORT SITUATION

The Netherlands is a highly successful exporter at the macro-level. This country has the second highest percentage (after Belgium) of GNP being exported in the industrialized world. Its average percentage of export growth since the 1950s underline this strong export performance.

Figure 11.1: Network of the Netherlands Export Promotion and Information Service (EVD)

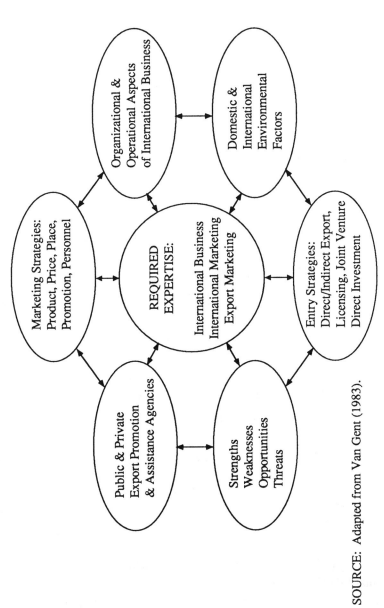

SOURCE: Adapted from Van Gent (1983).

Up to the first oil crisis of 1973 exports grew nearly twice as fast as the domestic economy. Thereafter, except for 1981/2, export growth continued to outperform domestic growth (Figure 11.2). Perhaps this is characteristic of a small open economy like the Netherlands. More and more countries are competing with their products in the international market place which leads to increased specialization in their areas of comparative advantage. Products that are no longer made domestically must be imported, which must be offset by higher levels of exports.

Figure 11.2: Average export growth (%)

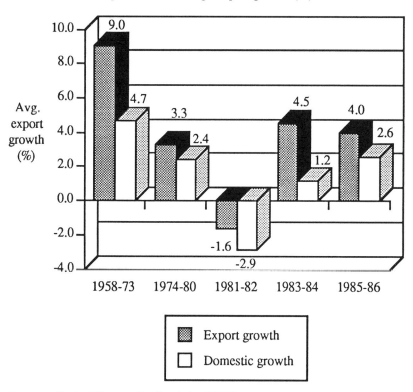

Source: Central Bureau for Statistics (CBS).

In 1970 exports were 62 billion Dutch guilders and in 1985, 130 billion in 1975 prices. However, while the value of exports doubled in this period, the distribution over markets remained nearly unchanged. Table 11.1 shows that Dutch exports are heavily concentrated with more than four-fifths destined for Western European countries.   Within Western Europe the main export markets are: West Germany (accounting for 28% of total exports); Belgium-Luxembourg (14%); France (11%); and the United Kingdom (10%). One may ask, whether Dutch exporters are myopic in their export policies foregoing potential opportunities outside of Western Europe? A related question concerns the extent to which public export promotion can bring about a change in this situation?

Next, a brief description of the types of products exported by the Netherlands is given and compared to the respective average of the ten E.E.C. countries.   Figure 11.3 shows the heavy concentration in Food & Agricultural Products (mainly Dairy & Meat products; Fruit and Vegetables) and Fuels (mainly Natural Gas), and the relatively low share of Machinery & Transportation Equipment. A major related concern of the Dutch government is how to compensate for the loss in export revenues for natural gas, once these reserves are depleted. With this backdrop on the profile of exports we now turn to the structure of export promotion.

Table 11.1: Dutch exports by region (%)

Region	1970	1985
Western Europe	81	82
Eastern Europe	2	1
Africa	3	3
North America	5	6
Central and South America	3	1
Middle East	2	3
Asia	3	3
Oceania	1	1
Total	100	100

Source: Central Bureau for Statistics (CBS).

Figure 11.3: Composition of Dutch and European Common Market exports by product category (%)

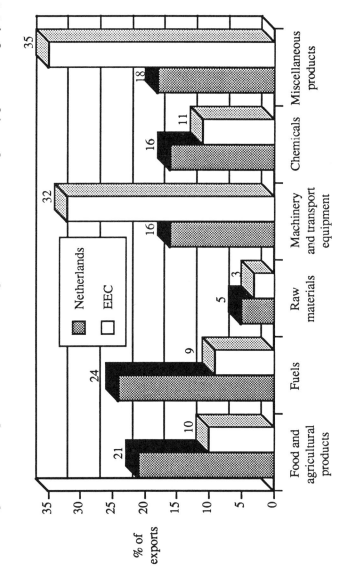

Source: Eurostat 1986.

THE EXPORT PROMOTION NETWORK IN THE NETHERLANDS

In the Netherlands, as perhaps in most countries, we see a link between the health of the economy and government intervention in the private sector. During the period 1960-1973 the country enjoyed considerable economic growth and increasing per capita income. Government intervention, at any level, was minimal. The period 1973-1984 was marked by a slowing of economic growth and a decrease in per capita income in real terms. The oil crises of 1973 and 1979 played a major role in this decline. Intervention, through increased taxes and regulations, was at an all-time high, aided by the fact that a succession of socialist governments had been in power during most of that time. It was also during this period that export and export promotion became a high priority. Since 1984, the Dutch economy has shown slow but gradual improvement under a conservative government. Intervention in the private sector has abated, however so have public expenditures, including funds for public export promotion (Kok 1987).

Direct public export promotion is the responsibility of Ministry of Economic Affairs, and is carried out through its Export Promotion and Information Service. The latter was founded in 1936, under the name "Economic Informations Service". As the name implied, its sole task was to provide information to help increase the country's exports. Stimulating demand for Dutch products abroad, or the export supply at home, were not part of its activities. However, in due course the service strengthened its ties with industry and the emphasis shifted from passively providing information to actively promoting exports, as well as coordinating export activities. These changes in policies and activities were expressed even more clearly when in 1982 its name was changed to "Export Promotion and Information Service" (EVD).

The EVD plays a central part in all public export development and promotional activities in the Netherlands. It utilizes the services and coordinates the export promotional activities of several other public and private agencies and organizations, as shown in Figure 11.4. In addition, the EVD and the other organizations maintain an information exchange amongst themselves about their services. To some extent, EVD acts as a clearing house for the purpose of promoting Dutch exports.

The EVD targets its services at Dutch companies which do not have the means to independently investigate and evaluate export markets and to undertake

Figure 11.4: Network of the Netherlands Export Promotion and Information Service (EVD)

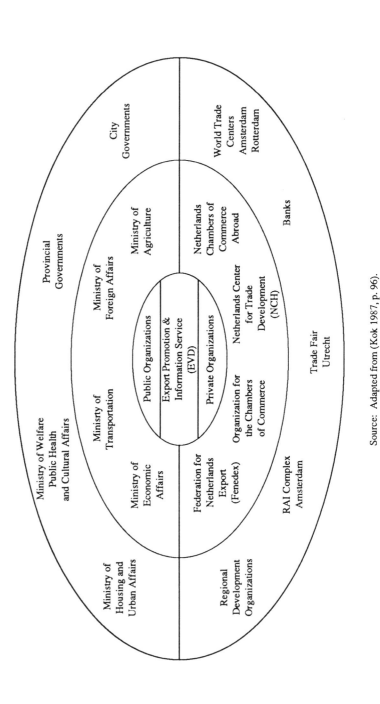

Source: Adapted from (Kok 1987, p. 96).

promotional activities to sell in those markets (EVD 1986). Its services can be divided into two types, namely: (1) Export Advisory Services, and (2) Export Promotional Services.

The first involves investigating and pursuing opportunities to sell products in existing and potential export markets. Contacts are maintained with, and assistance given to companies with the aim of developing and/or improving their foreign market position. Moreover, a constant concern of EVD is how foreigners think of the Netherlands. Continuous efforts are made to create a positive image of the country as a supplier of high-quality goods, services and know-how. In addition, EVD provides information about current developments in foreign markets, including the latest government rules and regulations. The organization maintains a large reference library with statistical information, country studies, market studies, trade journals, textbooks, directories, and a host of other reference material. This library is linked to many domestic and foreign data bases, and is accessible from terminals in most regional chambers of commerce. Included in the array of services the EVD has a series of publications aimed at domestic and international trade. For example, in 1986, 25 issues of Export Magazine were published and sold to subscribers and bookstores. The EVD is also involved in the development and performing of trade mediation (not, however, contractual disputes) between Dutch sellers and the foreign buyers to bring both parties together. EVD's Organization Chart (see Figure 11.5) shows the structural arrangement underlying the wide range of services provided.

The EVD defines export promotion as bringing together Dutch suppliers and potential foreign buyers. As noted, its export development and promotional activities are performed in close cooperation with several other institutions. For instance, EVD works closely with the Ministry of Foreign Affairs and its embassies and consulates around the world. The embassies are divided into political, economic, and technical sections and serve as important sources of information on foreign markets and entry conditions. The agricultural attaché at an embassy or consulate is responsible for promoting exports of Dutch agricultural products in cooperation with the Ministry of Agriculture. Here again, the EVD acts as a link between two government departments but always with the aim of developing and promoting exports. Another example of this linkage is the "Fairwind '86" project, where 50 manufacturers of high-tech nautical equipment presented their products in a dozen Far-Eastern ports, which were simultaneously being called upon by a detachment of the Dutch Royal Navy. Last year, the EVD organized the "Holland Trade Express", a large project

Figure 11.5: Organization chart of the Netherlands Export Promotion & Information Service (EVD).

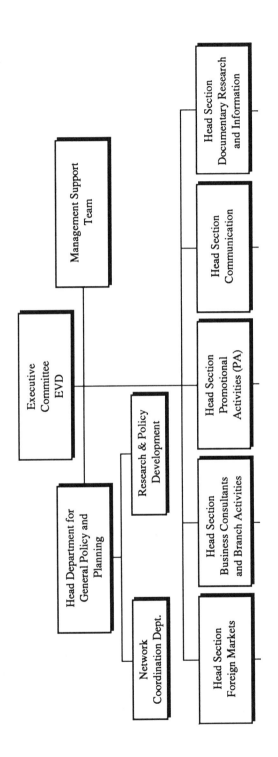

Source: (EVD 1986).

Figure 11.5: Organization chart of the Netherlands Export Promotion & Information Service (EVD). (cont'd)

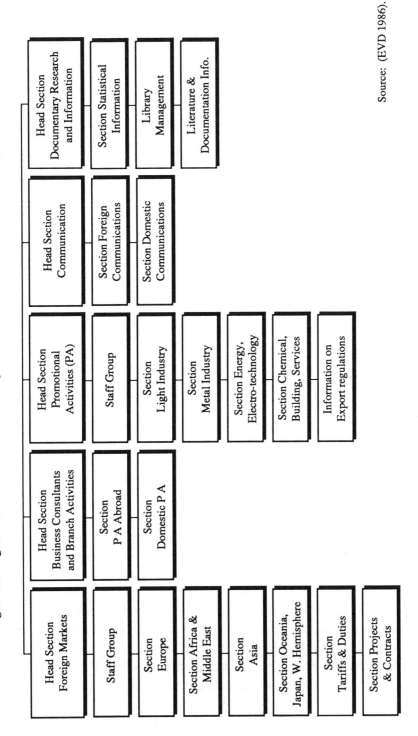

Source: (EVD 1986).

in the form of a promotional train which ran between Tokyo and Kobe. In 1989 preparations are underway for the commemoration of 380 years of uninterrupted trade relations between the Netherlands and Japan.

The most widely used promotional tool in 1986 was collective participation in international trade fairs and exhibitions. Other promotional activities included collective business trips; organizing product presentations; organizing seminars and symposia; setting up information booths and so-called Holland lounges. With the background on Dutch export promotion services we now turn to the surveys of their use and usefulness.

THE SURVEYS

In the Netherlands, the 1980's can be characterized as the decade where the total preoccupation with export development and promotion reached its highest peak. It seems that no previous period generated as many government and private sector studies, academic conferences, seminars, symposia, and a plethora of publications and papers, on how the country might sell its goods and services more effectively abroad. From this abundant material we selected three studies that deal, among other things, specifically with the effectiveness of public export promotion.

Before we begin our discussion we should mention which categories of firms were surveyed. The Netherlands is the home of several large multinationals such as Philips, Shell, Unilever, and Akzo. Although these companies make up a disproportionately large percentage of Dutch exports, they are not the typical target customer of the EVD. Besides, these firms have considerable in-house expertise in international business matters. For that reason, they are not included in the discussions below.

For the period 1976-1980 average annual export growth for large firms (100 + employees) had been 7.6 percent, whereas the small- and medium- size sector grew by 4.8 percent. During 1980-1985, the trend was reversed and small- and medium-size firms grew an average 11.5 percent versus 8.2 percent for the larger firms. One possible reason for this shift is a change in the composition of exports, i.e. a larger proportion of finished products made by smaller firms. For the previous 1976-1980 period, exports were concentrated in raw materials and intermediate products an area dominated by larger firms.

The first survey in our discussion was undertaken by the NMB bank of Amsterdam. In early 1980 a mail questionnaire was sent to 343 companies comprised of exporters and potential exporters. The latter group were firms that manufactured products for which there was a known demand evidenced by competitors already selling abroad. Firms were differentiated only according to size determined by the number of employees. Figure 11.6 shows that the survey found the following usage of export promotion and information services: EVD and commercial sections of embassies are mainly accessed by larger firms, while chambers of commerce appear to owe their relatively high use levels to their natural close relationship with the business community.

The second survey was undertaken by the Amsterdam-Rotterdam Bank in 1983 among 494 small and medium-sized (100 employees or less) exporting companies, in order to get a better picture of the problems associated with doing business abroad. The sample consisted of 27 percent manufacturers of intermediate goods, 28 percent manufacturers of finished goods, 24 percent wholesalers, and 21 percent service firms.

This survey showed that, on average, these firms do business in 4 countries. Half of them restrict themselves to operating within the European Economic Community (E.E.C.); 44 percent exports to E.E.C. countries *and* to other destinations inside and/or outside Europe, whereas only 6 percent exports to countries outside the E.E.C.. The larger the firm the greater the number of countries exported to and the farther the destination. Also, the farther the destination the more likely it is that exporting becomes the result of fortuitous circumstances (i.e., the result of an inquiry from a potential foreign buyer). Exporting to closer destinations is much more the result of systematic planning. These results, incidentally, correspond with the several export research studies that were undertaken in the 1970's (see, for example, Goodnow et. al. 1972, Simpson et. al. 1974, Wiedersheim-Paul et. al. 1978).

We would like to focus now on several problem areas in export management, namely: What are the typical start-up problems; what are typical current (on-going) problems; and what is the level of awareness of the various export assistance services. Table 11.2 and Figure 11.7 present the relevant information.

Figure 11.6: Use of various export promotion and information services (%)
(n=343)

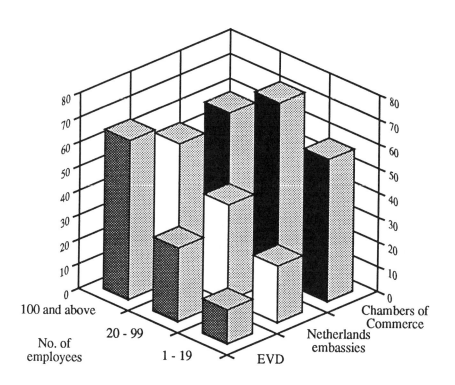

Source: NMB Bank.

Table 11.2: Problem areas for small- and medium-sized exporters – n=494

Type of export problem	Percent of respondents indicating major problem at: Start-up	Now
Finding the right source of information	8	4
Obtaining information about foreign markets	11	4
Obtaining information about foreign distribution (i.e., agents/importers)	18	10
Knowledge about customs regulations	15	6
Language problems (e.g. translating brochures)	8	5
Transportation problems (costs/volume)	15	10
Administrative (e.g. "red tape")	13	9
Financing	12	12
Insurance	2	2
Funds needed to enter new export market	5	5
Import restrictions	11	11
Quality standards and inspection	10	8
Reliability/Trustworthiness of foreign partners	21	18
Legal aspects (e.g. contracts, guarantees)	3	2
Foreign exchange fluctuations	6	17
Organization for export in own firm	2	1
Wage/Production costs too high	6	13

Source: Amsterdam-Rotterdam Bank.

Interestingly, for these sample firms the most significant problem is the reliability and/or trustworthiness of foreign partners (e.g., importers, agents, distributors abroad). Reliability and trustworthiness are personal characteristics which rarely come to light *prima facie*. One may also ask to what extent the EVD can play a role in the screening and selection process of potential trade partners that would optimize their relationship. This, in view of the relatively high percentage of firms which had difficulties obtaining information about foreign distribution at export start-up, and the fact that later on this problem apparently becomes less prevalent. A reverse situation is noted as far as foreign exchange fluctuations are concerned, which were minor at start up.

Figure 11.7: Awareness of export support organizations (n=360)

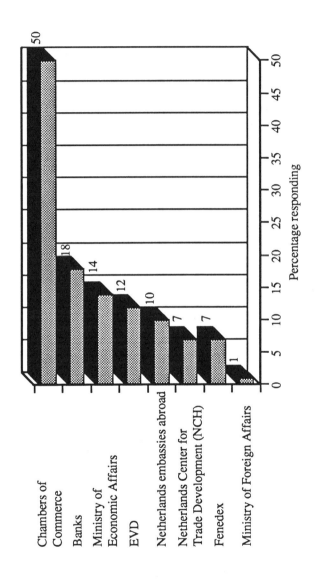

Percentage responding

Chambers of Commerce 50
Banks 18
Ministry of Economic Affairs 14
EVD 12
Netherlands embassies abroad 10
Netherlands Center for Trade Development (NCH) 7
Fenedex 7
Ministry of Foreign Affairs 1

Source: Amsterdam-Rotterdam Bank

Table 11.3 shows the extent of firms' awareness of services available from export support organizations. Of the 494 firms surveyed, 27 percent were unaware of any support organizations. The remaining 73 percent gave the responses shown. Chambers of commerce are by far the best known support organization, with firms much less aware of government services. This survey also looked into the question whether a firm, currently having export problems, was (1) aware of the export support organizations, and (2) had been in contact with any of the organizations.

Two recommendations were offered by this survey. First, it is desirable to have a clear and simple structure of the main public export promotion agency (EVD) in order to improve its approachability. Second, it is desirable to initiate the services of an "all-round" export specialist who will be able to analyze the entire export environment, rather than different persons giving separate advice (e.g. on documentation or product adaptation). This would require the person to have a higher level educational background (such as an M.B.A.) that the current norm at the agency.

Table 11.3: "Awareness of" and "Contact with" export support organizations by extent of export problems

	No export problems	Export problems to some areas	Export problems to all areas
Awareness of export support organizations	74%	68%	88%
No awareness of export support organizations (n=494)	26	32	12
Had contact with export support organizations	80	85	94
No contact with export support organizations (n=360)	20	15	6

Source: Amsterdam-Rotterdam Bank.

We now come to the final, third survey. In 1986, the EVD, in cooperation with the Netherlands Institute of Public Opinion (NIPO), interviewed decision-makers in 570 exporting companies drawn from the manufacturing, wholesaling and service sectors. The purpose of the study was to determine whether the services offered by the EVD corresponded with the needs of the exporting firms. In other words, need, awareness, and opinion of the services were of primary concern. It must be pointed out that only exporters were surveyed and other service providers such as chambers of commerce, universities, and so on were not included.

Size characteristics of respondent firms were as follows: 29 percent had fewer than 10 employees, 30 percent between 10-49, and 41 percent, 50 or more employees. A first step in improving the effectiveness and efficiency of the services offered, is determining the need for export promotion and information in general. Table 11.4, gives an indication of that need.

Table 11.4: Need for EVD export support services by firm size

Need	Size (Number of employees)		
	1 - 9 (n=165)	10 - 49 (n=173)	50+ (n=232)
Considerable need	29%	19%	34%
Average need	26	43	41
No need	43	36	23
No opinion	2	2	2
Total	100	100	100

Source: EVD/NIPO.

It is surprising that almost one-third of the companies surveyed had no need for export promotion and information in general. Remarkable is the fact that the largest "No need" response occurred in the smallest (1-9 employees) category. If growth over time is taken into consideration one would think that smaller firms are also younger firms with less export experience. However, it does correspond with the 1980 NMB survey (see Figure 11.6) as well as the EVD's own survey (see Table 11.5 below) which found a relatively small amount of users of its services among small companies. Apparently, these small firms tend to make greater use of local chambers of commerce for their export support needs as seen below. Another explanation would be that these small firms concentrate their efforts on nearby markets for which not much support and/or information is needed.

The next question deals with the specific services that are offered by the EVD, and firms' awareness of these services. Respondents consisted only of firms which knew the EVD at least by name. The sample size was thus reduced to 317. Table 11.6 gives the percentage of positive responses, in decreasing order, to the questions listed.

Table 11.5: Use of various export support services by company size

Export support organizations	Size (Number of employees)		
	1 - 9	10 - 49	50+
Chambers of Commerce	59%	68%	76%
Export consultant	23	31	39
Netherlands Chambers of Commerce abroad	23	34	45
EVD	15	18	53
Netherlands Center for Trade Development (NCH)	7	11	34
Fenedex	8	11	39

Source: EVD/NIPO.

The responses lead us to conclude that the EVD is mostly known as an organization which supplies general information about export markets and issues publications. Less than half of the respondents were aware that the EVD has a reference library. One would have thought such a source to be a good starting point in the search for information on new export opportunities.

Next, decision-makers were asked about their familiarity with and opinion of major EVD publications (see Table 11.7).

Table 11.6: Awareness of EVD Services (n=317)

Did you know that EVD...	Positive Response (%)
Supplies general information about export markets	88
Issues publications	85
Organizes Dutch trade missions abroad	71
Issues *Export Magazine*	68
Supplies information about export support from other government agencies	67
Supplies market information for specific products	62
Supplies information about import and customs regulations	62
Issues market reports	56
Stimulates firms to combine efforts to sell abroad	56
Grants export subsidies	52
Has a reference library	47
Issues export handbooks and catalogs	44
Organizes the reception of foreign trade delegations	43
Advises solutions to trade disputes	42

Source: EVD/NIPO.

Table 11.7: Awareness and opinion of selected EVD publications (n=317)

Publications	Aware (%)	Opinion (%)		
		Good	Average	Poor
Export Magazine	67	67	10	23
Holland Info	55	51	33	16
Country specials	39	70	13	17
Export catalogs	22	62	18	19
Quarterly Report of Export developments	21	55	27	18

Source: EVD/NIPO.

It seems that the best-known publication is Export Magazine, which is sent to subscribers and is sold in bookstores and at newsstands. Only a little over a third of the respondents were familiar with the "Country Specials", but the majority thought they were good. So here the problem may not be so much quality, but rather awareness and familiarity of the publications issued.

For a general opinion about service access and delivery we refer to Table 11.8, below.

Table 11.8: A general opinion about service access and delivery of EVD
n=317 (%)

Characteristics	Good	Average	Poor	No opinion
Independence	51%	15%	4%	29%
Accessibility	48	16	8	28
Efficiency	25	26	9	40
Objectivity	52	9	6	32
Usefulness of information	35	21	12	32

Source: EVD/NIPO.

It should concern EVD that efficiency (i.e., the expeditiousness with which requests for information are handled) and the usefulness of the information itself received low ratings. The same respondents were also asked how they viewed EVD in general as an organization that provides export support (Table 11.9).

The main potential problem apparent is that EVD is viewed as an organization which lacks the necessary practical knowledge about exporting. This implies that EVD is not involved enough in solving export problems and offering solutions to firms asking for assistance. In addition, from the response to the last statement one may conclude that assistance offered is not always based on up-to-date knowledge.

Table 11.9: General comments about the EVD - n=317

Comments about the EVD	Applicable	Not Applicable	No Opinion
An organization that helps firms solve export problems	79%	3%	17%
An organization where firms can get specific answers to export questions	60	16	24
An organization which prescribes exactly how to export	15	63	22
An organization where firms are sent "from pillar to post" with their enquiries	14	59	27
An organization with a lot of practical knowledge about export problems	49	20	32
An organization which lacks the speed necessary to keep up with current export problems	28	32	39

Source: EVD/NIPO.

Next, Table 11.10 gives satisfaction ratings of users of EVD services. These results imply relatively low usage of the facilities and services offered, but when utilized the satisfaction is generally high. The conclusion here is that by and large user expectations are being met, however, promotion of the services to potential users is clearly inadequate.

CONCLUSION AND RECOMMENDATIONS

What conclusions can be drawn from the Netherlands' export situation and its export promotion efforts? Mostly, we believe that the Netherlands' exports are too concentrated in terms of product category, and definitely in terms of foreign market region. At the macro-level, the Dutch seem very successful exporters, a closer look at the micro-level, however, reveals serious weaknesses. One may ask, what would happen if that one concentrated market for those few product categories would become threatened due to unforeseen economic and/or

Table 11.10: Use and satisfaction of selected EVD facilities and services
n=317

Facilities/services	Use	Satisfied	Not satisfied	No opinion
General export information	15%	78%	22%	-
Reference library	20	87	3	10%
Statistical information	14	96	4	-
Government regulation information	8	93	7	-
Industry experts	12	74	21	5
Country specialists	30	85	13	2
Fairs and exhibitions	21	79	18	3

Source: EVD/NIPO.

political forces? Are the products now offered by the Dutch, in step with the current developments in international trade? Are significant opportunities being missed? At the micro-level, it seems that the EVD has problems reaching companies, in their efforts to increase businesses' awareness of the export promotion and information package that they offer. The larger firms seem to make the most use of the services offered by the EVD, but they do also most of the exporting. New export growth has to come form the small and medium-sized firms. However, these smaller firms typically lack the necessary export knowledge and expertise. Studies, including the one of EVD/NIPO (1986) cited above, have shown that smaller companies often begin exporting as a result of fortuitous circumstances and exporting is rarely the result of systematic planning (see also Simpson & Kujawa 1974, de Mortanges 1983). Thus, it would appear that both government (i.e., the public export promotion agency EVD), as well as industry (i.e., small and medium-sized firms) lack the proper knowledge about what exporting actually entails. It is our opinion, that the theories and other knowledge developed in the academic fields of international business, international marketing, and specifically exporting can help. We believe that there is a definite need for a solid body of knowledge, which, for the lack of a better term, we call "Export Marketing". There is a need for this body of knowledge to be transferred from the often isolated domain of academia to both public agencies and the private business community involved in international business (see Figure 11.8). In the next section we offer a proposal as to how this may be done.

Export promotion in the coming years has to be able to survive in a business environment that will continue to change dramatically and dynamically. In order to present a picture of where international business has been, and where it is likely to go in the future, we utilize a framework put forth by Robinson (1981). Robinson distinguishes four general episodes. First, the post-war period 1945-1955 is characterized as a two-actor era (the firm itself and its foreign commercial constituencies). During the period 1955-1970 (the so-called "growth years") the domestic political impact of, and the domestic political response to, international corporate strategies enters the decision making process. With the involvement of the home government begins the three-actor era. Then during the 1970's and early 1980's ("the years of trouble") another actor enters the stage, namely the host government, which increasingly becomes a key variable in international business decisions (the four-actor era). The period of the supra-national organizations is called the multi-actor era in which the new international order will develop. Robinson expects that the main profit generator in international business will then lie in an efficient and accurate international information system. Information with regard to lowest-cost resources (e.g., money, manpower, machinery, raw materials, semi-finished and finished products) as well as information on opportunities where to employ these resources most profitably.

Although Robinson's scheme is based on U.S. events, his framework can also be applied to the European experience. If we juxtapose the role of academia in the Netherlands on the periods cited by Robinson, we can make the following observations. First, during 1945-1955 there is only a fragmented interest in international business, primarily from the area's of international economics and international law. This situation continues for the period 1955-1970. During the period 1970-1982 ("the trouble years") we see that multi-disciplinary studies are not yet integrated explicitly at the managerial level in industry, however international business theories and concepts slowly begin to permeate the management of public export promotion. From 1982 to the present we see the results of the numerous export conferences, seminars, symposia, coupled with the plethora of writings on export behavior. Finally, there is an integration of relevant concepts, methods, and techniques from different disciplines to specialized interdisciplinary "solid bodies of knowledge", such as international marketing, international accounting and finance, international organization, etc. Students of international business begin to enter the work force.

Figure 11.8: The export triad

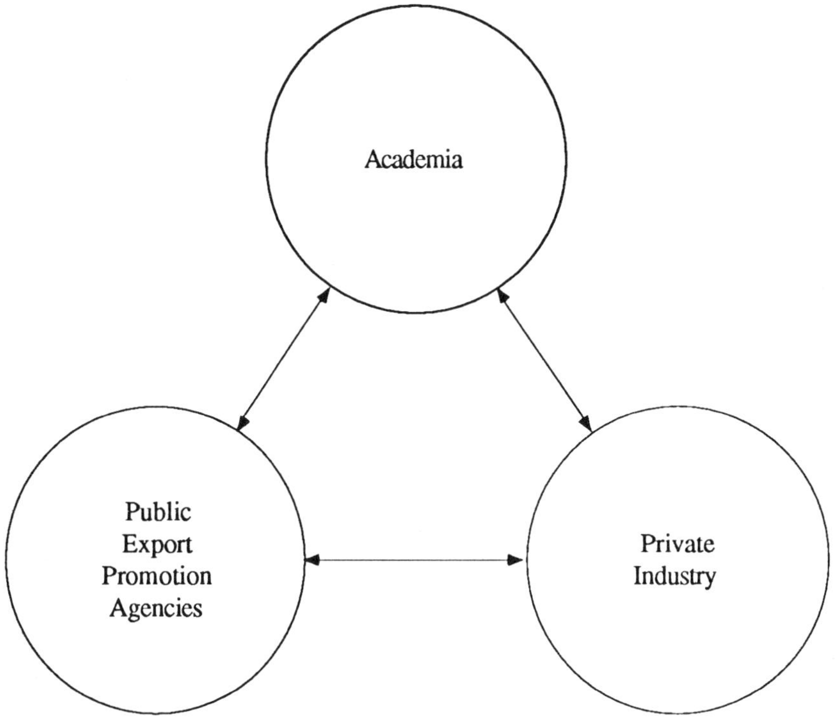

Source: Prepared by authors.

Enter 1992

After 1992, a complete commercial integration of European Economic Community (E.E.C.) is expected.   How will this affect public export promotion? It would seem that with a "borderless" Western Europe, and given that most Netherlands' exports end up in neighbouring countries, the role of the EVD may be greatly reduced. It is conceivable the agency needs to redefine its mission, rethink its strategies, and adjust its operations to cope with the fact that what used to be international is now (more or less) domestic. A potentially important role would help firms adjust themselves to a new European business environment, first of all by providing information.

In the Netherlands and other European countries export promotion agencies have been investing in data banks containing information about opportunities in Europe after 1992. A special Euro-Data bank has been developed by the Netherlands Ministry of Economic Affairs with, for example, informations about the "new" E.E.C. in general, which measures have been taken so far to eliminate obstacles to the movement of goods and capital, and a list of the functions of the many E.E.C. organizations that have in-house expertise in various subject areas. At the E.E.C.-level special offices have been established to assist small and medium-sized firms not only to give information but also to provide opportunities for obtaining regular financing as well as venture capital. The "Business Cooperation Network" provides support in the search for suitable joint venture partners, and the ICONE system will supply technical information about technical standards in different countries.

From the above examples it is clear that the interaction between public export agencies and the business community is a very dynamic one in terms of the constant (and often severe) changes that are occurring. Successful interaction, in this case, requires considerable knowledge/expertise in the areas depicted in Figure 11.1. It is no longer sufficient for public export promotion agencies to provide possible answers to export questions. Because most small and medium-sized firms are inexperienced in international trade it is essential that the agencies themselves provide the questions as well. It implies an interaction between agency and client from the earliest stages of the export process and requires a thorough knowledge of the client's internal and external business environment. A way to achieve this degree of expertise would correspond with the establishing of the all-round export specialist as was recommended earlier as a result of the survey by the Amsterdam-Rotterdam Bank. Such a person will be more of a hands-on consultant/manager instead of a distant supplier of information. His (or her) role and work will be complemented by the vast amount of data and information he has at his disposal in the various forms described above. Both agency and client will have to think polycentrically, instead of ethnocentrically necessitated by the changes occurring because of a more commercially integrated Europe.

In the above triangle (Fig. 11.8), the role of universities and business schools is to contribute to the optimization of the triad by transforming "export marketing" into a solid body of knowledge. This knowledge is to be anchored in the broader fields of knowledge of international business and international marketing. Then special emphasis has to be given to the education of current and future managers operating within the triad. The aim is a new systematic way of thinking about export management and export promotion, which gives the opportunity to define problems at a level better suited to cope with the dynamics of present international competition. Therefore, the results of the above surveys, with respect to the effectiveness of public export promotion, should be seen in a different perspective. Managers can only partly define the effectiveness of export promotional activities; export promotion has to define what the criteria are for efficient and effective export management and then measure the results of their actions against these criteria.

REFERENCES

Alexandrides, C.G. and George P. Moschis (1977). *Export Marketing Management*, New York: Praeger Publishers.

Amsterdam-Rotterdam Bank (1983). Report on "Greater Export Opportunities for Small and Medium-sized Firms" (January).

Bersee, H. (1987). "NIPO enquete: optimisme bij Nederlandse exporteurs", *Export Magazine*, (February 7).

Bilkey, Waren J. (1978). "An Attempted Integration of the Literature on the Export Behavior of Firms," *Journal of International Business Studies*, vol. 9, pp. 33-46.

Czinkota, Michael R. and David A. Ricks (1981). "Export Assistance: Are We Supporting the Best Programs? *Columbia Journal of World Business*, (Summer), pp. 31-47.

de Graaf (1983). "Exportondersteuning voor midden- en kleinbedrijf", Report from the World Trade Centre, Rotterdam, (May).

de Mortanges, Charles Pahud (1983). "A Study of the Export Decision in Small Manufacturing Firms in the San Francisco Bay Area", Unpublished Master's Thesis, California State University, Sacramento.

Dik, W. (1982). *Exportnota*, Nederlands Ministerie van Economische Zaken.

EVD (1986). (Netherlands Export Promotion & Information Service), Conference Report on "Export: Research and Policy", The Hague.

EVD (1986). (Netherlands Export Promotion & Information Service), *Annual Report*.

Goodnow, James D. and James E. Hansz (1972). "Environmental Determinants of Overseas Market Entry Strategies", *Journal of International Business Studies*, (Spring), pp. 33-50.

Hibbert, Edgar P. (1985). *The Principles and Practice of Export Marketing*, London: Heinemann.

Jeannet, Jean Pierre and Hubert D. Hennessey (1988). *International Marketing Management*, Boston: Houghton-Mifflin Co.

Kok, A. (1987). *Export Management*, Boston: Kluwer-Nijhoff.

Lagerweij, J. (1986). "NIPO's export monitor: bedrijven optimistisch over buitenlandse afzet" *Export Magazine*, (May 14).

NMB Bank (1979). *Annual Report*.

Malekzadeh, A.R. and S. Rabino (1986). "Manufacturers' Export Strategies", *International Marketing Review*, (Winter), pp. 125-141.

Medland, D. (1987). "How the British Overseas Trade Board Can Help Exporters", *The Financial Times*, (September 8).

Reid, Stan D. (1981). "The Decision-Maker and Export Entry and Expansion", *Journal of International Business Studies*, (Fall), pp. 101- 112.

Robinson, Richard D. (1981). "Background Concepts and Philosophy of International Business from World War II to the Present", *Journal of International Business Studies*, (Spring/Summer), pp. 13-17.

Simpson, Claude L. and Duane Kujawa (1974). "The Export Decision Process: An Empirical Enquiry", *Journal of International Business Studies*, (Spring), pp. 107-117.

Van den Berg, T. (1986). "Exporterend midden- en kleinbedrijf in industrie en groothandel", Economisch Instituut van het Midden-en Kleinbedrijf, (September).

Van Gent, Aart P. (1983). *Internationale Bedrijfskunde, Internationale Marktkunde, en Exportkunde*, Breukelen: Nijenrode.

_____ and Gerald M. Hampton, eds. (1983). *Marketing Aspects of International Business*, Boston: Kluwer-Nijhoff.

_____ and Scheurleer, F.A.F. (1986). *Internationaal Ondernemingsbeleid* Amsterdam: Meulenhoff Educatief.

Verhoeven, J. (1985). "Het exportgedrag van het midden- en kleinbedrijf" Economisch Instituut van het Midden- en Kleinbedrijf, (October).

Wiedersheim-Paul, F., Hans C. Olson, and Lawrence S. Welch (1978). "Pre-Export Activity: The First Step in Internationalization", *Journal of International Business Studies*, Vol. 9, pp. 47-58.

Wijdeveld, T. (1985). "Kan Nederland meer markegericht exporteren?", *Management Team.*

Wiltink, K. (1985). "Midden- en kleinbedrijf steeds groter in export", *Export Magazine*, (December 18).

PART IV

A Case For Successful Intervention: Some New Initiatives

INTRODUCTION

The two chapters in Part IV discuss initiatives that differ from the services and programs so frequently found in export promotion. In Chapter twelve, Clarke describes the evolution of a strategic approach to export promotion and development in Northern Ireland. The program was conceived to overcome the business community's seeming reluctance to turn to public organizations for advice and assistance. A second objective was to cultivate a proactive export orientation among Northern Ireland companies. This study shows encouraging results from a well-conceived and effectively communicated program.

Onto and Hamley report in Chapter thirteen on export development efforts in the Australian state of Victoria. This joint government/education initiative focuses on upgrading the international business skills of management in specific high export potential sectors. This training involves learning by doing, including a period spent conducting research overseas. Early results show a measure of export success—both in terms of sales and long-term commitment to foreign marketing.

A second educational initiative is discussed by Bell and Murray. This joint program is offered by the industrial training authority in the Republic of Ireland and the Northern Ireland Department of Economic Development, and has as its goal assisting Irish companies to enter the E.E.C.. Recent graduates are brought into "host" companies to develop their own export marketing skills and the competitive competence of their host. The program incorporates foreign market study and research. To date some 100 companies have sponsored participants and the program has been expanded to cover markets outside Europe.

The strength of each of the initiatives examined in Part IV is that they foster positive attitudes towards export assistance and emphasize the skill and knowledge aspects that are so vital in international marketing.

CHAPTER TWELVE

Changing Small Firms' Attitudes to Exporting: A Case Study of Successful Intervention

W.M. Clarke[*]

SUMMARY

Recent research suggests that the attitudes of key decision-makers at the level of the individual firm are of critical importance in the export development process. The chapter describes and evaluates the efforts of a government-funded body (Industrial Development Board for Northern Ireland) to increase exports by positively influencing the attitudes and thus the behaviour of small firms located in a politically-troubled and economically weak region of the United Kingdom.

The circumstances and nature of the decision-making process leading to the introduction of a specific action programme are the focus of the chapter. Surveys of senior executives of small firms undertaken immediately prior to and 30 months after its introduction suggest the programme to be successful. Lessons for public organizations engaged in export promotion are suggested, including adoption of a proactive facilitating role at the local level, emphasis on motivating business to use support services by influencing the attitudes of key decision makers towards public organizations.

[*] University of Ulster, Jordanstown.

INTRODUCTION

Export development is a key feature of economic policy for the great majority of governments throughout the world, regardless of whether they are rich or poor, capitalist or socialist. Many governments have established state-funded organizations to facilitate the process, and have developed a complex system of export support measures and mechanisms. A broad similarity of approach in the export promotion policies of the major Western industrialized nations has been noted (Seringhaus 1987).

There is now available a substantial volume of empirical research into the exporting activities of smaller firms, including recent work relating to the Netherlands (Verhoeven 1988), Singapore (Cheong & Chong, 1988), Sweden (Kaynak et. al. 1987), Great Britain (Piercy 1983), Canada (Seringhaus 1986) and a comparative study of the USA and Canada at regional level (Kaynak & Kothari 1984). Miesenbock (1988) has reviewed a large number of studies and concludes that at least two common problems exist in relation to governmental export stimulation measures. First, the majority of small firms are superficially aware of the availability of export support, but are much less clear on the detail of specific schemes. Second, many small firms believe that the specific support measures available in their own region are either insufficient, or unsuited to their needs.

Several other closely-related themes appear in the literature with such frequency that they would appear to possess a more general, world-wide validity. These may be summarized in the following terms:

1. Exporting is a dynamic process and the support needs of firms change as they accumulate expertise and experience (see for example Cannon & Willis 1983, Olson and Wiedersheim-Paul 1978).
2. It is incorrect to think of small exporters as a homogeneous group, and treat them accordingly; in fact the support needs of firms are diverse (Cheong & Chong 1988, Seringhaus 1987).
3. Government support is often not tailored to the varying and changing needs of small exporters. For example, in their comparative study of small firms in Texas and Nova Scotia, Kaynak & Kothari (1984) identified in both regions a low awareness and usage of the export assistance programs and incentives on offer, and concluded that government agencies should

shoulder additional responsibilities. In the case of Ireland, Bradley (1985) has argued that there has been a failure to recognize that macro policy support does not necessarily percolate down to the level of individual firm. Buckley (1983) suggests that British export support policies do not work well at the bottom end of the size spectrum.

4. The attitudes, motivation, characteristics and abilities of the key decision-maker at the level of the individual firm is the critical factor in determining whether or not it decides to export, and its success or otherwise in attempting to do so. Much research effort has been devoted to investigating various aspects of this basic phenomenon (see Miesenbock 1988, for a useful summary), and various models of the process have been suggested (for example, Bilkey & Tesar 1977, Cavusgil 1980, Czinkota & Johnston 1984, Dichtl et. al. 1984). Thomas & Araujo (1985) have reviewed theories of export behaviour and conclude that whilst export behaviour and foreign market entry decisions can be understood as innovation adoption behaviour, the export development process is determined at each stage by the interaction between the firm and the individual characteristics of managers. They also observe that the research they review suggests that government policy designed to stimulate exports should not be confined to macro-level inducements but should be aimed at directly influencing decision makers in individual firms. This chapter describes and evaluates the efforts of a government funded body to do so.

The chapter first considers the political and economic problem against which the export promotion effort is positioned, this is followed by a description of the suggested solution. A discussion of the process and implementation and consideration of the effectiveness of the program follow. Finally, conclusions are offered.

THE PROBLEM

A number of studies completed in recent years have analyzed the basic structural weaknesses of the region's economy along the following lines.

An Open Economy

Northern Ireland is an integral part of the UK, which has traditionally implemented policies designed to minimize impediments to trade. In consequence, a very high proportion of the goods and services consumed locally are imported, either from other regions of the UK or from further afield. Implementation of the Single European Act, scheduled for 1992, will inevitably increase further the pressures of foreign competition on local businesses.

A Peripheral Economy

Geographically the region is located in the top left-hand corner of Europe, relatively far removed from major potential markets. Unlike other regions of the UK, firms based in Northern Ireland have the problem of crossing not one but two stretches of water before reaching the heartland of Continental Europe. Quite apart from the resulting additional burden of transport costs, there is no doubt that the perceived "psychic distance" is much greater than the actual physical barriers encountered.

A Small Economy

It is self-evident that the level of demand created by a domestic market of one million people is inadequate to sustain large-scale operations. Export development is the only viable option for local companies aiming for growth. Indeed, it may be argued that exporting is essential to the survival of many of them.

A Dependent Economy

Northern Ireland has been described as an economy whose current prosperity is largely a function of the level of subsidy provided by the UK central government, supplemented more recently by contributions from the European Community via the Social and Regional Funds. Some evidence in support of this view is provided by the fact that 45 percent of total employment is provided by public sector organizations. Another aspect of dependency arises from the fact that many local businesses are subsidiaries of larger firms based elsewhere. In consequence, major strategic decisions are often taken in the context of overall corporate policy without regard to local needs.

It is said that prolonged dependency of this kind over many years has resulted in the lack of an enterprise culture, and that local businessmen are more inclined to look to government rather than to their own efforts to ensure their survival and prosperity. The local business community has been described as isolationist, protectionist and parochial.

At the level of the indigenously-owned individual firm, it has been alleged that the great majority of them are:

- financially weak;
- provincial/introverted in outlook; and
- chronically short of management expertise, particularly in marketing and exporting.

THE SOLUTION

The initiative to adopt a new and imaginative approach to the resolution of these problems was taken by public officials within the regional administration, specifically in this case the Department of Economic Development (DED) and the Industrial Development Board for Northern Ireland (IDB). To some extent their actions were in response to a groundswell of informed public opinion within the region that something radical was needed to respond adequately to a steadily deteriorating economic situation, combined with a realization that the resources required to do so could only be provided by government. Within the broader context of policy formulation, it is also interesting to note that the specific measures here described were devised and implemented at regional level. Clearly, these measures could not have been introduced without the approval of central government; the necessary approval was given because the economic development of Northern Ireland has long been a major regional policy objective of successive UK governments, and because it was believed that the measures proposed were likely to be cost-effective. Thus the policy response adopted may be described as a modified top-down initiative, originating within the regional administration in response to the perceived needs of the local business community.

Given the constraints imposed by the realities of the problem briefly outlined above, the solution adopted throughout the 1980's has been to concentrate efforts on strengthening and expanding the existing industrial base, whilst at the same time maintaining efforts to attract new investment from abroad. Within the region, primary responsibility for providing and monitoring institutional and infrastructural measures to promote economic growth rests with the Department of Economic Development, the aims of which have been stated as:

- to strengthen the regional economy and provide self-sustaining employment;
- to support existing employment where it is cost-effective to do so;
- to provide the institutional and infra-structural services essential to the region's economic development; and
- to manage all programmes efficiently and effectively, and progressively transfer DED resources from economic support to economic strengthening activities.

The long-term policy objective is stated as being to transform the region from an economy dependent on external funding, ideas and initiatives into a resilient economy (Fell 1987). A resilient economy is characterized as:

- building on its own resources and strengths;
- having a diversified industrial base;
- accepting and indeed initiating positive change rather than resisting it;
- being outwardly directed rather than isolationist, protectionist or parochial;
- providing support at the personal level to the unemployed through opportunities for rehabilitation, remotivation and retraining as well as for personal enterprise.

These aims and objectives have been vigorously pursued by the DED using a wide range of innovative and imaginative measures. One such measure was the establishment in September 1982 of the Industrial Development Board for Northern Ireland. The primary basic objective of the IDB is clearly indicated by its name.

In addition to a role in seeking inward investment, the IDB assumed responsibility for implementing a number of schemes designed to provide financial and other assistance to existing firms. In relation to export promotion, the Board was designated as a regional office of the British Overseas Trade Board, the UK government's primary agency for providing export support. Within the IDB, a Trade Development Branch was established to make available the full range of BOTB services to firms located in Northern Ireland. These included a scheme aimed at encouraging firms to undertake market research in foreign markets and the organization of visits by groups of companies through trade missions to selected overseas markets. Trade Development Branch had limited manpower and funding, and no specific marketing/exporting development function. Although local participation in, for example, trade missions was actively encouraged, its basic stance was largely re-active. Enquiries and approaches from firms were dealt with as promptly and efficiently as possible, but at this initial phase of the Board's operation no major effort was made to actively generate increased exporting within the local business community.

After widespread consultations with a broad cross section of local industry and commerce, the trade unions and higher education, the IDB adopted a medium-term strategy which set out a series of specific objectives for the period 1985-90. These include:

- to continue to give first priority to the modernization and expansion of the region's existing industrial base;
- to place increased emphasis on the development of marketing skills and a market-led philosophy in all client companies, in order to encourage a higher level of export activity;
- to move increasingly towards a sector-based approach, seeking out companies which are prepared to work together with the Board in developing expansion plans.

Thus, top management within the IDB recognized early on as a major strategic problem requiring urgent attention the need for export development through better marketing at the level of the individual firm. Equally important, resources were allocated to try and do something positive about it. In 1983 the Board established a Marketing and Trade Support Division with a remit to address these identified needs pro-actively and without delay. The Division's response to this challenge provides a classic example of sound public sector marketing.

THE PROCESS

It is useful to abstract from the detail the process followed by the public body concerned. A number of sequential steps may be clearly identified.

1. Problem recognition – the fact that an export-promotion problem existed, and a preliminary diagnosis of its main elements needed, emerged at a very early stage in the Board's evolution.

2. Top-management commitment – the active and whole-hearted support of senior officials both in the Board and in its "parent" government department was crucial to subsequent effective action at grass-roots level.

3. Resource Allocation – a measure of the commitment to solve the problem was the decision to provide the resources, both human and financial, needed to address it effectively including, crucially, the assignment of a talented individual capable of doing so.

4. Strategy Formulation – the problem was not tackled in an ad hoc, piecemeal way, but on the basis of a broad strategic action plan derived from appropriate research and observation of the realities of the situation. This strategy has the objective to (a) encourage local firms to export; (b) increase their awareness of the assistance provided by the Board; (c) facilitate their use of these various types of assistance; and (d) encourage them to adopt a planned and co-ordinated long-term approach to export development.

5. Detailed Tactical Planning – there is clear evidence that as much attention was paid to the details of presentation and promotion as to the mechanics of the various measures adopted.

6. Effective Implementation – none of the above could have contributed to the progress made without efficient and effective day-to-day action by the officials concerned.

7. Evaluation and Evolution – the action programme described was not seen as a static one-off effort; rather it was (and is) dynamic, in the sense that the measures adopted are critically evaluated and adapted to changing circumstances, with new elements introduced as gaps in provision are identified and lessons learnt from experience.

IMPLEMENTATION

Marketing Support Division

The senior executive given the responsibility of heading this Division was well qualified for the task, and had just returned from a period of secondment to the British Consulate General's Office in Los Angeles. The personality and abilities of the individual concerned are in fact of critical importance to what subsequently transpired.

A major element in his initial response to the task set was to identify more precisely the nature and details of the general problem, through a process of formal and informal research. It rapidly became apparent that communications between the Board and its customers (ie. the companies it seeks to serve) were not entirely satisfactory. Managers often complained that they found it difficult to obtain information about exporting and trade support activities. At the heart of the problem was a certain vagueness about who exactly one should contact in what was perceived to be a large and bureaucratic government body. The solution devised was very simple, and has been very effective.

Contact

In September 1984 the Division began to mail out to companies on a monthly basis a one-page news-sheet providing basic information on a wide range of matters related to marketing development and export promotion. This news-sheet is in fact called "Contact". Its key features are:

- brevity and simplicity – recognizing that busy company executives have neither time nor inclination to plough through lengthy and detailed documentation presented in "official" jargon; and
- a personal touch – every item in Contact no matter how short, ends with the name and telephone number of a specific person within the Division, sometimes with a photograph of the individual concerned.

One measure of the success of this very simple initiative is that initially it was mailed to about 700 firms each month, its circulation has since increased to about 3,500. A more important measure is essentially qualitative, in terms of its contribution to changing the image of the Division (and of the

Board) from that of a typical bureaucratic government department into a much more positive presentation of a group of people who can help, and want to do so (Figure 12.1).

The Marketing Development Grant Scheme

Ongoing IDB research had revealed a number of key elements within the underlying basic problem:

- a lack of awareness on the part of many senior executives of the need to improve their marketing and develop their exports;
- in consequence, an unwillingness to make effective use of the assistance measures already available;
- a tendency for the relatively few firms which were making use of the assistance available to do so in a fragmented and ad hoc fashion, with little or no planning or co-ordination; and
- a feeling that this latter problem was at least in part due to the fact that the assistance measures then available were themselves somewhat ad hoc, fragmented and not comprehensive in their scope.

It was therefore decided to make a major effort to overcome these impediments by devising an integrated scheme of assistance aimed specifically at providing firms with an incentive to radically and rapidly improve their marketing expertise and hence their exporting capability. The Marketing Development Grant Scheme was launched in September 1985 (after prolonged negotiations with central government). Its key feature is that any company embarking on a marketing programme which includes certain approved activities could obtain financial assistance for up to 40 percent of the costs incurred, subject to a maximum of £30,000 a year. The approved activities include:

- employment of an independent consultant to conduct a marketing audit reviewing the company's basic strategies and organizational structure;
- export marketing research, including purchase of published materials, costs of research commissioned from an independent agency, and travel and accommodation costs incurred by an employee of the company visiting a foreign market for the purpose of gathering information;

Figure 12.1: "Contact" news-letter

Marketing Support Division   No. 4   1988

►► REMINDER ◄◄

SELLING IN THE SINGLE MARKET - WEST GERMANY
Companies are reminded of the seminar which will take place on 5 October in the Business Centre, Belfast International Airport.

A team of speakers is being assembled to advise and assist companies interested in the UK's largest trading partner in Europe.

West Germany is a lucrative but tough marketplace where opportunities prevail for the determined entrepreneur.

Details of the Seminar (and fees) are available from Nualin Gillespie, Export Development Branch, Ext 310.

1992: THE SINGLE EUROPEAN MARKET
In conjunction with IDB and LEDU, and as part of a UK wide awareness programme, a DTI Breakfast Conference on 1992: Single European Market will be held in Northern Ireland on Tuesday 8 November.

The opportunities and challenges of the Single European Market will affect all companies, and not just those with export business. Everyone must prepare for the new trading environment, so do plan to attend this conference.

The number of places is limited. If you are interested in attending please *contact* Rosemary Wade, Export Development Branch, Ext 309 by 11 October 1988.

RECENT REPORTS ON OVERSEAS MARKETS
Overseas Market Reports and Briefing Notes received recently in the Export Development Branch include:-

USA	Machine Tools;
Spain	Machine Tools;
Portugal	Machine Tools;
Spain	Selling Clothing;
Canada	Pleasure Craft;
Canada	CAD/CAM and Robotics; and
Canada	Computer Softwear

To obtain your copy of any of the above please *contact* Nualin Gillespie, Export Development Branch, Ext 310.

TRADE MISSION TO MIAMI AND CARIBBEAN BASIN

With some 36% of US exports to Latin America and the Caribbean passing through South Florida ports, Miami is unrivalled as a focus for sales, customer servicing and warehousing for exports to the Caribbean. Miami is also a convenient entry point for the vast growing Florida market. The 4th largest state in the Union with a popultion of 11.5 million (3.5 million in south Florida) and growing by 900 new arrivals daily, Florida offers excellent market prospects for Northern Ireland companies in such diverse fields as hi-tech equipment and components, medical care, food, beverage and giftware.

The Caribbean, where tourism is probably the region's largest single industry, also presents significant export opportunities for local companies. Barbados for example has a target of 442,000 stop-over tourists next year and this year the number of cruise ship passengers has increased by 60.0 per cent, the majority coming from Britain and the rest of Europe. In the Bahamas the Inter-American Development Bank has approved a US$6m loan to the Bahamas Development Bank to support productive projects in agriculture, fishing, industry and tourism.

To take advantage of these opportunities IDB is to mount a Trade Mission to Miami and the Caribbean in February 1989. This will be preceded by a seminar which will provide specific advice and guidance on trade opportunities in Florida and the Caribbean. The seminar will be co-hosted by the Caribbean Trade Advisory Group and will be held in Belfast on 17 November 1988 (venue to be arranged).

If you are interested in attending the seminar or if you wish to participate in the Trade Mission please *contact* Pearse Lawlor, Trade Development Branch, Ext 328.

DOUBLE OPPORTUNITY
TRADE MISSION TO KOREA AND JAPAN

IDB will sponsor a trade mission for Northern Ireland companies to include both South Korea and Japan next April.

In 1987 UK exports to South Korea reached an all time high of £427 million — representing an increase of more than 48% over the 1986 figure. Increasingly South Korea is also being regarded as a base from which to target other Pacific Basin markets.

This will be the first time an IDB supported trade mission has visited South Korea. The inclusion of Japan is a direct result of the success of the IDB trade mission in April 1988.

You will not want to miss this opportunity to visit both of these markets and full details of the trade mission and preparatory seminar and workshops will be published shortly.

Dates for the Trade Mission are:-

    10-14 April 1988   South Korea; and
    17-21 April 1988   Japan.

To record your interest and for further information *contact* Alan Dunn, Director Exports, Ext 331.

LOCAL SOURCING EXHIBITIONS

The Local Sourcing Unit will be in attendance at the Med Tech Exhibition in the Northern Ireland Business Centre, London from 11-22 October, at Enquiry '88 in the RDS, Dublin from 18-22 October and at the 'Selling to the Public Sector' in Ballymena Town Hall on 25 October. Staff will highlight the opportunities available through local sourcing and demonstrate the Northern Ireland Product and Services Capability Register.

If you would like further information *contact* Anne Trundle/Michaela Bell, Local Sourcing Unit, Ext 376/378.

- participation in trade fairs or exhibitions, including both staff costs and the cost of renting space;
- design costs incurred in respect of brochures, catalogues and other items of sales literature, point of sale material, preparation of promotional videos, advertisements, mail shots and incentive schemes;
- development costs associated with designing or re-designing packaging material;
- test marketing of a new product or service in existing markets, or of an existing product or service in new markets;
- customer visits to the company's premises;
- employment of a consultant to assist in preparation of a strategic export marketing plan;
- recruitment and re-location of key marketing/sales personnel.

As a matter of deliberate policy, certain elements are not eligible for assistance under the scheme. For example, no assistance is provided in respect of the media costs of advertising, partly on grounds of cost (given that even a relatively simple television advertising campaign can be very expensive indeed) and partly in order to emphasize to firms that advertising alone is no instant panacea guaranteeing successful market entry. In the case of publicity material, print costs are not eligible for assistance, primarily in order to force firms to consider carefully what quantity of a particular item of sales literature they really need, and what exactly they intend doing with it.

The 40/30 Plan

The way in which the Marketing Development Grant Scheme was promoted is perhaps of greater interest in the context of this chapter than the details of its operation. Firstly, it was given an imaginative and easily-remembered brand name summarizing its key features – the 40/30 Plan. Considerable thought went into designing the printed publicity material associated with it. An attractive, good quality brochure was produced, setting out the key features of the scheme, and the benefits of participation. The language used was deliberately simple, avoiding detailed treatment of the intricacies of the scheme and the bureaucratic jargon which so often makes material emanating from public bodies inherently unreadable. A user-friendly application form was included, requiring the minimum rather than the maximum of information needed to initially process a proposal. Clarity of presentation and communications effectiveness were the primary objectives of brochure design, but an important subsidiary objective was to demonstrate by example what a good piece of publicity material should look like.

The brochure was initially mailed to the Chief Executive of all companies eligible for IDB assistance. Subsequently, senior executives of IDB embarked on a series of speaking engagements throughout the region, including several "workshops" organized specifically to promote the scheme. Opportunities to present it on local radio and television where actively sought. IDB "client executives" (ie. staff assigned to act as the primary link with a number of firms) were instructed to "sell" the 40/30 Plan to the companies for which they were responsible, and in the main did so enthusiastically. The scheme was also advertised extensively in the local press, both initially and in a series of reminders spread over the subsequent 2-year period.

The 40/60 Plan

The initial 40/30 Plan was successful in that it was rapidly taken up by a large number of firms. However, the Board was concerned that many companies were not adopting a structured long-term perspective based on a coherent strategy, although there were signs that a number of them were beginning to do so. To encourage this, a revised and expanded version of the initial plan was introduced in April 1988, providing 40 percent grants up to a maximum of £60,000 a year, and marketed as the 40/60 Plan (Table 12.1).

Access to 40/60 is restricted to firms which have developed, or are in process of developing, a detailed strategic marketing plan. In a sense, companies will graduate to 40/60, having been introduced to the concept of strategic marketing planning through participation in 40/30. An important element in both schemes is the pro-active relationship being forged between the board and its "client" companies (see Figure 12.2). The Board's chairman (McDowell 1987, p. 16) has expressed this philosophy in the following terms:

> IDB sees itself as a major agent of change in creating an
> enterprise culture, and is now accepting a leadership role in
> helping companies to see how they can individually move
> forward, both in terms of improving their competitiveness, and

expanding their operations with the creation of viable long-
term jobs.

Companies are being encouraged to look further ahead in
respect of their own futures, and to raise their sights from the
local to the international level.

Other Measures

In addition to the 40/30 and 40/60 Plans, a number of other measures
aimed at achieving the overall basic objective are being implemented, including:

Research and Development Grant Scheme. An integral part of
the Board's philosophy is to ensure that firms adopt a policy of continuous new
product development and adaptation. This scheme enables them to recoup up to
50 percent of expenditure on approved research and development work related to
the introduction of new products or processes for manufacture or application
within Northern Ireland. The availability of this scheme has also been
vigorously promoted, and the uptake has shown a significant improvement as a
result (Table 12.2).

Design Clinics. Recognizing that good design is essential for
success in export markets, and that some local companies appeared to be
somewhat deficient in this key area, the board has recently organized a number of
"design clinics". These are two-day events held in provincial locations and
conducted by staff of a leading London-based design house. Participants are first
given a brief presentation on the principles of good design and how these might
be beneficially applied in practice. Each company then receives a free 2-hour
consultation focused on their own specific design problems (pre-registration of
companies well in advance of the event is essential, so that the consultant can be
briefed on the broad nature of the issues likely to arise). Subsequently the
company is supplied with a detailed report on the product design/marketing
problems identified, and how these might be tackled. A full costing of possible
future work required is included; at that point it is up to the company to decide
whether or not it wishes to proceed.

Figure 12.2: Pro-active export promotion

Table 12.1: Marketing development grant scheme

	1985/86	1986/87	1987/88
Companies assisted (no.)	124	203	189
Grant offered (£m)	£1.1	£1.9	£2.1
Grant paid (£m)	£0.5	£1.0	£1.6

Source: Industrial Development Board for Northern Ireland.

Initial feedback indicates that the clinics have been of considerable value to those companies participating in them.

Table 12.2: Research and development grant scheme

	1985/86	1986/87	1987/88
No. of projects assisted	120	157	173
Grants offered (£m)	6.4	8.3	7.8
Related expenditure (£m)	16.4	22.7	22.1

Source: Industrial Development Board for Northern Ireland.

Trade Missions. The practice of organizing visits to foreign markets for small groups of companies had been for many years a feature of local efforts to increase exports. However more recently a more positive and pro-active approach has been adopted. Here again client executives have been encouraged to "sell" the idea of participation to companies with which they have links. Forthcoming missions are highlighted in the "Contact" news sheet. In response to a specific problem expressed by some companies (that they are given too little warning of future trade missions, and do not have sufficient time to organize their participation) a two-year calendar of planned missions is now sent to every company. A trade mission "consultative forum" was held – all companies which had ever participated in a trade mission were invited to discuss their experiences, and their views on shortcomings/possible improvements.

Some valuable lessons were learned from this exercise. The geographical scope of the trade mission programme has been extended in order to introduce companies to markets which they might not ordinarily consider on their own – for example, China and the USSR. A simple measure of the success of these various initiatives is that 5 years ago on average about 10 companies were involved in the typical trade mission, compared with 18 to 20 firms now (see Table 12.3). A recent mission to Sweden and Finland involving 23 companies resulted in firm and potential orders in excess of £3m.

Inward Trade Missions and Import Substitution. As well as organizing visits abroad by local companies, the Board regularly arranges for representatives of large British and foreign companies to visit Northern Ireland and give presentations of their purchasing requirements to possible local suppliers. In addition, efforts have been made to try and ensure that large companies located in the region use local sources for their requirements, as far as possible.

Table 12.3: Participation in trade missions

	1985/86	1986/87	1987/88
No. of missions	5	11	10
Number of companies participating	46	80	129
Value of orders taken (£m)	£9.5	£12.2	£21.8

Source: Industrial Development Board for Northern Ireland.

Distance Learning. Efforts have also been made to facilitate the development of marketing expertise within existing firms. Conventional training courses have been organized on topics such as "Strategic Marketing", "Exporting", and "Selling Techniques". The initial take-up rate for these events was rather disappointing, but the Division responded vigorously to this apparent lack of interest. One issue of the news sheet "Contact" included a hard-hitting editorial entitled "Marketing Training Not for Us"; subsequently, the training package was re-designed and "sold" to companies by telephone and personal contacts. However, it became clear that a significant number of managers could not be persuaded to take part in events of this kind. The excuse usually given was the difficulty of finding the time needed to do so (Table 12.4).

Here again an innovative and imaginative approach has been adopted. In association with a leading management training institution, the Board developed a distance learning package comprising videos, case studies and a work-book. This was made available to companies at a nominal fee (£350), and to date just under 100 have been sold. The initial package was aimed at the larger firms; more recently (June 1988) an alternative package geared to the needs of smaller firms has been introduced.

Table 12.4: Use of export development services

	1985/86	1986/87	1987/88
No. of companies participating in export seminars	76	206	247
Number of overseas market enquiries received	N/A*	916	975

Note: * – not available.
Source: Industrial Development Board for Northern Ireland.

EFFECTIVENESS

The measures outlined above have been outstandingly successful in changing basic attitudes to marketing and exporting throughout the region. It may be argued that this success has at least in part been due to the fact that the climate was right – the time had come for the basic idea to be taken up on a large scale within the local business community. Awareness of the need to increase exports through the application of sound marketing principles had been building up over a number of years. Membership of the European Community and growing competition within it is a fact of life which could not be ignored.

The opinion leadership effect of government ministers, officials, academics and others repeatedly emphasizing the need for action should not be under-estimated nor should the role-model impact provided by local self-made success stories. Nevertheless the stimulus to act appears to have come from the imaginative and innovative efforts of the public officials concerned who, in effect, marketed marketing and exporting.

Quantitative measurements of this success are provided by statistics of participation rates in the various schemes referred to. More than 500 companies were assisted under the Marketing Development Grant Scheme during the first three years of its operation (Table 12.1), and more than 400 new product development projects were assisted under the Research and Development Grant Scheme during the same period (Table 12.2). Three times as many companies participated in outward trade missions during the third year of the programme compared with the number who did so in its first year (Table 12.3). The number of companies participating in export development seminars also increased substantially, and just under 1,000 enquiries concerning overseas markets are processed annually (Table 12.4).

An alternative measure is provided by surveys of managers' attitudes conducted in December 1985 and in June 1988. The data obtained in the first of these surveys was collected by means of personal interviews with senior managers in 75 companies based in the region. Quota controls were set to ensure that the sample of firms was representative of the region in terms of industrial sector; respondents within each sector were selected randomly. Using a standard scaling technique, respondents were invited to agree/disagree with various statements designed to reveal their attitudes to exporting, and to the IDB. The same individuals were contacted again by mail three months later, and invited to re-complete essentially the same questionnaire. Inevitably, some of the executives involved in the original survey had moved on and could no longer be contacted. In a few cases it could not be established with an acceptable degree of confidence that the same individual had responded to both enquiries; these replies were rejected as invalid. A total of 52 of the original 75 respondents completed the second stage of the enquiry. Mean attitudinal scores in respect of each statement for both enquiries were computed and compared using a standard t-test. The results of this exercise reveal a statistically significant positive change in attitudes in many cases (see Tables 12.5 and 12.6).

Table 12.5: Attitudes to exporting

Statement:		Strongly Disagree	Disagree	Agree	Strongly Agree	Mean Scale Value
				Number of firms		
Export business is essential to the long-term survival of any Northern Ireland based manufacturer	1985	3	31	19	22	+0.35
	1988	2	5	21	18	+1.04 *
There are so many problems with exporting that it is not worth the effort involved	1985	28	30	8	5	-0.96
	1988	8	34	3	1	-0.97 n.s.
Export business is usually more profitable than the domestic business	1985	8	40	13	6	-0.46
	1988	4	27	12	1	-0.47 n.s.
If you want to get into exporting there is plenty of support available from the Government	1985	4	24	39	4	+0.21
	1988	2	11	27	6	+0.56 n.s.

Notes: Sample size - 1985: 75; 1988: 52.
Scale values - Strongly disagree: -2, Disagree: -1, Agree: 1, Strongly agree: 2.
Statistical Test: T-test, 2-tailed; significance of the difference in scale values: * = p<.01, n.s. = not significant.

Source: Prepared by author.

Table 12.6: Attitudes to export assistance

Statement:		Number of firms				Mean Scale Value
		Strongly Disagree	Disagree	Agree	Strongly Agree	
In general the IDB is doing a good job in helping local firms to export if they want to	1985	1	19	45	1	+0.39
	1988	1	8	32	6	+0.72 n.s.
The export assistance provided by the IDB is very well tailored to the needs of Northern Ireland firms	1985	11	25	12	0	-0.73
	1988	2	14	21	1	+0.13 *
The IDB is too bureaucratic - its staff behave like civil servants rather than businessmen	1985	1	24	24	21	+0.57
	1988	3	27	11	2	-0.42 *
You never seem to get the help you need when you contact the IDB	1985	3	52	14	0	-0.64
	1988	6	29	6	0	-0.85 n.s.
The support services offered by the IDB do not live up to the expectations created by their publicity	1985	0	32	22	5	0
	1988	6	26	9	1	-0.64 *

Notes: Sample size - 1985: 75; 1988: 52.   Scale values - Strongly disagree: -2, Disagree: -1, Agree: 1, Strongly agree: 2.
          Statistical Test: T-test, 2-tailed; significance of the difference in scale values: * = p<.01, n.s. = not significant.
Source: Prepared by author.

It is unfortunately not possible to obtain precise data on changes in the volume and value of exports. The difficulty arises because a substantial proportion of the region's exports are routed via Great Britain; in consequence it is impossible to ascertain with any degree of certainty what proportion of the goods exported from Northern Ireland are destined for customers located in other parts of the United Kingdom as opposed to overseas. However the limited data available indicates a definite and substantial improvement in export trade over the period in question.

Moreover, the outcomes noted above have been achieved with a relatively modest outlay of public funds. Costs were covered by a diversion of resources within the Board's overall subvention, and were not incremental. The major costs involved were in fact the salaries of the staff concerned, and the sums paid to firms under the various schemes discussed. Details of the actual direct marketing costs of the programme described are not available, but these cannot have been substantial – design and printing of a few thousand brochures, a limited amount of regional press advertising, and the organization of seminars workshops and "clinics". Given that the salary costs would have been incurred anyway regardless of whether the officials concerned performed their tasks well or badly, and that a healthy uptake of the support measures available was in a sense the object of the exercise, it would appear that on this occasion the public funds were spent effectively when the costs of the programme are set against the income and employment benefits accruing, both immediately and in the longer term.

CONCLUSIONS

It was noted in the introduction to this chapter that the attitudes of key decision-makers at the level of the individual firm are of critical importance in export development. The specific example discussed suggests a number of valuable lessons for public organizations engaged in export promotion.

First, the provision of a complex infra-structure of financial incentives and other assistance measures is not in itself sufficient to ensure that export development takes place. An active willingness on the part of business managers to make use of the services available, and some knowledge of how to do so, is also essential. If substantial numbers of them are unable or unwilling to export for whatever reason, the only possible strategy for an export promotion organization to adopt is to seek to change negative attitudes of this kind. In attempting to do so, some knowledge, perhaps intuitive, of the processes involved in generating attitudinal change is required.

Second, it is possible for a public body to change the attitudes of key decision-makers, and thus influence their behaviour. However this requires the commitment of adequate resources, and a sustained effort over a substantial period of time. It also requires expertise, imagination, enthusiasm and flexibility on the part of the officials concerned, who must pro-actively market their services to the companies which are in effect their customers.

Third, if the necessary alteration in basic attitudes to exporting can be achieved, difficulties caused initially by a lack of marketing and exporting know-how are more easily overcome. If managers can be motivated to pursue a policy of export development, they themselves will take whatever steps are necessary to acquire the detailed knowledge they need.

Fourth, initiatives of this kind are more likely to be successful if they are designed and implemented at a regional level, in response to local conditions and needs, rather than imposed by central government.

Fifth, perhaps the most basic lesson to be drawn from the experience described is that publicly-funded organizations concerned with export development are more likely to achieve a measure of success by adopting a pro-active, facilitating role. A passively bureaucratic and prescriptive stance is unlikely to be effective in changing attitudes and thus influencing behaviour.

REFERENCES

Bilkey, W.J. and G. Tesar (1977). "The Export Behaviour of Smaller-sized Wisconsin Manufacturing Firms", *Journal of International Business Studies*, Vol. 8, No. 1, pp. 93-98.

Bradley, M.F., (1985). "Key Factors Influencing International Competitiveness", *Journal of Irish Business and Administrative Research*, Vol. 7, No 2, Winter.

Buckley, P.J. (1983). "Government in Industry Relations in Exporting: Lessons from the United Kingdom", in M.R. Czinkota, Ed., *Export Promotion: The Public and Private Sector Interaction*, New York: Praeger Publishers, pp. 89-109.

Cannon, T. and M. Willis (1983) "The Smaller Firms in Overseas Trade", *European Small Business Journal* 1, 3, pp. 45-55.

Cavusgil, S.T., (1980). "On the Internationalisation Process of Firms", *European Research*, Vol. 8, pp. 273-281.

Cheong, W.K. and K.W. Chong (1988). "Export Behaviour of Small Firms In Singapore", *International Small Business Journal*, 6, 2, pp. 34-41.

Czinkota, M.R. and W.J. Johnston (1981). "Segmenting U.S. Firms for Export Development", *Journal of Business Research*, Vol. 9, No. 4, pp. 353-365.

Dichtl, E., M. Leibold, H.G. Koglmayr and S. Muller (1984). "The Export Decision of Small and Medium-sized firms: a Review", *Management International Review*, No. 2, pp. 49-60.

Fell, D., (1986). "Northern Ireland: Building a Stronger Economy", *Business Outlook and Economic Review*, Vol. 1, No. 3, December, pp. 22-25.

Kaynak E. and V. Kothari (1984). "Export Behaviour of Small and Medium-Sized Manufacturers; Some Policy Guidelines for International Marketers", *Management International Review*, No. 2, pp. 61-69.

Kaynak, E., P.W. Ghauri, and T. Olopson-Bredenlow (1987). "Export Behaviour of Small Swedish Firms", *Journal of Small Business Management*, Vol. 25, No. 2, April, pp. 26-32.

McDowell, E. (1987). "The Industrial Development Board for Northern Ireland and the Future", *Business Outlook and Economic Review*, Vol. 2, No. 1, April, pp. 15-18.

Miesenbock, K.J. (1988). "Small Businesses and Exporting: A Literature Review", *International Small Business Journal*, Vol. 6, 2, pp. 42-61.

Olson, C.H. and Paul F. Wiedersheim (1978). "Factors Affecting the Pre-Export Behaviour of Non-Exporting Firms", in Ghertman, Michel and James Leontiades, Eds., *European Research in International Business*, Amsterdam: North-Holland Publishing Company, pp. 283-305.

Piercy, N., (1983). "Export Marketing Management In Medium-Sized British firms", *European Journal of Marketing*, Vol. 17, No. 1, pp. 48-67.

Seringhaus, F.H.R., (1986). "The Role of Information Assistance in Small Firms Export Involvement", *International Small Business Journal*, Vol. 5, No. 2, pp. 26-36.

Seringhaus, F.H.R. (1987). "Export Promotion: The Role and Impact of Government Services", *Irish Marketing Review*, Vol. 2, pp. 106-116.

Thomas, M.J. and Araujo (1985). "Theories of Export Behaviour: A Critical Analysis", *European Journal of Marketing* 19, 2, pp. 42-52.

Verhoeven, W. (1988). "The Export Performance of Small and Medium sized enterprises in the Netherlands", *International Small Business Journal*, Vol. 6, 2, pp. 20-33.

CHAPTER THIRTEEN

Two Educational Initiatives in Public Support for Export

"The Victorian Export Market Development Program, Australia."
John Onto and Nigel Hamley*

"The European Marketing Program, Northern Ireland/Republic of Ireland."
Jim Bell and Maurice Murray†

SUMMARY

This chapter examines two recent initiatives to boost export activity. In both cases, these represent a major departure from existing support methods and consequently reflect some dissatisfaction with these. The initiatives have a heavy educational component to them. These are not traditional educational programs, however, but involve "learning by doing". Although these initiatives are sufficiently new to rule out any definitive evaluation, the early results are promising and suggest others might think along similar lines.

INTRODUCTION

    In this chapter, two recent public sector programs are described. Although the main purpose of both programs is educational, other related objectives are of some considerable importance. The programs are an interesting

    *   Georgetown University, Washington, D.C., and Centre for International Business, Monash University, Clayton, Melbourne, respectively.
    †   University of Ulster at Jordanstown.

addition to the support services available to exporters. Each program is described below, beginning with the context that helps explain its establishment, then moving on to specific program details, and ending with some preliminary assessment of effectiveness.

THE VICTORIAN EXPORT MARKET DEVELOPMENT PROGRAM, AUSTRALIA

The Context

In November, 1986, the Victorian State Government approved an extensive package of industry support schemes, including the Export Market Development Program. This package was the outcome of an in-depth review of the State economy, begun shortly after the election of the Labour Party in 1982.[1] Since Victoria is a major manufacturing State, emphasis was placed on the development of a stronger exporting base with consideration given to the role that might be played by the education sector.

As part of this process, the International Business Centre at Chisholm Institute for Technology (CIT) was invited by the Victoria Department of Management and Budget to look at the viability of a State backed export development program aimed at upgrading the international business skills of executives in high export potential industries, as well as the best design for such a program. The research process was a simple one; a program model was developed and then discussed in a series of interviews with business executives, and academics with international marketing and executive training expertise.

On the basis of these interviews and the considerable support that emerged, CIT submitted a proposal for an "Export Market Development Program" with both learning content and process recommendations. This was approved and a two-year commitment made by the State Government, with

---

[1] The Labour Party was returned to government in Victoria after some 30 years in opposition. In 1983, the Australian Labour Party (ALP) won the federal election. As in Victoria, this signalled the end of an era of Liberal (conservative) Party domination. The ALP inherited a difficult, potentially disastrous economic situation; a fiscal deficit approaching $8 billion (8.3% of GNP), a balance of payments deficit of $170 million annually (2.3% of GNP), inflation of around 11.5% per annum and unemployment of 8.9%. Despite considerable apprehension on the part of the business sector regarding the election of Labour governments, traditional stereotypes have been shattered with privatization and free market policies pursued.

overall responsibility vested in the Department of Industry, Technology and Resources (DITR), and program implementation to be carried out by the International Business Centre at CIT.

The Program

Early recognition was given to the need to not only "teach" international marketing, but to build long term commitment within the client organization to the goal of penetrating foreign markets; thus attitude change was identified as being an integral part of the process. This was important for several reasons. First, "new to export" companies tend to underestimate the human, financial and time commitment required for international marketing. Therefore, the greater the investment required from participants, the more likely that they would stick with the plan when confronted with inevitable obstacles. Second, the export function is often a peripheral activity aimed at selling excess capacity or capitalizing on advantageous currency fluctuations. The goal of the Export Market Development Program then was to move the function into the mainstream of corporate strategic planning.

The determination to see these necessary attitude changes along with export education led to a systems approach to the program, which proceeded from the selection to the evaluation phase. At each phase, attention was given to communication with and involvement by senior management of the participant companies.

The program is conducted in three phases: training and preparation; overseas research; and business planning. The objectives of the training and preparation phase are to:
1. Provide a background in international marketing
2. Acquaint participants with the marketing planning process
3. Identify target markets
4. Complete secondary market research.

The educational content focuses on outlining in detail the international marketing model, building networks, information collection techniques, area studies and export marketing success stories. The educational process emphasizes the use of session leaders with practical international marketing experience as well as academics with international experience. Other elements include work by participants as they begin to develop their marketing plan, and intensive interaction with the program director. Throughout this process, participants are made aware of government resources available for exporters.

To date, this phase has taken place over six, two-day sessions with intensive assignment work between sessions typically involving research into the participant company and its potential target markets. At the end of phase one, participants have a clear idea of what is required for success in their target market together with an appreciation of additional data needs that will be collected through primary research when they visit the target market in phase two.

The overseas research phase is an intensive period of immersion in the target market of up to four weeks. Armed with a clear understanding of information requirements, an initial list of scheduled meetings and a marketing plan (beginning to take shape but still with significant gaps), the participant is encouraged to meet with a wide range of organizations – distribution channel members, advertising agents, market researchers, transportation companies, banks, accountants, customers and, where possible, competitors. The objective is to systematically gather information that could not otherwise be acquired yet is basic to the development of the business plan. It should be stressed that the generation of sales is not the goal of this stage although sales have frequently been achieved.

The third phase completes the training activity and requires the preparation and presentation by the participant of a detailed "business plan" for entry to the selected foreign market. This plan is presented to senior management of the participant's organization, senior members of the managing government department (DITR) and the program director. The organization's progress in implementation is then monitored very closely by the program director.

As indicated above, commitment by senior management to the project is considered a major contributing factor to the successful completion of this business plan. A number of strategems were developed to boost such commitment. First, applications for the program had to be signed by the chief executive (CEO) of the corporation or in the case of large multidivisional companies, the divisional CEO. Second, although heavily subsidized by the State Government, companies are required to pay a participation fee (see below). Third, the CEO is invited to a function at the end of phase one and briefed on the progress and process to date. Fourth, and perhaps most important, the CEO's presence is required at the presentation of the business plan at which time continuing support for the implementation of the plan is sought.

The total cost of the program which involves two intakes of 10-12 participants is $410,000. This is funded by a State Government contribution of $290,000 and participating company fees of $5,000 each. The participating companies also are responsible for all expenses incurred during the overseas phase of the program. They also face the additional (considerable) cost of releasing participants from the demands of their everyday job so as to take part in the three-month long program.

Preliminary Assessment

The first program involved 11 companies and case evidence points to some good degree of success. Three examples are provided below.

A medium-sized scientific instruments manufacturer focusing primarily on the education sector had export sales of A$500,000 in 1986-87. Export orders total A$4 million for 1988. These will be shipped to a wider range of countries and the company attributes increased confidence in its pricing, packaging and supply strategies to the Export Market Development Program. Increased order sizes are another result, with one product line having increased from 100 to 1,000 units per order. Some 10 additional jobs have been created as a result of increased exports. A horticulture firm sold its entire output of blueberries to a West German customer as a result of the field visit during phase two. This order was worth A$340,000. The managing director of an animal waste products company returned from phase two, his first overseas trip ever, with order for A$600,000 per month – their first export sales.

In total, 80 percent of the participants on the program achieved over A$100 million in new exports, and the four pilot Export Development Programs commissioned by the Victorian Government were considered an outstanding success to the extent that the Government continued its funding for a further two years at the end of the initial contract.

Export successes that have been achieved include exporting:

to Canada	• Confectionary
	• Heating & Ventilation Equipment
to China	• Tallow
	• Electric Generating

Equipment
to Denmark, Norway & Sweden	• Processed Garlic
to Europe and United States	• Pharmaceuticals
to Italy	• Office Furniture
to Japan	• Furniture
	• Giftware
	• Opals
	• Processed Meat
	• Petfood
	• Smoked Salmon
	• Dried Wild Flowers
to Korea and Taiwan	• Veterinary Products
to New Zealand	• Vehicle bodies
to United Kingdom	• Software
to United States &	
United Kingdom	• Computerized Photocopiers
to United States	• Robotics
	• Farm Machinery
	• Fish
	• Clothing & Knitwear

The concept of the 3-phase program – training, marketing research at home and overseas, and business planning – has now been recognized as a highly cost effective method of export enhancement in Australia. This approach has been adopted by a number of other tertiary institutions; notably Monash University, Centre for International Business, which has received Federal funding for further programs and is now the leading centre in this field in Australia.

The major problem the program has experienced is, that whilst it is recognized as being beneficial and cost effective, it relies heavily on ad hoc funding and subsidy from various government agencies. It is highly unlikely that, in Australia, the program could be marketed to industry on a full cost recovery basis, as Australia, unlike a number of other countries, lacks an export ethos or culture.

It is important to note that the program focuses on the development and implementation of long-term marketing strategies rather than immediate sales. To have achieved these short-term results is therefore very encouraging and justifies the government support provided.

Three concluding comments might usefully be made. First, there has been a temptation in some organizations to see the program as an excellent vehicle for personal development for the individual nominated. Clearly, this is an important byproduct but it is only that. Organizations must be made to see that the Export Market Development Program is the start of a process that requires a long term commitment and must be built into its overall strategy. The more ways in which CEOs can be brought into the process the greater the chance that they will commit to their nominee and the market strategies he/she is proposing. The commitment of the participant company to the program is, therefore, critical. Second, the company's support for the person selected is also important. There is a paradox that must be confronted during the selection of participants. By definition, if a top line executive is nominated, that is just the person likely to be called on to deal with emergencies at the office (and so is called off the program). This has an obvious disrupting effect which is quite serious, because implementation of the business plan depends very much on continuous involvement and championship of the process. Third, our initial experience suggests that there is merit in aiming for some program homogeneity, either in terms of the industries that participants are drawn from or the markets they are targeting. This would help to focus phase one more tightly and facilitate a more supportive network during phase two. We believe that learning would be accelerated and deepened throughout the program with such an approach.

THE EUROPEAN EXPORT MARKETING PROGRAM, NORTHERN IRELAND/REPUBLIC OF IRELAND

The Context

The importance attached to developing export competence among smaller firms is reflective of the economic conditions prevailing in Ireland. These circumstances are briefly elaborated in order to place the program in context and to highlight similarities and differences between the two countries.

The Republic of Ireland has a small home market and a small-firm dominated indigenous economy. Much of the economic growth achieved through the last decades has been as a result of the successful attraction of mobile investment. Aggregate export performance is strong, exceeding $15 billion or 64 percent of GDP in 1987 and the contribution of small indigenous firms is increasing. However, policymakers express concern that multinationals and foreign owned subsidiaries account for 70 percent of total exports. A decline in the number and size of mobile investment projects suggests that the contribution of smaller firms will become increasingly important.

Northern Ireland, fiscally and politically part of the United Kingdom, also has a small-firm base and a small local market. Traditionally dependent on the UK mainland market, its problems have been exacerbated by a decline in traditional industries such as textiles and shipbuilding. The departure of multinationals in a period of global recession has been compounded by the difficulty in attracting mobile investment due to political unrest. As a regional economy, precise export performance is difficult to quantify because statistics are incorporated in the aggregate UK trade figures. In these circumstances, developing the indigenous base and improving the export performance of smaller firms is regarded by policymakers as a major priority.

The Program

The European Export Marketing Program, a joint initiative of AnCO, the industrial training authority in the Republic of Ireland and the Northern Ireland Department of Economic Development (DED), is designed to assist Irish companies to enter the European market or expand their existing operations (see Figure 13.1 for details).

Participants, usually recent business or language graduates, are matched with "host" companies for the duration of the 41 week program. In the current year 25 companies/participants are involved, 15 from the Republic of Ireland and 10 from Northern Ireland. Companies and participants are integrated in a training and development program which has the dual objective of developing the export marketing skills of the participant and the competitive competence of their "host" firms (see Figure 13.2).

Once participating companies have agreed upon a suitable project, participants are interviewed, selected and "matched" to "host" companies. Great care is taken to ensure that the participant's skills in terms of qualifications, languages and prior experience meet company requirements, as they have the final decision on selection. A senior company executive is nominated as the contact link with the participant, he/she attends the company workshops and undertakes to support the participant throughout the program.

Figure 13.1: Providers and intermediators associated with the
European Export Marketing Programme

Role	Organization	
Management, promotion, administration, funding	AnCO (Republic of Ireland industrial training authority)	Northern Ireland Dept. of Economic Development
Market information/support	Irish Export Board	Industrial Development Board Northern Ireland
Programme leader	Irish Institute for European Affairs	
Programme consultant	Centre D'etudes en Gestion Internationale, Universite Catholique de Louvain	
Selection and matching of companies/participants	Frank Coyne and Associates*	University of Ulster

Note: * Also responsible for the Dublin Training Programme.
Source: Prepared by authors.

The first workshop, attended by participants and company executives, provides a framework for export development and advice in preparing project specifications. These are reviewed, revised and developed during the training program in Dublin. The objective of this intensive four-week module is to prepare participants by inculcating fundamental business concepts and diagnostic skills and to assist them locate sources of market information. Participants are introduced to the services of the Irish Export Board and the Northern Ireland Industrial Development Board and are encouraged to make extensive use of information and support provided by these agencies. The second workshop focuses on the strategic role of marketing strategy. This is followed by a five-week module of in-company training. During this period the project specification is further developed.

The remainder of the program is based in Europe. The third module is based at the Irish Institute of European Affairs in Louvain and includes intensive training in export marketing. Inputs on exporting research, planning and strategy, the marketing mix for exporting, cross-cultural communications and doing business in Europe are supplemented by intensive language courses designed to meet each participant's needs and level of competence. A pilot study in the Belgian market is designed to test the participant's ability to practically apply export principles and concepts. Successful completion is a prerequisite for undertaking the major project in the target market. Two workshops take place during this module, the second in Louvain coincides with an interim review. At this stage each company finalises its project specification, reviews the participant's progress and receives advice on financing export development and utilising government support packages.

Figure 13.2: Structure of European Export Marketing Programme

Week number	Participant program	Company program
	Participant selection	Company selection
Module 1		Workshop 1
1-4	Dublin Training Program	Workshop 2
Module 2		
5-9	In-Company Training	
Module 3		
10-17	Louvain Training Program Part 1	Workshop 3
18-21	Louvain Training Program Part 2	
22	Interim Report No. 1	Workshop 4
Module 4		
23-29	European Marketplace Fieldwork Part 1	
30	Interim Report No. 2	Workshop 5
31-38	European Marketplace Fieldwork Part 2	
39-41	Report Finalization and Career Planning	
	Program Conclusion	Workshop 6

Source: Prepared by authors.

During the final 18 week module, each participant conducts field investigations in a selected target market, reporting back to the Irish Institute and their companies on a weekly basis. As well as providing detailed progress reports identifying key contacts and action required, they also itemise their expenses and prepare an itinerary for the following week. Any action points are quickly followed-up by the company. An interim review and the fifth workshop in Louvain ensure that research is progressing according to plan and enables the concluding research phase to be fine-tuned. Having completed the field research, each participant prepares a written report and a verbal presentation for the final workshop.

During the program, participants receive a modest training allowance and subsistence from AnCO or DED. Each company also contributes IR£3,000 (about $5,000) to cover expenses incurred during the field research. While AnCO and DED in their capacity as training authorities expect that at least some of the participants will be offered permanent employment, there is no obligation on companies to offer positions, or indeed, on participants to accept any such offers.

Preliminary Assessment

The European Export Marketing Program offers real benefits for the small firms involved. They stand to obtain additional resources at modest cost, receive step-by-step advice on exporting and develop a long-term strategy for new markets without disrupting day-to-day operations. Individual participants learn new skills in a structured setting, are exposed to the social and business culture of new markets and generally have an opportunity to "showcase" themselves to the sponsoring firm or to others they come into contact with during the program. At a macro-level, the enhancement of exporting skills should increase the competitive competence of Irish firms over time. Greater and more effective usage of export support services is a further outcome of the program.

Given that export development is regarded as a long-term process and the relative youth of this program, the quantification of success is difficult. However, some preliminary research undertaken on 1986, 1987 and 1988 permits an initial assessment to be made.

Perhaps the most tangible measure of success is provided by the career choices made by participants completing the program. Table 13.1 shows that 75 percent or more of the program participants pursued careers in marketing either with their "host" company, another Irish company, or one based in Europe. The latter of these career paths is not a stated goal of the Program but demonstrates the calibre of the participants, in that they came to the attention of European firms during the field work phase. Brief case histories provide another indication of the program's success (see Table 13.2). Again, a good level of achievement is indicated. Although some companies may have gone into Europe anyway, the program accelerated this process for many firms. In other cases, many companies would not have attempted the exercise without the resources and support provided. The long-run impact of the program remains to be seen; some will undoubtedly generate substantial export business whereas others may do little more than improve their domestic performance as a consequence of foreign market exposure.

A final measure of success is the response by AnCO and DED to demand for such initiatives. Programs in progress during 1989 include:

1. A fourth European Export Marketing Program involving 25 companies, which was considerably over-subscribed.
2. A third East Coast U.S.A. Program with a similar approach and structure, which began in November 1988.
3. A third U.K. program, exclusively for companies in the Republic of Ireland.

Table 13.1: Employment of participants on program completion

Nature of employment/ position	1986 (n=24)		1987 (n=24)		1988 (n=24)	
Marketing in "host" company	8	(33%)	10	(42%)	16	(66%)
Marketing in another Irish firm	7	(29%)	6	(25%)	3	(13%)
Marketing in European firm	3	(13%)	2	(8%)	2	(8%)
Other*	6	(25%)	6	(25%)	3	(13%)

Note: * Includes a number of participants who obtained employment in other areas, emigrated or are self-employed.
Source: Prepared by authors.

4. A new West Coast U.S.A. Program involving 10 companies.

5. A small pilot program targeting the Canadian market.

Table 13.2: Case histories of companies involved in the programme

Sector	Outcomes
Clothing and textiles	Three companies have appointed agents or representatives in Europe.
Food and drink	To date, seven companies have entered new markets.
Industrial products	Two companies, currently seeking standards approval for the German market, are already doing significant business in France. A number of firms on the 1988 program have recently secured new business in Belgium, Holland and West Germany.
Medical/pharmaceutical	Five of six companies hired their participant, all are currently involved in new market development (not only in Europe).
High technology	In the electronics and information technology fields, three companies have entered or expanded export markets. Another two are currently involved in joint venture discussions with potential European partners.

Source: Prepared by authors.

In total, these initiatives are providing export market development and training for about 100 companies and participants. The source of greatest encouragement to policymakers is that many companies, having experienced the benefits, are making provision in their budgets to sponsor participants on future programs. Indeed, there is clear evidence to suggest that many companies now consider the programs to be an integral element in their strategic planning and corporate development.

DISCUSSION*

An earlier comment was made that, to some extent, the initiatives described in this chapter suggest some dissatisfaction with existing forms of export promotion assistance provided by public organizations. Certainly, studies demonstrate that levels of awareness, use and satisfaction with assistance programs are typically low (Seringhaus & Rosson, 1990). Considerable room exists then for improved program design and delivery. The Australian and Irish educational initiatives seem to overcome two of the problems that bedevil existing export promotion assistance – their passive nature and lack of a strategic imperative.

Considerable government and other public organization effort goes into making export information available and offering promotional support schemes. This is helpful but will not necessarily lead to export involvement, especially for companies that lack critical skills and resources. Hull and Hjern (1987) suggest that "intermediation" can be useful here:

> By linking firms lacking the wherewithal to tackle their problems of development and actors suited to tackling them, effective intermediation can counteract the predominantly passive delivery strategy of many resource providers.

Intermediation is evident in the Irish and Australian programs. Essentially, these initiatives are strong because a motivated person is dedicated to work on a company's behalf and, with help from program personnel, learns how to access information and resources critical to problem-solving.

A second strength of the Australian and Irish initiatives is that they acknowledge the long-term, strategic nature of export involvement. With a few notable exceptions (eg., Sweden), most nations offer a plethora of export promotion options to companies, with seemingly little tracking or control over the selections that are made. Sweden takes a more strategic approach to company export assistance, requiring that a long-term plan is developed and that the program assistance fits into this overall scheme. The Australian and Irish educational initiatives operate along the same lines, encouraging companies to look beyond the immediate to a point some years in the future when exporting could well be a major source of revenues and profits.

---

*   Written by the editors.

Because they address some of the weaknesses of current export promotion programs and do this in a very powerful action-learning setting, the Australian and Irish initiatives offer much promise. Early indications point to some success, paving the way for other similar offerings elsewhere.

REFERENCES

Hull, C. and Hjern, B. (1987). *Helping Small Firms Grow: An Implementation Approach*, New York: Croom Helm.

Seringhaus, F.H. Rolf and Philip J. Rosson (1990). *Government Export Promotion: A Global Perspective*, London: Routledge.

PART V

Export Promotion and Public Organizations: Present and Future Research

INTRODUCTION

The final chapter provides an assessment of present research on public organizations and export promotion as well as looking to the future. It is hoped that more sustained research will be done in this very important area.

CHAPTER FOURTEEN

Export Promotion and Public Organizations: Present and Future Research

Philip J. Rosson and F.H. Rolf Seringhaus[*]

INTRODUCTION

Public organizations can and do play a useful role in export promotion and development. Smaller companies benefit from these organizations' programs because they help reduce the barriers standing in the way of foreign market involvement and expansion. A comprehensive review of export programs in various parts of the world was presented in the previous 13 chapters, and is supplemented by the discussion in the Appendix. In this chapter the present body of research knowledge is briefly assessed. This naturally leads to suggestions for future work in this area.

AN ASSESSMENT OF PRESENT RESEARCH

Increasing research attention has been paid to the role of public organizations in export promotion and development in recent years. This research has different emphases and takes different forms. Research tends to be carried out either with a supplier or user emphasis. Thus, on the supply-side, the programs of public organizations are evaluated on a periodic basis. In many cases this is a mandatory process to ensure that public funds are being put to good use. In other cases, the evaluation is not mandated but auditing of

---

[*]   Dalhousie University, Halifax and Wilfrid Laurier University, Waterloo respectively.

operations is considered good management practice. These evaluations or audits are conducted either internally or contracted out to independent consultants, and the proprietary nature of these reports mean that they seldom enter the public domain.[1] In contrast, research studies with a user emphasis are very often published and so are readily available. These studies are usually carried out by academics whose interest in the internationalization of companies means that they examine export programs of public organizations as part of this process.

Different forms of export promotion and development research are found. Because supplier-side research is concerned with program impact, a fairly narrow range of study types is found here. A typical research approach is that of program benefit-cost analysis, with an attempt made to determine the payoff in exports[2] from program expenditures. Public organizations are also interested in "softer" measures of impact and so frequently employ survey techniques in evaluation studies. This means that they include data on, for example, company use of programs, actions resulting from program use, and attitudes towards aspects of program design and delivery. These programs tend to be evaluated at different times (say on a staggered five-year basis) and employing varying methods (often because a new consultant is used). This makes comparisons across programs and the tracking of impacts over time a very difficult undertaking.

Due to a wider range of interests, greater diversity is seen in user-side studies. As noted above, many academic researchers are concerned to examine why and how companies internationalize, and the factors and organizations that are influential in this process. Among the typical studies resulting are those focusing on: characteristics differentiating companies that export from those that do not; export barriers faced by companies and how these are overcome; strategies associated with successful exporting; and, patterns of foreign market development. Public organization activities often feature in these analyses. The variety in topics examined is matched by a diversity of treatments—ranging from simple descriptive "armchair" accounts to prescriptions for companies and public organizations based on the "scientific" examination of large data-sets. Most of these studies are conducted with small budgets which constrain their design and execution. Consequently, academic studies are usually restricted to low-cost data

---

[1] The results speak to the efficiency and effectiveness of specific programs and the organization in general.

[2] This analysis sometimes incorporates "multiplier effects" in an attempt to go beyond an impact measurement stated solely in terms of export sales.

collection methods (mail surveys outnumber all others), limited coverage (regional or sectoral samples), and less-than-adequate survey administration (available help is used).

Perhaps the main point to be made about existing research is that, with few exceptions, public organization and (largely) academic researchers operate in isolation – each conducting their studies independently of the other.[3] This is unfortunate in that much could potentially be achieved through greater collaboration. Public organizations bring resources, data availability, and practical insight to any collaboration whereas academics offer know-how in export theory, research methods, and bring a broad export perspective to bear on particular study topics. With this general comment in mind, we now suggest a number of areas that warrant greater emphasis in future research endeavours.

FUTURE RESEARCH DIRECTIONS

There are two glaring gaps in our current knowledge about the involvement of public organizations in export promotion and development. First, relatively little has been written outside the developed world, and second, there is a shortage of published material from the supply-side. This situation requires attention. A third research matter is that of methodology. Better and more varied practice is advocated here.

The Developing World

As this volume attests, the literature is dominated by developed world experiences where comprehensive programs have been in operation for a number of decades. Although there is room for additional research and program improvement in the First World, a greater need exists to understand developing country experiences—what is currently being done and how this might be improved. There are fairly obvious reasons for the present imbalance in research effort and knowledge, but a greater emphasis on the Third World is in order. Programs are clearly in operation on the continent of Africa, but what is known about them?

---

[3] Exceptions are found as seen from Chapter 8.

If the developing country literature is largely silent, there is only a whisper about export promotion and development in newly industrializing countries (NICs). What little has been written is from the standpoint of public policy and infrastructure development, rather than programs operating at the company level.[4] The NICs provide an interesting case, falling as they do between the rich, industrial countries of the West and the poorer, developing countries of the South. The contribution of public organization export programs in Singapore, South Korea, Brazil and other nations deserve more attention.

We should also mention the countries of the Second World. As the old regimes in Eastern Europe are replaced by governments that are more democratic and embrace freer market principles, the state's role regarding exports is changing. For example, whereas foreign trade organizations used to be the focal point for all export activity in the USSR, responsibility has now shifted to enterprises and relevant Ministries. This change creates an opportunity for important research, as do changes throughout the Eastern bloc, because it is probable that these countries will develop different approaches to export promotion and development as the years unfold.

As well as studies from outside the developed world, there is a need for comparative research. Multi-country research is always expensive, time-consuming and difficult to bring to fruition. Yet there is much to be gained from such efforts. We noted in Chapter one that there are considerable similarities in the export promotion programs offered in developed countries but that at the same time contrasting approaches (loose coordination versus strategic emphasis) and organizational arrangements (government-led versus private sector-led) exist. We also know that the level of funding varies considerably across these nations. This provides a fertile ground for comparative studies that could unearth useful findings about the effectiveness and efficiency of alternative methods (Seringhaus & Botschen 1990).

Research on the Supply-Side

A number of research topics would yield helpful information in this area. The first point to be made is that we are hard-pressed to come up with a single piece of public organization export research aside from those of national governments and quasi-government bodies (the International Trade Centre at

---

[4] Keesing and Lall (1988) is an exception.

UNCTAD/GATT, for example). Therefore, it seems an opportune time for a study of the role and impact of these organizations, say the chambers of commerce in Germany, or the World Trade Centre network in the U.S.. Rather than being a passing comment in some other piece of research, it would be useful to see the contribution of organizations such as these separately examined.

Whether it is government or some other public organization, export promotion decision-making is ignored in the literature. As a result, we have no real idea of how these organizations develop their export promotion and development policies, strategies and programs, or how these are implemented and evaluated.[5] For example, researchers on the user-side often are critical about government programs, arguing that these are not targeted to the most appropriate companies or that the wrong participants are chosen for a trade mission or fair. This may or may not be the case. If it is, there may be some good reason for the decisions and choices that are made that is presently being missed. This same point extends to the notion of program "success" and "failure". Using data from Chapter eleven by way of example, our instinct is that the finding "49 percent of companies make no sales at trade fairs up to 12 months after and beyond" reflects failure. Yet government officials we have presented this argument to do not necessarily agree. Clearly, there are "different views of the world" in operation here. Our point then is that the dearth of published "supply-side" studies and limited interaction among various researchers creates something of a knowledge vacuum.

Another supply-side issue that merits attention concerns organizational change. In various countries there are moves afoot to modify the traditional forms of export promotion and development. In Chapter two, for example, it was noted that many states in the U.S. have developed extensive programs to supplement or replace federal initiatives. In other countries, certain public organization functions are being privatised, either because of a change in political philosophy, reduced budgets, or for both of these reasons. These examples illustrate export promotion dynamics. Again, we have not seen any studies that analyze and assess the outcomes of such change, from a public organization or company standpoint.

---

[5] We should also recognize that exports are no longer the sole concern of public organizations in developed countries. As the emphasis shifts from export promotion to efforts to create a fitter economy to compete in the 1990s and beyond, imports, inward investment and in-licensing of technology are on the agenda of many organizations, government departments in particular.

Methods: Realism, Precision and Variation

Public organization programs are being examined more carefully today than ever before. However, even better methods and analysis are required. The business environment is complex, with numerous factors and bodies influencing the decisions made and results achieved. Research studies deal with such complexity through simplification. At the results stage, however, researchers often draw the most sweeping conclusions from their work. More caution is in order, as is better framing of the research undertaken. An understanding of the export process in companies and of public organization programs is essential to good research. This seems absent from some studies.

The main method used in present studies is the mailed questionnaire or telephone interview of a medium-sized sample (40-100 companies). In a sense this is too large a sample to enable an in-depth understanding to be developed of the matter under study and, if there are several sub-groups to be explored, too small a sample to permit more than rudimentary statistical analysis. Therefore, active consideration should be given to more small and large-scale samples to satisfy the separate purposes noted. We argue that if the researcher wishes to study the role played by public organization programs in the decision of companies to begin exporting, there is more to be gained from personally interviewing say 30 companies than using a questionnaire mailed to 200 companies. In contrast, when the research question involves considering several industrial sectors, a mail or telephone survey of 200 or more companies is probably ideal. This may seem an obvious point but seems to elude many researchers who appear to opt for methods that are convenient.

If the role and impact of public organization export programs is to be properly determined, precise measures and appropriate data analysis is essential. Progress is being made as energy and thought is focused on this problem. However, when researchers skip from one study field to another (many consultants and a good number of academics fall into this category), this effort is diluted. The question of program impact is a particularly thorny one, made difficult by the numerous variables at play, measurement problems, and different dimensions of impact (Seringhaus & Rosson 1990).

A wider array of research approaches could be employed. For example, case analysis is a method with potential. This technique has yielded very useful insight in other research settings (Hakansson 1982) and there is no reason why this should not apply here. A case study of a government-led foreign trade mission could considerably enrich the literature, as might other topics. Longitudinal research is also desirable. Public organization export programs tend to lend support at a particular point in time, but the hope is that there will be some lasting effect (e.g. a sponsored trade fair exhibit in a new foreign market will pave the way for distribution arrangements and eventual sales). In fact, our argument is that the overriding objective of export programs should be skill and knowledge development—an investment that pays off over time. Therefore, longitudinal methods offer much potential.

As can be seen, there is considerable room for further study of public organizations in the field of export development and promotion

REFERENCES

Hakansson, Hakan (1982). *International Marketing and Purchasing of Industrial Goods: An Interaction Approach*, Chichester: Wiley.

Keesing, Donald B. and Sanjara Lall (1988). "Marketing Manufactured Products from Developing Countries: Information Links, Buyers' Orders and Institutional Support," Paper presented at UNU/WIDER Conference on New Trade Theories and Industrialization in Developing Countries, Helsinki, August.

Seringhaus, F.H. Rolf and Botschen, Guenther (1990). "Cross-National Comparison of Export Promotion Services and their Usage by Canadian and Austrian Companies," In Hans Mühlbacher and Christoph Jochum, Eds. *Advanced Research in Marketing*, Vol. II, European Marketing Academy, Innsbruck, Austria, 1563-82.

Seringhaus, F.H. Rolf and Rosson, Philip J. (1990). *Government Export Promotion: A Global Perspective*, London: Routledge.

APPENDIX

Public Support Programs for Export Development

Export promotion efforts vary across different countries as to their comprehensiveness, strategic orientation, and involvement of public and private sectors. This Appendix provides a flavour of the heterogeneity that exists. We begin by providing an overview of export support in three countries – the U.S., Austria and Singapore. These choices enable us to describe a government-based export system, a private sector-based system, and a developing country approach to export support, respectively. The Appendix concludes with a summary of the types of public organizations involved in export development. Derived from an ITC survey undertaken in 1988, this once again reinforces the diversity of approaches that are found around the world.

U.S.A.

The main source for export promotion support at the national level is the U.S. Department of Commerce (DOC) and its International Trade Administration (ITA) Division. The export support structure and system at the federal level have been criticized as insufficient in terms of providing comprehensive and relevant assistance to potential and actual exporters. It is out of this situation that widespread and substantial export development and support efforts have arisen at the state level, which are discussed in Chapter two of this book. Given the discussion in Chapter two, here we limit ourselves to export promotion at the national level. Four main types of assistance are available: (1) Market identification statistics – which highlights attractive export markets as well as emerging market opportunities; (2) market research studies – in the form of detailed evaluations of opportunities, either country or product-based; (3) market contact services – through services providing sales leads, identified individuals, background information on foreign prospective buyers; and (4) product and services promotion – in the form of trade missions and international trade fairs, catalogue and video exhibitions, international publications.

Some 48 ITA district offices as well as 19 branch offices are located across the U.S. to provide information as well as professional export consulting to the business community. Each office is capable of providing information about trade and investment opportunities abroad, foreign markets for products and services, services to both locate and evaluate overseas buyers and representatives, and export-related seminars and conferences. Foreign commercial services are available through 126 offices in some 66 countries. Foreign offices are vital in data collection, market analysis and providing organizational support for promotional activities. They work closely with the domestic ITA offices to satisfy the specific needs of exporters.

Some of the major ITA programs geared to exporters are:

1. Automated Information Transfer System

    This is a computer-based network linking all ITA offices and provides access to up-to-date market information.

2. Trade Opportunities Program (TOP)

    U.S. Foreign Commercial Service posts transmit information on export opportunities to TOP on a daily basis. Subscribers to TOP specify the products or services they export and receive the appropriate leads from TOP head office daily.

3. New Product Information Service

    A Commercial News U.S.A. magazine containing new U.S. products available for export is distributed widely to business and government leaders in foreign countries.

4. Export Contact List Service

    ITA maintains a computerized Foreign Trade Index with more than 140,000 import agents, distributors, service organizations, manufacturers, and retailers (covering some 143 countries), as a source of contacts for exporters.

5. World Traders Data Reports

    Business reports with background information on potential foreign trade contacts, prepared by commercial officers abroad.

6. Agent/Distributor Service

Provides names of foreign agents or distributors with a declared interest in handling specific U.S. products. ITA officers conduct 'on-site' searches to locate qualified representatives.

7. Overseas Trade Fairs

ITA sponsors participation by U.S. firms in international trade fairs and assists with the organizational and marketing tasks.

8. Commerce Assistance on Specific Markets

ITA's international policy unit provides commercial and economic information on most U.S. trading partners.

9. Comparison Shopping

A customized service where foreign office staff conduct on-site interviews about specific marketing and representation aspects of exporting particular products.

10. Foreign Buyer Program

Exporters can meet qualified foreign buyers at trade shows in the U.S.. The DOC promotes such shows worldwide and invites foreign buyer delegations, manages an international business centre and brings buyers and sellers together.

11. Overseas Trade Missions

Group visits to foreign markets are organized for executives of U.S. firms. The agenda is organized by DOC and include meetings with influential government and business representatives.

12. Matchmaker Events

Matchmaker Trade Delegations provide introductions to new markets through short overseas visits. The objective is specific and limited, namely to match a U.S. firm with a representative or prospective joint venture/licensee partner.

As well as these ITA services and programs, other institutions such as the EXIMBANK and the Foreign Credit Insurance Association provide services to exporters to cope with various forms of foreign market financial risk. These include various kinds of financing vehicles, loan guarantees, and insurance coverage.

In recent years export development and promotion initiatives have grown rapidly at the state level so that most states now maintain offices and programs to promote exporting (See Chapter two). These often provide similar types of assistance to that available through DOC and ITA, although more closely tailored to the particular industrial and business base of the state in question (Jain 1990, Czinkota & Ronkainen 1990).

AUSTRIA

The Austrian export promotion system is largely private sector-based so that aside from some aspects of export financing, the government has no involvement in the system. The basic goals of the export promotion system are to:

- increase competitiveness;
- increase level of export involvement;
- aim for a positive international trade balance;
- emphasize exports as a medium for economic growth.

The Bundeswirtschaftskammer is the key institution through which export support is provided to the business community. This non-governmental organization requires that all business enterprises are members and it finances a large part of its operations through membership fees. While the organization is a national chamber of commerce, its structure and mandate are very comprehensive. Nine provincial Landeskammern focus on regional interests of the business community, while the head office is the umbrella organization and plays a major role in providing export promotion services. The latter are available through two branches, the Economic Development Institute and the Trade Policy Department. All phases of the exporting process are targeted through programs that include information services and publications, export consulting, training and seminars, various promotional events. Services are available for a fee or require cost participation on part of the user (Seringhaus & Botschen 1990).

The export promotion system extends beyond Austria's borders through trade commissioner offices attached to consulates in foreign countries. Bilateral chambers abroad also add a further support structure to the system. Tables A.1 and A.2 offer a detailed listing of the two branches of the Bundeswirtschaftskammer.

In addition to the export support by the Bundeswirtschaftskammer, various industry associations which maintain provincial branches assist the business community with services such as export statistics, procedures, documentation as well as customized market research. Industry associations also often assist with contacts between buyers and sellers at home and abroad, and arrange study visits as well as trade missions to export markets. Banks are intensively involved in export financing and also offer some limited information services to clients. Their information services usually are restricted to reports on markets and export opportunities, however, their foreign branches provide advice to exporters. Banks maintain close contact with government and regulatory bodies and provide export seminars to relay pertinent information to the business community.

Overall, the Austrian export promotion system appears to operate in an integrated and strategically-focused way, that is its programs and services emphasize the needs of small and medium-sized companies and the different levels of export involvement.

SINGAPORE

The Singaporean government has been pursuing an economic development policy that has been based on developing technically skilled capital-intensive industries with a distinct export focus. Because of the importance of exports to the economic development of the country, export promotion is essentially a constituent component of economic development policy. The Trade Development Board (TDB)[1] is the main organization concerned with export promotion. Its status is one of an autonomous organization whose governing body is made up of equal numbers of private and public sector directors. The TDB's mandate is explicit in that it is the only institution responsible for export promotion of products and services and the promotion of trade generally, and maintains, in addition to the Head Office, some 15 foreign offices.

Two thrusts of export promotion support are evident. First, planning and production, second, marketing of products and services. Planning and production support is provided through professional advisory organizations in the form of consultation, rather than through emphasis on printed materials, as is the case in many other countries. Governmental tax subsidies encourage 'export enterprises' to enhance their production and technological capacity. Marketing

---

[1]   This resulted from the amalgamation of the Department of Trade with the Ministry of Trade and Industry in 1982/83.

Table A.1: Export promotion services of the Bundeswirtschaftskammer: Economic Development Institute

Service	Explanation
Export magazines	For particular sectors
Consulting to companies	To rationalize and improve management of operations
Support for individual exhibitors	Participation of individual exporters in foreign trade fairs and exhibitions
Academie of Export	Various courses on foreign trade
Export publications	Promotion of publications for the marketing of Austrian products abroad
Subsidy of travel costs	To support foreign travel of company staff, must be conversant with language of target market
Foreign language study	Support of foreign language training for company personnel
Joint promotion and advertising	Support of promotion and advertising campaigns of industry and trade-associations
Group exhibits	Official participation in foreign trade fairs and exhibits
Innovation service	Consulting on product innovation and new markets
Sales ads and brand advertising	Support for advertisements aimed at increasing exports
Trade fairs	Comprehensive consulting concerning information and participation in trade fairs
Information on fashion trends	The fashion secretariat provides details on trends and targeted sales efforts
Standards	The Standards Institute provides information on Austrian and foreign standards
Austrian seal of quality and origin	Testing, certification and promotion of quality standards
Technical information	Information on wide range of technical topics
Contribution to transportation costs	Support of shipping of exhibited goods from non-European events
Packaging	Packaging advice for export
Sales activities in department stores	Sales exhibits in cooperation with foreign partners for Austrian consumer products

Table A.2: Export Promotion Services of the Bundeswirtschaftskammer:
Trade Policy Department

Service	Explanation
Austrian Bulletins	Publications of foreign offices which also include specific requests of companies free of charge
Training of assembly and service personnel	Cost subsidy for personnel from developing countries
Credit information	Through foreign offices for a fee
Individual export consulting	In-house consulting on contact establishment with prospective customers
Accounts receivable collection	Through all foreign offices
Joint ventures or consortia abroad	Financial support for small and medium-sized firms
Consulting through sector desks	Export guarantees and financing problems
International bidding and contract opportunities	Provision of documentation through foreign offices
Contact development	Contacts with foreign prospects for Austrian goods
Financing	Financing of equipment in industrial countries and export-related investment in developing countries
Market research	Internal studies for support for studies by market research firms
Planning for export	Varied support for export planning
Information	Pertaining to foreign market
TELESELEKT	Data collection on foreign trade firms
Data bank on global trade	Statistical analysis of data of UN member countries as basis for market research
Trade missions and buyer-seller meetings	Group travel for contact establishment and individual meetings with buyers and distributors abroad

support is provided by the TDB and frequently involves other institutions. For example, the Singapore Manufacturer's Association supports member firms' participation in trade fairs. Fairs of interest are cleared through TDB, thus entitling participants to claim generous expenses associated with such promotional activities. The TDB carries out export promotion activities on a regular basis, as shown in Table A.3.

Financial support is available through the Monetary Authority of Singapore through short-term discounting of letters of credit which exporters have received from customers. The Export Credit Insurance Corporation provides coverage for both commercial and political risks. Export financing, unlike many other countries, is only available through the private banking sector.

Further export promotion support is available through the Singapore Chinese Chamber of Commerce and Intraco, a state trading company established to provide small business access to export markets. Intraco provides product development advice and is keen to introduce new companies with sophisticated products to export markets. Overall, export promotion in Singapore reflects the mentality that international business activity is 'the way of business' as opposed to separating international from domestic business orientation (National Swedish Industrial Board 1985, ITC 1988).

TYPES OF PUBLIC ORGANIZATION AND INSTITUTIONAL FORMAT

Numerous types of organizations and institutions are responsible for foreign trade and export promotion activities. Whatever the nature and responsibilities of each of these institutions, there are some basic conditions that must be met to enable them to operate successfully and to implement the foreign trade policy and export promotion programs as effectively as possible. Among the basic conditions necessary are:

1. Each organization's responsibilities must be clearly defined;
2. The formulation of these responsibilities and the resulting activities should not lead to conflicts between organizations
3. There must be good co-ordination mechanisms between organizations.

Many organizations, in addition to government ministries, are involved in trade promotion. They include trade promotion boards and councils, standard and regulatory organizations, banks and other financial institutions, producers' associations and chambers of commerce. These organizations, usually autonomous, provide the means by which trade policies are realized. Ideally, they

Table A.3: Regular Export Promotion Activities of the Trade
Development Board

1. PRODUCT AND MARKET PROMOTION DEVELOPMENT
   Export supply studies
   Identification of export constraints
   Preparation of product profiles
   Preparation of market profiles
   Analysis of opportunities in foreign markets
   Complete market studies
   Identification of export potential for development
   Export promotion programs on a product basis
   Trade information service
   Selective dissemination of information
2. SPECIALIZED SUPPORT SERVICES TO EXPORTERS
   Export procedures and documentation
   Guidance for export financing
   Marketing
   Product adaptation
   Export packaging
   Publicity
   Direct training
   Export of services
3. ACTIVITIES ABROAD
   Participation in trade fairs
   Organization of sales missions
   Invitation to foreign buyers
4. SUPPORT TO ACTIVITIES OF OTHER ENTITIES
   Training programs of specialized schools
   Free zones promotion or administration
   Motivational campaigns
   Economic studies/advisory service to the Government
   Support to small and medium enterprises
   Promotion of joint export mechanisms
   Quality control and standardization programs
   Export packaging improvement

Source: Profiles of Trade Promotion Organizations, ITC, International Trade
Centre UNCTAD/GATT, Geneva, 1988.

should complement each other, create an environment for trade to flourish, and enable the importer or exporter to obtain the services required.

For many reasons, developing countries have a great variety of institutions performing trade functions whose responsibilities also vary widely from one country to another. Table A.4 shows this heterogeneity in organizations and functions. Despite the variations, however, it is possible to state which type of organization is best suited for certain activities. These organizations are marked with a ✔ in the table while ✗ shows which organizations actually perform the function. It should be stressed, however, that the final decision on structure should be based on the circumstances prevailing in the country and the resources available to it.

A trade or export promotion program should be a comprehensive mix of consistent policies and organizations. Weakness in any one of these will jeopardize the effectiveness of the others and may render the entire program ineffective. Formal co-ordination between organizations and policies is rare, the situation in many countries generally representing merely an accretion of government decisions over a number of years.

Where export promotion has been regarded as successful, despite the informality of linkages, the programs have been found to be responsive to market conditions, to the needs of importers and exporters, and to the possibilities offered by new products and technologies.

Table A.4: Public organizations and their foreign trade
and export promotion functions

	Type of public organization										
Functions related to foreign trade and export promotion:	CM	PO	FTC	CB	MF	MT	MFA	TPO	SI	BS	TS
Policy recommendations:											
on exports		√	×	√	×	×	×	√	×		×
on imports		√	×	√	×	×	×	√	×		×
Policy-making:											
on exports	×	×	√	×	×	×	×	×			
on imports	×	×	√	×	×	×	×	×			
Policy implementation:											
Control functions:											
on exports				×	×	√		×	√		
on imports				×	×	√		×	√		
Export promotion:											
Domestic promotion activities				×	×	×		√	×	×	
Advisory services to exporters						×		√	√	×	
Commercial representation abroad							×	√			
Trade fairs and missions						×	×	√	×		×
Incentives: establishment	×	×	√	×	×		×	×			
granting			√	√			×				
Export credit	×	×	×	×	×		√		√		
Export credit insurance			×		×		×	√	√		
New export development							×	√	√	×	
Training							×			×	×

Table A.4: Public organizations and their foreign trade
and export promotion functions (cont'd)

Functions related to investment	CM	PO	FTC	CB	MF	MT	MFA	TPO	SI	BS	TS
Policy recommendations	✓	✗	✗	✓	✗		✓			✗	
Policy formulation	✓	✗	✗	✗	✗						
Control functions	✓		✗	✗	✗		✗	✓			
Studies and profiles	✓				✗		✓	✓		✗	
Promotion	✗				✗		✓	✓			

Type of public organization

CM   Council of ministers and/or monetary council
FTC   Foreign trade council or equivalent
MF   Ministry of finance
MFA   Ministry of foreign affairs
TPO   Trade promotion organization
BS   Banking and financial system
TS   Trade sector

PO   Planning organization: board or ministry
CB   Central bank
MT   Ministry of trade, commerce or development (divisions other than TPO)
SI   Specialized institution such as foreign trade institute, export credit insurance company, packaging institute, standards institute, etc.

Note: ✗ shows organization found to perform the function.
      ✓ indicates the organization which seems best suited to perform the function.

Source: Monograph on the Role and Organization of Trade Promotion, ITC International Trade Centre UNCTAD/GATT, Geneva, 1986, p. 5.

REFERENCES

Czinkota, Michael R. and Ilkka A. Ronkainen (1990). *International Marketing*, 2nd. Ed., Hinsdale, Il.: The Dryden Press.

ITC (1988). *Profiles of Trade Promotion Organizations*, Geneva, International Trade Centre UNCTAD/GATT.

Jain, Subhash C. (1990). *International Marketing Management*, 3rd. Ed., Boston: PWS-Kent Publishing Company.

National Swedish Industrial Board (1985). *Export Promotion by Governments in Nine Countries*, Stockholm.

Seringhaus, F.H.Rolf and Günther Botschen (1990). "Cross-National Comparison of Export Promotion Services and their Usage by Canadian and Austrian Companies", in Hans Mühlbacher and Christoph Jochum, Eds. *Advanced Research in Marketing*, Vol. II, European Marketing Academy, Innsbruck, Austria, pp. 1563-82.

REFERENCES

Alexandrides, C.G. and George P. Moschis (1977). *Export Marketing Management*, New York: Praeger Publishers.

Amsterdam-Rotterdam Bank (1983). Report on "Greater Export Opportunities for Small and Medium-sized Firms" (January).

Anjaria, Shailendra J., Kirmani, Naheed and Petersen, Arne B. (1985). *Trade Policy Issues and Developments*, International Monetary Fund, Washington, D.C.

Artavia, Robert, Forrest D. Colburn and Iván Saballos (1987). "De Sustitución de Imprtanciones a Promoción de Exportaciones: Lecciones de Costa Rica," *Revista INCAE*, Vol. 1, No. 1, pp. 44-52.

Balassa, Bela (1979). "Export Incentives and Export Performance in Developing Countries: A Comparative Analysis", in Barend A. de Vries, *Export Promotion Policies*, World Bank Staff Working Papers, No. 313, Washington, D.C., The World Bank, pp. 20-28.

Balassa, Bela (1984). "The Process of Industrial Development and Alternative Development Strategies," Essays in International Finance, No. 141, 4-11, as reprinted in *Leading Issues in Economic Development*, Gerald T. Meier, Ed., Oxford: Oxford University Press.

Barrett, Nigel J. and Ian F. Wilkinson (1985). "Export Stimulation: A Segmentation Study of the Export Problems of Australian Manufacturing Firms," *European Journal of Marketing*, Vol. 19, No. 2, pp. 53-72.

Bauerschmidt, Alan, Daniel Sullivan and Kate Gillespie (1985). "Common Factors Underlying Barriers to Export: Studies in the U.S. Paper Industry" in *Journal of International Business Studies*, vol. 16, no. 3, pp. 111-123.

Bekerman, Marta (1986). *Promotion de Exportaciones. Una Experiencia Latinoamericana: El caso de Brasil.*, Comercio Exterior, vol. 36 No. 5, Mexico.

Bello, Daniel C. and Hiram C. Barksdale (1986). "Exporting at Industrial Trade Shows," *Industrial Marketing Management*, Vol. 15, pp. 197-206.

Bendow, Bruce (1981). "Before You Enter a Trade Fair," *International Trade Forum*, (October-December), 10-13, pp. 28-30.

Bersee, H. (1987). "NIPO enquete: optimisme bij Nederlandse exporteurs", *Export Magazine*, (February 7).

Beyfuss, J. (1984). "Formen staatlicher Exportfoerderung", in E. Dichtl and O. Issing, Eds., *Exporte als Herausforderung fuer die deutsche Wirtschaft*, Koeln: Deutscher Instituts verlag GmbH.

Bilkey, W.J. (1978). "An Attempted Integration of the Literature on the Export Behavior of Firms", *Journal of International Business Studies*, Vol 9, Summer, pp. 34-46.

Bilkey, W.J. and G. Tesar (1977). "The Export Behaviour of Smaller-sized Wisconsin Manufacturing Firms", *Journal of International Business Studies*, Vol. 8, No. 1, pp. 93-98.

Bittante, E. (1985). "I servizi reali a sostegno dell internazionalizzazione: una analisi comparata dell intervento pubblico", *Commercio*, No. 21, pp. 149-175.

Bonaccorsi, A. (1987). "L'attivita esportativa delle piccole e medie imprese in Italia: una rassegna delle indagini empiriche", *Economia e Politica Industriale*, No. 54, pp. 229-267.

Bonoma, Thomas V. (1983). "Get More Out of Your Trade Shows," *Harvard Business Review*, (January/February), 75-83.

Borchert, M. (1977). *Aussenwirtschaftslehre – Theorie und Politik*, Opladen: Westdeutscher Verlag.

Bradley, M.F., (1985). "Key Factors Influencing International Competitiveness", *Journal of Irish Business and Administrative Research*, Vol. 7, No 2, Winter.

Braudel, Fernand (1981). *The Structures of Everyday Life*, New York: Harper and Row.

Brezzo, Roberto and Isaak Perkal (1983). "The Role of Marketing Incentives in Export Promotion: The Uruguayan Case," *Export Promotion*, Michael R. Czinkota et al., Eds., New York: Praeger, 227-40.

British Food Export Council (1987). *Let's Get the Most out of Britain*, London.

British Overseas Trade Board (1987). *British Overseas Trade Board Report 1986*, London.

Brooks, M.R. and P.J. Rosson (1982). "A Study of the Export Behavior of Small and Medium-Sized Manufacturing Firms in Three Canadian

Provinces," in M.R. Czinkota and G. Tesar, Eds., *Export Management: An International Context*, Praeger Publishers, New York, pp. 39-54.

Buckley, P.J. (1983). "Government in Industry Relations in Exporting: Lessons from the United Kingdom", in M.R. Czinkota, Ed., *Export Promotion: The Public and Private Sector Interaction*, New York: Praeger Publishers, pp. 89-109.

Bulmer-Thomas, V. (1979). "Import Substitution vs. Export Promotion in the Central American Common Market," *Journal of Economic Studies*, 6 (2), 182-203.

Business Facilities (1987). March, pp. 51-59.

Business Week (1986). "The Hollow Corporation", 3 March.

Cahiers francais no. 229 (1987). *Le Commerce International*, Paris.

California Economic Development Corporation, Pacific Rim Task Force (1986). California and the Pacific Rim Sacramento, Cal.: California Economic Development Corporation, Appendix IV, p. 2.

Cannon, T. (1977). "Developing the Export Potential of Small Firms: The Role of Government and Banking Services", Sixth Annual Conference of the European Foundation for Management Development, Paris.

Cannon, T. and M. Willis (1983) "The Smaller Firms in Overseas Trade", *European Small Business Journal* 1, 3, pp. 45-55.

Cavusgil, S. Tamer (1984). "Differences Among Exporting Firms Based on Their Degree of Internationalization." *Journal of Business Research*, Vol. 12, No. 2, pp. 195-208.

Cavusgil, S. Tamer and John Nevin (1981). "Internal Determinants of Export Marketing Behaviour," *Journal of Marketing Research*, 18 (February), 114-119.

Cavusgil, S.T., (1980). "On the Internationalisation Process of Firms", *European Research*, Vol. 8, pp. 273-281.

CENPRO (1983). "Ley Costarricense de Incentivos a las Exportaciones," Mimeographed document, Centro para la Promoción de las Exportaciones e Inversiones, San José, Costa Rica.

Ceris, Finpiemonte (1981). *Strutture di intermediazione e assistenza sui mercati esteri per le piccole e medie imprese*, Milano: F. Angeli.

Chapman, N. (1986). "Why the FFB is Flying the British Flag in Europe", *Marketing Week*, (October), pp. 50-53.

Cheong, W.K. and K.W. Chong (1988). "Export Behaviour of Small Firms In Singapore", *International Small Business Journal*, 6, 2, pp. 34-41.

Christensen Carl H., Angela da Rocha and Rosane Kerbel Gertner (1987). "An Empirical Investigation of the Factors Influencing Exporting Success of Brazilian Firms", *Journal of International Business Studies*, Fall, pp. 61-77.

Cohen, Stephen S. and John Zysman (1987). *Manufacturing Matters*, New York: Basic Books.

Colaiacovo, Juan Luis (1982). "Export Development in Latin America", in Michael R. Czinkota and George Tesar, Eds. *Export Policy: a Global Assessment*, New York: Praeger Press, pp. 102-111.

Commonwealth of Puerto Rico, Economic Development Administration (1985). "Foreign Trade Zones and Federal Insular Bonded Warehouses", San Juan: EDA, p. 1.

Couretas, John (1984). "'Unknown Prospect' Unmasked at Trade Shows," *Business Marketing*, (July), p. 33.

Cox, Jonathan M., Robert S. Ciok and Ian K. Sequeira (1986). "Trade Show Trends," *Business Marketing*, (June), p. 142 *et passim*.

Crescini, M. (1986). "Le politiche di sostegno delle esportazioni nelle Marche: un'indagine quantitativa", *Economia Marche*, No. 2.

Crespy, Guy (1988). *Strategies et Competitivites Dans L'industrie Mondiale*, Observatoire des Strategies Industrielles, Ed. Economica, Paris.

Cullwick, T.D.C. and J.P. Mellallieu (1981). "Business Attitudes to Government Export Services and Export Marketing Behaviour", *New Zealand Journal of Business*, Vol. 3, pp. 33-54.

Cunningham, M.T. and R.I. Spigel (1971). "A Study in Successful Exporting", *British Journal of Marketing*, Vol. 5, (Spring), pp. 2-12.

Czinkota, M.R. (1982). *Export Development Strategies*, New York: Praeger Publishers.

Czinkota, M.R. and W.J. Johnston (1981). "Segmenting U.S. Firms for Export Development", *Journal of Business Research*, Vol. 9, No. 4, pp. 353-365.

Czinkota, Michael R. and David A. Ricks (1981). "Export Assistance: Are We Supporting the Best Programs? *Columbia Journal of World Business*, (Summer), pp. 31-47.

Czinkota, Michael R. and George Tesar, Eds. (1982). *Export Management: An International Context*, New York: Praeger Press.

Czinkota, Michael R. and Ilkka A. Ronkainen (1990). *International Marketing*, 2nd. Ed., Hinsdale, Il.: The Dryden Press.

Czinkota, Michael R. and Wesley J. Johnston (1983). "Exporting: Does Sales Volume Make a Difference?" in *Journal of International Business Studies*, vol. 14, no. 1, pp. 147-153.

De La Torre, Jose (1971). "Exports of Manufactured Goods from Developing Countries: Marketing Factors and The Role of Foreign Enterprise", *Journal of International Business Studies*, Vol. 2, No. 1, Spring, pp. 26-39.

De Vries, Barend A. (1979). *Export Promotion Policies*, World Bank Staff Working Papers No. 313, Washington D.C.

de Graaf (1983). "Exportondersteuning voor midden- en kleinbedrijf", Report from the World Trade Centre, Rotterdam, (May).

de Mortanges, Charles Pahud (1983). "A Study of the Export Decision in Small Manufacturing Firms in the San Francisco Bay Area", Unpublished Master's Thesis, California State University, Sacramento.

de Souza, Linda-Mar, Angela Schmidt and Juan L. Colaiacovo (1983). "Pre-Export Behaviour: An Analysis of the Variables Influencing the Decision Process" in Michael R. Czinkota, Ed. *Export Promotion: The Public and Private Sector Interaction*, New York: Praeger Press, pp. 227-240.

Dhawan, K.C. and L. Kryzanowski (1978). *Export Consortia, A Canadian Study*, Montreal: DEKEMCO Ltd.

Diamantopoulos, A. and K.N. Inglis (1988). "Identifying Differences Between High and Low-Involvement Exporters", *International Marketing Review*, Vol. 5, No. 2, pp. 52-60.

Dichtl, E., M. Leibold, G. Koglmayr and S. Muller (1984). "The Export Decision of Small and Medium-sized Firms: A Review" in *Management International Review*, vol. 24, no. 2, pp. 49-60.

Dik, W. (1982). *Exportnota*, Nederlands Ministerie van Economische Zaken.

Dominguez, Luis V. and Cristina Vanmarcke (1987). "Market Structure and Marketing Behaviour in LDCs: The Case of Venezuela," *Journal of Macromarketing*, 7 (Fall).

Donges, Juergen B. and James Riedel (1977). "The Expansion of Manufactured Exports in Developing Countries: An Empirical Assessment of Supply and Demand Issues", *Weltwirtschaftliches Archiv*, Band 113, Heft 1, pp. 58-85.

Dymsza, William A. (1983). "A National Export Strategy for Latin American Countries: in Michael R. Czinkota, ed., *U.S. – Latin American Trade Relations: Issues and Concerns*, New York: Praeger Press, pp. 5-25.

Economist (1987). "A Survey of the World Economy", Sept. 26, pp. 6-56.

Economist (1989a). "Japan and the Third World," June 17, pp. 25-28.

Economist (1989b). "A Survey of the Yen Block: Together under the Sun," July 15, pp. 5-20.

Economist (1989c). "A Survey of the Third World: Poor Man's Burden," September 23, pp. 25-39.

Economist (1990). "GATT Brief – The American Connection," April 21, pp. 85-6.

Edmunds, John (1984). "Pórtico S.A." Case, Centre for Documentation and Exchange of Cases, INCAE, Alajuela, Costa Rica.

Espansione (1983). No. 162, November.

Evans, David and Parvin Alizadeh (1984). "Trade, Industrialization and the Visible Hand," *Journal of Development Studies*, 21 (October), 22-46.

EVD (1986). (Netherlands Export Promotion & Information Service), *Annual Report*.

EVD (1986). (Netherlands Export Promotion & Information Service), Conference Report on "Export: Research and Policy", The Hague.

Faria, A.J. and J.R. Dickinson (1985a). "What Kinds of Companies Use Trade Shows Most – And Why?," *Business Marketing*, (June), p. 150 *et passim*.

Faria, A.J. and J.R. Dickinson (1985b). "Behind the Push to Exhibit at Trade Shows," *Business Marketing*, (August), p. 99, 100, 102.

Federexport (1988). *Consorzi export in Italia*, Roma: Confindustria.

Fell, D., (1986). "Northern Ireland: Building a Stronger Economy", *Business Outlook and Economic Review*, Vol. 1, No. 3, December, pp. 22-25.

Forbes (1987). "States Look Abroad", April 20, p. 13.

Ford, David (1986). "Export Development From the Third World: A Structure for the Analysis of Buyer-Seller Relationships," Staff Paper, National Centre for the Export-Import Studies, Georgetown University, Washington, D.C.

Fornasari, C. (1986). "Primi risultati di una indagine campionaria sulle imprese esportatrici modenesi", in M.L. Fornaciari Davoli-G. Pini, *Piccole e medie imprese ed esportazioni*, Milano: Fiuffre.

Frances, Antonio (1987). *La Empresa Manufactura Venezolana y las Exportaciones No Tradicionales*, Papel de Trabajo PTI-1987-11 Caracas: Instituto de Estudios Superiores de Administracion.

Garcia Bianco, J.L. (1985). La Politica de Promoción Comercial Española., Información Comercial Española no. 624-625, Madrid.

Gerbi Sethi, M. (1979). *Imprese italiane di fronte alle esportazioni*, Milano: F. Angeli.

Gerbi Sethi, M. (1982). *Piccole e medie imprese di fronte alle esportazioni* Milano: F. Angeli.

Glastetter, W. (1979). *Aussenwirtschaftspolitik*, Koeln.

Goodnow, J. and J.E. Hanz (1972). "Environmental Determinants of Overseas Market Entry Strategies" in *Journal of International Business Studies*, Spring, pp. 33-60.

Granell, Francesc (1979). *La Exportación y los Mercados Internacionales*, Hispano Europea, Barcelona.

Griffing, John (1984). "The Other Deficit: A Review of International Trade in California and the U.S.", Sacramento, Cal.: Senate Office of Research, November.

Gronhaug, K. and T. Lorentzen (1983). "Exploring the Impact of Government Export Subsidies", *European Journal of Marketing*, Vol. 17, No. 2, pp. 5-12.

Hakansson, Hakan (1982). *International Marketing and Purchasing of Industrial Goods: An Interaction Approach*, Chichester: Wiley.

Hartland-Thunberg, Penelope and Morris Crawford (1982). *Government Support for Exports*, Lexington, Mass.: Lexington Books.

Hatter, Victoria L. (1985). *U.S. High Technology Trade and Competitiveness*, Washington, D.C.: U.S. Department of Commerce, February, Staff Report, International Trade Administration.

Hesse, Helmut (1972). "Promotion of Manufactured exports as Development Strategy of Semi-Industrialized Countries: The Brazilian Case", *Weltwirtschaftliches Archiv*, Band 108, Heft 2, pp. 236-255.

Hibbert, Edgar P. (1985). *The Principles and Practice of Export Marketing*, London: Heinemann.

Hillman, Jordan Jay (1982). *The Export-Import Bank at Work*, Westport, Connecticut: Quantum Books.

Hoffman, Ellen (1988). "Overseas Sales Pitch", *National Journal*, 16 January, p. 132.

House of Commons (1980). "Proceeding of the Special Committee on a National Trading Corporation", First Session of the Thirty-Second Parliament, Issue No. 29.

Hull, C. and Hjern, B. (1987). *Helping Small Firms Grow: An Implementation Approach*, New York: Croom Helm.

I.C.E. (1986). "La struttura delle esportazioni italiane", Roma.

IMF (1988). *Exchange Arrangements and Exchange Restrictions 1988.* Washington, D.C.: International Monetary Fund.

Instituto Español de Comercio Exterior (1988). *Servicios a la Exportación*, Madrid.

Instituto Nacional de Fomento de la Exportación (1985). *Objetivos y Programas*, Madrid.

INTAL (1971). *El Desarrollo Integradeo de Centroamérica en las Presente Década.* San José: Instituto para la Integración de América Latina.

Isham, Robert C. (1985). "The China Trade Show," *Sales and Marketing Management*, October 7, p. 50, 52-3.

ITC (1986a). *Selected Export Promotion Organizations: Structures, Functions and Activities*, International Trade Centre UNCTAD/GATT, Geneva, Sept. 25.

ITC (1986b). *Trade Promotion Institutions: Monograph on the Role and Organization of Trade Promotion*, International Trade Centre UNCTAD/GATT, Geneva.

ITC (1988). *Profiles of Trade Promotion Organizations*, Geneva, International Trade Centre UNCTAD/GATT.

Jackson, Graham I. (1981). "Exporting--From the Importer's Viewpoint," *European Journal of Marketing* 15 (October), 3-125.

Jain, Subhash C. (1990). *International Marketing Management*, 3rd. Ed., Boston: PWS-Kent Publishing Company.

Jeannet, Jean Pierre and Hubert D. Hennessey (1988). *International Marketing Management*, Boston: Houghton-Mifflin Co.

Johansson, Jan and Jan-Erik Vahlne (1976). "The Internationalization Process of the Firm--A Model of Knowledge Development and Increasing Foreign Market Commitment," *Journal of International Business Studies*, 8 (Spring-Summer), 23-32.

Johnson, Chalmers Ed. (1984). *The Industrial Policy Debate,* San Francisco: IPC Press.

Joint Economic Committee, Congress of the United States (1986). *Technology and Trade: Indicators of U.S. Industrial Innovation*, Washington, D.C.: U.S. Government Printing Office, 14 July.

Jung, Woo S. and Gyu Lee (1986). "The Effectiveness of Export Promotion Policies: The Case of Korea", *Wiltwirtschaftliches Archiv*, Band 122, Heft 2, pp. 341-357.

Kamath, Shyam, Philip J. Rosson, Donald Patton and M. Brooks (1987). "Research on Success in Exporting: Past, Present, and Future", in Philip J. Rosson and Stanley D. Reid, Eds. *Managing Export Entry and Expansion*, New York: Praeger Press, pp. 398-421.

Kaynak E. and V. Kothari (1984). "Export Behaviour of Small and Medium-Sized Manufacturers; Some Policy Guidelines for International Marketers", *Management International Review*, No. 2, pp. 61-69.

Kaynak, E., P.W. Ghauri, and T. Olopson-Bredenlow (1987). "Export Behaviour of Small Swedish Firms", *Journal of Small Business Management*, Vol. 25, No. 2, April, pp. 26-32.

Kaynak, Erdener (1982). *Marketing in the Third World*, New York: Praeger.

Kedia, Ben L. and Jagdeed S. Chokar (1986). "An Empirical Investigation of Export Promotion Programs," *Columbia Journal of World Business*, 21 Winter, 13-20.

Keesing, Donald B. and Sanjara Lall (1988). "Marketing Manufactured Products from Developing Countries: Information Links, Buyers' Orders and Institutional Support," Paper presented at UNU/WIDER Conference on New Trade Theories and Industrialization in Developing Countries, Helsinki, August.

Kerin, Roger A. and William L. Cron (1987). "Trade show Functions and Performance: An Exploratory Study," *Journal of Marketing*, Vol. 51 (July), pp. 87-94.

Kok, A. (1987). *Export Management*, Boston: Kluwer-Nijhoff.

Konopacki, Allen (1985). "Capturing Power Buyers on the Trade Show Floor," *Meetings and Conventions*, Special Piedmont Supplement, Vol. 10, pp. 42-52.

Krebs, G. (1977). *Angewandte Aussenwirtschaftstheorie und -Politik*, Koeln: Fachhochschule.

Lagerweij, J. (1986). "NIPO's export monitor: bedrijven optimistisch over buitenlandse afzet" *Export Magazine*, (May 14).

Lanzara, R. (1987). "Strategic Differentiation and Adaptation among Small and Medium-Sized Italian Exporting Manufacturers", in P.J. Rosson and S.D. Reid, Eds, *Managing Export Entry and Expansion*, New York: Praeger, pp. 41-53.

Lanzara, R. (1988). "I rapporti strategici con le imprese conciarie", in R. Varaldo, Ed., *Il sistema delle imprese calzaturiere*, (Torino, Giappichelli editore), pp. 41-53.

Lanzara, R. and R. Sbrana (1984). "Export Trade: Government Policies and Italian Small Firms", in *Economia Aziendale*, Volume III, Number 2, August, pp. 117-30.

Lee, Woo-Young and John J. Brasch (1978). "The Adoption of Export as an Innovative Strategy," *Journal of International Business Studies*, 9 (Spring-Summer), 85-93.

Lefevre, D. (1970). *Staatliche Ausfuhrfoerderung und das Verbot wettbewerbsverzerrender Beihilfen im EWG Vertrag*, Baden-Baden.

Lilien, Gary (1982). "A Descriptive Model of the Trade-Show Budgeting Decision Process," *Industrial Marketing Management*, Vol. 12 (February), pp. 25-9.

Luis, Luis R. (1982). "Macroeconomic Management and Export Promotion in Latin America" in Michael R. Czinkota and George Tesar, Eds. *Export Promotion: A Global Assessment*, New York: Praeger Press, pp. 35-42.

Luttwak, Edward N. (1987). *Strategy: The Logic of War and Peace*, Cambridge: Harvard University Press.

Machado, Carios (1988). "Export Assistance: Yes or No?. And if Yes, What Kind?" Symposium on the Importance of Trade Promotion and Assistance, Washington D.C.

Magaziner, Ira C. and Robert B. Reich (1983). *Minding America's Business*, New York: Vintage Books.

Malekzadeh, A.R. and S. Rabino (1986). "Manufacturers' Export Strategies", *International Marketing Review*, (Winter), pp. 125-141.

Manzanares, Rafael (1983). "Instrumentos de fomento de la exportación", Información Comercial Española, Julio-Agosto, Madrid.

Mayer, C.S. and J.E. Flynn (1973). "Canadian Small Business Abroad: Opportunities, Aids and Experiences", *Business Quarterly*, (Winter), pp. 33-47.

McDowell, E. (1987). "The Industrial Development Board for Northern Ireland and the Future", *Business Outlook and Economic Review*, Vol. 2, No. 1, April, pp. 15-18.

McFarlane, G. (1978). "Scots Queen's Award Winners Don't Excel", *Marketing*, (April), pp. 27-32.

Medland, D. (1987). "How the British Overseas Trade Board Can Help Exporters", *The Financial Times*, (September 8).

Meliani, R. (1988). "Il marketing internazionale delle imprese produttrici di macchine per il legno", unpublished Tesi di laurea, Dipartimento di Economia Aziendale, Universita' Degli Studi di Pisa.

Miesenbock, K.J. (1988). "Small Businesses and Exporting: A Literature Review", *International Small Business Journal*, Vol. 6, 2, pp. 42-61.

Ministerio de Industria y Energia (1987). *España en Europa, un Futuro Industrial*, Madrid.

Morawitz (1981). *Why the Emperor's New Clothes Are Not Made in Colombia*, New York: Oxford University Press.

Morici, Peter (1984). *The Global Competitive Struggle: Challenges to the United States and Canada*, Washington, D.C.: National Planning Association.

NASDA - National Association of State Development Agencies (1984). "NASDA State Export program Database", Washington, D.C.: NASDA, August, p. 1.

National Governors Association (1986). Committee on Economic Development and Technological Innovation, "Revitalizing State Economies", (prepared by Marianne Clarke) Washington, D.C." National Governors Association, February.

National Swedish Industrial Board (1984). *Export Promotion by Governments in Nine Countries*, Stockholm.

New York Times (1987). "The Clamour for Competitiveness", 14 January.

New York Times (1988). "A New Spirit of Cooperation", 14 January.

NMB Bank (1979). *Annual Report*.

Obey, David and Paul Sarbanes, Eds. (1986). *The Changing American Economy*, New York: Basil Blackwell.

OECD (1987). *The Export Credit Financing Systems in OECD Member Countries*, Paris.

Office of the President (1984). *The State of Small Business*, Washington, D.C.: U.S. Government Printing Office.

Ohmae, Kenichi (1985). *Triad of Power*, New York: Free Press.

Olson, C.H. and Paul F. Wiedersheim (1978). "Factors Affecting the Pre-Export Behaviour of Non-Exporting Firms", in Ghertman, Michel and James Leontiades, Eds., *European Research in International Business*, Amsterdam: North-Holland Publishing Company, pp. 283-305.

Parsonm, M. and P. Foster (1978). "Notes on the Motivation and Methods of the Small Exporter", *Industrial Marketing Digest*, Vol. 3, No. 2, pp. 130-135.

Piercy, N. (1981a). "British Export Market Selection and Pricing," *Industrial Marketing Management*, 10 (October), 287-97.

Piercy, N. (1981b). "Company Internationalization: Active and Reactive Exporting," *European Journal of Marketing*, 15 (Spring), 107-16.

Piercy, N. (1983). "Export Marketing Management In Medium-Sized British firms", *European Journal of Marketing*, Vol. 17, No. 1, pp. 48-67.

Pilcher, Dan (1985). "State Roles in Foreign Trade", *State Legislatures* 11(4) April, p. 19.

Piore, M.J. and C.F. Sabel (1980). "Italian Small Business Development: Lessons for U.S. Industrial Policy", in J. Zysman and L. Tyson, eds, *American Industry in International Competition*, Ithaca: Cornell University Press, pp. 391-421.

Quaglia, F. (1986). "Politiche regionali di sostegno all export: un confronto tra diversi modelli organizzative, *Economia Marche*, No. 2.

Rabino, S. (1980). "An Examination of Barriers to Exporting Encountered by Small Manufacturing Companies", *Management International Review*, Vol. 20, No. 1, pp. 67-73.

Ram, Rati (1985). "Exports and Economic Growth: Some Additional Evidence", *Economic Development and Cultural Change*, Vol. 33, pp. 415-425.

Reid, S. D. (1981). "Managerial and Firm Influences on Export Behavior," *Journal of the Academy of Marketing Science*, 11 (Summer), 323-332.

Reid, S. D. (1981). "The Decision-Maker and Export Entry and Expansion", *Journal of International Business Studies*, (Fall), pp. 101- 112.

Reid, S. D. (1984). "Information Acquisition and Export Entry Decisions in Small Firms", *Journal of Business Research*, Vol. 12, (June), pp. 141-157.

Reid, S. D. (1987). "Export Strategies, Structure, and Performance: An Empirical Study of Small and Italian Manufacturing Firms", in

Managing Export in P.J. Rosson and S.D. Reid, Eds, *Managing Export Entry and Expansion*, New York: Praeger, pp. 335-357.

Reid, Stan D. and Charles C. Mayer (1980). "Export Behaviour and Decision Maker Characteristics: An Empirical Investigation," *Marketing 1980: Marketing Excellence in the 1980's*, ed. by V. Jones, University of Calgary, 298-307.

Reid, Stan D. and Philip J. Rosson (1987). "Managing Export Entry and Expansion: An Overview," in Philip J. Rosson and Stanley D. Reid, Eds., *Managing Export Entry and Expansion*, New York: Praeger, p. 6.

Requeijo, Jaime (1987). *Introducción a la Balanza de Pagos de España*, Madrid.

Resmini, L. (1987). "Efficacia dei servizi pubblici a sostegno dell internazionalizzazione", *Commercio*, No. 27, pp. 157-179.

Rhee, Young Whee (1985). *Instruments for Export Policy and Administration. Lessons from the East Asian Experience*, World Bank Staff Working Papers No. 725, Washington D.C.

Robinson, Richard D. (1981). "Background Concepts and Philosophy of International Business from World War II to the Present", *Journal of International Business Studies*, (Spring/Summer), pp. 13-17.

Root, Franklin R. (1971). "A Conceptual Model for Export Promotion Strategy at the National Level", *Foreign Trade Review*, July-Sept., pp. 184-194.

Root, Franklin R. (1971). "The Elements of Export Promotion," *International Trade Forum*, July-September, pp. 118-21.

Root, Franklin R. (1974). "Conceptual Foundations for the Strategy of a Government Export Promotion Agency", *Foreign Trade Review*, January-March, pp. 326-338.

Root, Franklin R. (1978). *International Trade and Investment*, 4th Edition, South-Western Publishing Co., Cincinnati.

Rosecrance, Richard (1985). *The Rise of the Trading State*, New York: Basic Books.

Rosson, Philip J. and Stanley D. Reid, Eds. (1987). *Managing Export Entry and Expansion*, New York: Praeger Press.

SBA - U.S. Small Business Administration, Office of Advocacy (1984). *State Export Promotion Activities*, Washington, D.C.: USGPO, October, p. 2.

Schmitz, Hubert (1984). "Industrialization Strategies in Less Developed Countries: Some Lessons of Historical Experience", *Journal of Development Studies*, Vol. 21, No. 1, October, pp. 1-21.

Schwartz, Hugh (1988). "The Potential Role of Behavioral Analysis in the Promotion of Private Enterprise in Developing Countries", *Columbia Journal of World Business*, Spring, pp. 53-56.

Schydlowsky, Daniel M. (1986). "The Macroeconomic Effect of Nontraditional Exports in Peru," *Economic Development and Cultural Change*, 34, 490-508.

Scott, Bruce R. and George C. Lodge, Eds. (1985). *U.S. Competitiveness in the World Economy*, Boston: Harvard Business School Press.

Scott, W.G. (1983). "Imprese minori: esportare per crescere", *L'impresa*, No. 1, pp. 21-28.

Scottish Council Development and Industry (1988). *Programme 1988*, Edinburgh.

Scottish Development Agency (1988). *Annual Report 1987*, Glasgow.

Secchi, C. (1983). "Radiografia della PMI che opera con l'estero", *L'impresa*, No. 1, pp. 29-36.

Secretaria General Técnica del Ministerio de Industria y Energia (1985). *Análisis Comparativo de las Ayudas Públicas a la Exportación en la CEE y en España*, Madrid.

Sekely, William S., Louis Capella and J. Markham Collins (1987). "Determining Information Needs of Exporters: A Segmentation Approach", *Issues in International Business*, vol. 4, no. 1, Spring, pp. 1-6.

Sequeira, Carlos and Iván Saballos (1987). "HILASAL" (A), (B) and (C) Case, Centre for Documentation and Exchange of Cases, INCAE, Alajuela, Costa Rica.

Seringhaus, F.H. Rolf (1983). "Government Export Marketing Assistance in the Early Phase of the Internationalization Process of the Firm", paper presented at the Ninth Annual Conference of the European International Business Association, Oslo.

Seringhaus, F.H. Rolf (1985). "Private/Public Sector Interaction: How Effective is Export Assistance by Government". Proceedings of the Annual Conference of the European Marketing Academy (Bielefeld, West Germany), pp. 119-128.

Seringhaus, F.H. Rolf (1986). "The Impact of Government Export Marketing Assistance," *International Marketing Review*, Vol. 3, No. 2, pp. 55-66.

Seringhaus, F.H. Rolf (1986/87). "The Role of Information Assistance in Small Firms' Export Involvement", *International Small Business Journal*, Vol. 5, No. 2, Winter, pp. 26-36.

Seringhaus, F.H. Rolf (1986a). "Empirical Investigation of Awareness, Use and Impact of Export Marketing Support by Government in Manufacturing Firms", in K. Moeller and M. Paltschik, Eds., *Contemporary Research in Marketing*, Vol. 1, European Marketing Academy, Helsinki, p. 249-267.

Seringhaus, F.H. Rolf (1986b). "Market Entry and the Impact of Export Marketing Assistance: A Conceptual Approach to Causal Modelling", *The Finnish Journal of Business Economics*, Vol. 35, No. 4, pp. 275-285.

Seringhaus, F.H. Rolf (1987). "Do Experienced Exporters have Market Entry Problems?", *Finnish Journal of Business Economics*, 4 (1987), 376-388.

Seringhaus, F.H. Rolf (1987). "Export Promotion: The Role and Impact of Government Services", *Irish Marketing Review*, Vol. 2, pp. 106-116.

Seringhaus, F.H. Rolf (1987). "The Role of Trade Missions in Export Expansion: a Comparison of Users and Non Users", in P.J. Rosson and S.D. Reid, eds, *Managing Export Entry and Expansion*, New York: Praeger, pp. 187-198.

Seringhaus, F.H. Rolf (1987a). "Export Promotion: The Role and Impact of Government Services," *Irish Marketing Review*, Vol. 2, pp. 106-116.

Seringhaus, F.H. Rolf (1989a). "Export Promotion Organizations as International Marketing Tool in Developing Countries," in George J. Avlonitis, Nikolaos K. Papavasiliou and Athanasios G. Kouremenos, Eds., *Marketing Thought and Practice in the 1990s*, Vol. 1, Proceedings of the European Marketing Academy, Athens, pp. 215-229.

Seringhaus, F.H. Rolf (1990). "Program Impact Evaluation: Application to Export Promotion", *Evaluation and Program Planning*, Vol. 13, No. 3, in press.

Seringhaus, F.H. Rolf and Günther Botschen (1990). "Cross-National Comparison of Export Promotion Services and their Usage by Canadian and Austrian Companies", in Hans Mühlbacher and Christoph Jochum, Eds. *Advanced Research in Marketing*, Vol. II, European Marketing Academy, Innsbruck, Austria, pp. 1563-82.

Seringhaus, F.H. Rolf and Philip J. Rosson (1990). *Government Export Promotion: A Global Perspective*, London: Routledge.

Shaw, Harry J. (1986). "Coping with the Foreign-Aid Pinch", *Wall Street Journal*, 15 July.

Sheth, Jagdish N. and Hanns-Martin Schoenfeld (1980). "How to Succeed in Export Marketing: Some Guidelines", in Jagdish N. Sheth and Hanns-Martin Schoenfeld, Eds., *Export Marketing: Lessons from Europe*, Bureau of Economic and Business Research, University of Illinois, Champaign, Ill., pp. 185-202.

Siegel, S. (1956). *Nonparametric Statistics for the Behavioural Sciences*, Intern. Ed, Tokyo: McGraw-Hill Kogakusha, Ltd.

Silva, F. (1979). "L'impresa esportatrice", *Giornale degli economisti*, No. 1, pp. 35-65.

Simpson, C.L., D.A. Roy and D.L. Loudon (1981). "Use and Perception of External Support Facilities in the Initial Export Activity Among Smaller Manufacturing Firms in the Southeastern United States", presented at the Annual Meeting of the Academy of International Business, Montreal, October, pp. 15-17.

Simpson, Claude L. and Duane Kujawa (1974). "The Export Decision Process: An Empirical Enquiry", *Journal of International Business Studies*, (Spring), pp. 107-117.

Sloan, Alfred P. Jr. (1963). *My Years with General Motors*, Garden City, N.Y.: Doubleday.

Sodersten, Bo (1982), *International Economics*, Hong Kong: The MacMillan Press Ltd.

South Carolina General Assembly. Legislative Audit Council (1985). *Review and Assessment of the State's Economic Development Activities*, Columbia, S.C.: General Assembly, p. 108.

Standing Commission on the Scottish Economy (1988). *Interim Report*, Glasgow: Fraser of Allander Institute.

Suntook, F. (1978). "How British Industry Exports", *Marketing*, (June), pp. 29-34.

Sylvester, Kathleen (1988). "Exporting Made Easy (Or How States and Cities are Selling Products Overseas)", *Governing* 1(4), January, pp. 41-42.

Task Force for a Long-Term Economic Strategy for Michigan (1984). *The Path to Prosperity*, Lansing: Cabinet Council on Jobs and Economic Development, November, Chapter 11.

Tesar, George and Jesse S. Tarleton (1983). "Stimulation of Manufacturing Firms to Export as Part of National Export Policy" in Michael R. Czinkota, Ed. *Export Promotion: The Public and Private Sector Interaction*, New York: Praeger, pp. 33-35.

The President's Commission on Industrial Competitiveness (1985a). *Global Competition: The New Reality*, vol. I, Washington: U.S. Government Printing Office.

Thomas, M.J. and Araujo (1985). "Theories of Export Behaviour: A Critical Analysis", *European Journal of Marketing* 19, 2, pp. 42-52.

Thurow, Lester (1980). *The Zero-Sum Society*, New York: Basic Books.

Tolchin, Martin and Susan (1988). *Buying into America*, New York: Times Books.

Tookey, D.A. (1964). "Factors Associated with Success in Exporting", *The Journal of Management Studies*, vol. 1, (March), pp. 48-66.

U.S. Department of Commerce (1988). "Export Now. It Makes Good Business Sense", *Business America*, Washington D.C.

UNCTAD (1982). *Incentives for Industrial Exports*, New York: United Nations Conference on Trade and Development.

United Stated Department of Commerce (1987). *1986 U.S. Foreign Trade Highlights*, Washington, D.C.

Ursic, Michael L. and Michael R. Czinkota (1984). "An Experience Curve Explanation of Export Expansion," *Journal of Business Research*, 12, 159-68.

Van den Berg, T. (1986). "Exporterend midden- en kleinbedrijf in industrie en groothandel", Economisch Instituut van het Midden-en Kleinbedrijf, (September).

Van Gent, Aart P. (1983). *Internationale Bedrijfskunde, Internationale Marktkunde, en Exportkunde*, Breukelen: Nijenrode.

Van Gent, Aart P. and Gerald M. Hampton, Eds. (1983). *Marketing Aspects of International Business*, Boston: Kluwer-Nijhoff.

Van Gent, Aart P. and Scheurleer, F.A.F. (1986). *Internationaal Ondernemingsbeleid* Amsterdam: Meulenhoff Educatief.

Varaldo, R. (1987). "Le industrie con prevalenza di piccole imprese nella realta produttiva italiana", in *Scritti di Economia Aziendale per Egidio Giannessi*, pp. 1169-1186.

Varaldo, R. (1987). "The Internationalization of Small and Medium-Sized Italian Manufacturing Firms", in P.J. Rosson and S.D. Reid, Eds, *Managing*

Export Entry and Expansion, New York: Praeger Publishers, pp. 203-222.

Verhoeven, J. (1985). "Het exportgedrag van het midden- en kleinbedrijf" Economisch Instituut van het Midden- en Kleinbedrijf, (October).

Verhoeven, W. (1988). "The Export Performance of Small and Medium sized enterprises in the Netherlands", *International Small Business Journal*, Vol. 6, 2, pp. 20-33.

Vernon, I. and J. Ryans (1975). "The Awareness and Selection of an Export Incentive: The DISC Case", *Baylor Business Studies*, (February- April), pp. 19-26.

Vogel, Ezra (1985). *Comeback,* New York: Simon and Schuster.

Wall Street Journal (1984). "Exporting Chaos", May 20, p. 80.

Wall Street Journal (1985). "Quiet War Rages on Technology's Front Line", 24 December.

Wall Street Journal (1986). "U.S. Economy Grows Ever More Vulnerable to Foreign Influences", 27 October.

Wall Street Journal (1987a). "States Launch Efforts to Make Small Firms Better Exporters", 2 February.

Wall Street Journal (1987b). "State Foreign Trade Figures Finally Becoming Clearer", 7 July, p. 31.

Wall Street Journal (1987c). "Foreign Trade Zones and Many Companies Stir Up Criticism", September 30, p. 1.

Walters, Peter G.P. (1983). "Export Information Sources – A Study of Their Usage and Utility", *International Marketing Review*, Vol. 1, Winter. pp. 34-43.

Weinrauch, J. Donald (1984). "Role and Utilization of Trade Shows for International Trade," *Proceedings*, Southern Marketing Association, New Orleans, November 14-17, pp. 284-287.

Welch, L.S. and P. Joynt (1987). "Grouping for Export: An Effective Solution", in P.J. Rosson and S.D. Reid, Eds., *Managing Export Entry and Expansion*, New York: Praeger Publishers, pp. 54-70.

Westphall, Lee E., Yung W. Rhee, Garry Pursell (1981). "Korean Industrial Competence: Where It Came From," World Bank Staff Paper No. 469, The World Bank, Washington, D.C.

Wheeler, Colin (1988). "Stimulating the Scottish and United Kingdom Economies through Export Promotion Programmes", Symposium on the Importance of Trade Promotion and Assistance, Washington D.C.

Wiedersheim-Paul, F., Hans C. Olson, and Lawrence S. Welch (1978). "Pre-Export Activity: The First Step in Internationalization", *Journal of International Business Studies*, Vol. 9, pp. 47-58.

Wijdeveld, T. (1985). "Kan Nederland meer markegericht exporteren?", *Management Team.*

Wiltink, K. (1985). "Midden- en kleinbedrijf steeds groter in export", *Export Magazine*, (December 18).

World Bank (1987). *World Development Report 1987*, Oxford University Press, New York.

Zagnoli, P. (1984). "D.P.R. 902/1976 e L. 240/1981 e loro applicazioni in Toscana", paper presented at the Conference on *L'innovazione tecnologica nell' impresa toscana*, Chianciano Terme, October.

INDEX